The Creative Community Builder's Handbook

How to Transform Communities Using Local Assets, Art, and Culture

by **Tom Borrup** with Partners for Livable Communities
Foreword by Robert McNulty

FIELDSTONE
ALLIANCE

SAINT PAUL
MINNESOTA

Special thanks to the McKnight Foundation for support
of the research, writing, editing, and production of this work.

Fieldstone Alliance is committed to strengthening the performance of the nonprofit sector. Through the synergy of its consulting, training, publishing, and research and demonstration projects, Fieldstone Alliance provides solutions to issues facing nonprofits, funders, and the communities they serve. Fieldstone Alliance was formerly Wilder Publishing and Wilder Consulting departments of the Amherst H. Wilder Foundation. If you would like more information about Fieldstone Alliance and our services, please contact Fieldstone Alliance at

800-274-6024
www.FieldstoneAlliance.org

Edited by Vincent Hyman
Text designed by Kirsten Nielsen
Cover designed by Rebecca Andrews

Second printing, March 2009
Manufactured in the USA

Library of Congress Data

Borrup, Tom, 1954-
  The creative community builder's handbook : how to transform communities using local assets, art, and culture / by Tom Borrup ; with Partners for Livable Communities ; foreword by Robert McNulty.
      p. cm.
  Includes bibliographical references and index.
  ISBN-13: 978-0-940069-47-3
  ISBN-10: 0-940069-47-4
  1. Community development--United States. 2. Community leadership--United States. 3. Cultural policy. I. Partners for Livable Communities. II. McKnight Foundation. III. Title.
  HN90.C6.B685 2006
  307.1'4068--dc22
                        2006010900

Cover Images:

A mother and daughter duo take part in In the Heart of the Beast Puppet and Mask Theatre's May Day Parade. Photo by Gayla Ellis.

Yak parade-style puppet by Andrew Kim from In the Heart of the Beast Puppet and Mask Theatre's 2001 May Day Parade. Photo by Gayla Ellis.

Downtown aerial view of Providence, Rhode Island during a WaterFire event. Photo by Thomas Payne, copyright 2003, WaterFire Providence.

"Strutin." A painting by artist Ta-coumba Aiken.

About the Author

TOM BORRUP has been a leader and innovator in nonprofit cultural and community development work for over twenty-five years. His consulting, writing, and teaching explore intersections between culture, art, community building, civic engagement, urban design, town planning, and the active use of public space. Based in Minneapolis and Miami Beach, Tom consults with foundations, nonprofits, and public agencies across the United States. He has written many articles for publications in the arts, city planning, and philanthropy. Many of these articles can be accessed at www.communityandculture.com/writing.html.

Tom explored the topic of this book as a fellow in the Knight Program in Community Building at the University of Miami School of Architecture in 2002, and through a St. Paul/Travelers Leadership Initiatives in Neighborhoods grant during 2002 and 2003. As executive director of Intermedia Arts in Minneapolis from 1980 until 2002, he developed a cross-disciplinary, cross-cultural organization recognized nationally for its innovative work engaging artists and other cultural assets in its diverse urban community.

From 1994 to 2003, Tom served on the board of the Jerome Foundation, a progressive funder of emerging artists in New York City and Minnesota, serving two terms as chair. He also served eight years on the board of the San Francisco–based National Alliance for Media Arts and Culture, including two terms as co-president. Throughout his career, Tom has actively served on funding and policy review panels for institutions including the Rockefeller, Ford, Wallace, and Andy Warhol foundations, the National Endowment for the Arts, and the Corporation for Public Broadcasting.

He has been an invited speaker for the American Association of Museums, the Planners Network, Grantmakers in the Arts, Americans for the Arts, and many other organizations. Tom teaches for the graduate program in arts administration at Saint Mary's University of Minnesota and for the Institute for Arts Management at the University of Massachusetts. He received his bachelor's degree in liberal arts from Goddard College, and continued there to receive his master's degree in communications and public policy.

About Partners for Livable Communities

Partners for Livable Communities (PLC) is a nonprofit organization that promotes quality of life, economic development, and social equity.

Partners for Livable Communities fosters livable communities through technical assistance, leadership training, workshops, charettes, research, and publications. Using these techniques, PLC helps communities envision bold futures, unleash vital new resources, and build vigorous public-private coalitions that, in combination, strengthen communities, their residents, and their economies. More than 1,200 individuals and groups from all sectors—local, state, national, international, public, private, nonprofit, philanthropy, and media—make up PLC's resource network. These groups share and build innovative ideas on livability and community improvement.

Partners for Livable Communities has a long and distinguished history in the use of culture, heritage, design, and the humanities to help people reclaim their neighborhoods. PLC was a direct outcome of a national conference on inner-city neighborhoods, hosted by the National Endowment for the Arts in New York City in 1975. Urged by then-NEA chair Nancy Hanks, a consortium of conferees concerned with livability and the built environment became officially incorporated in August 1977. Robert McNulty served as organizer-strategist in the creation of the organization, and continues as the president of PLC to this day.

In 1993, PLC began an extensive developmental program called Culture Builds Community, which aims to systematically place cultural assets within the portfolio of community development efforts. The project began in New York City under the sponsorship of CitiGroup Foundation with Citi-Group grantees. It expanded to work with the Enterprise Foundation, the Neighborhood Reinvestment Corporation, the William Penn Foundation, the Kellogg Foundation, the Ford Foundation, and others. Nationwide in scope, the program gave rise to a publication, *Culture Builds Communities*, that inspired this book.

Partners for Livable Communities has a board of thirty-five women and men from politics, banking, journalism, and community affairs. This board sees Partners as a resource center to help communities become more livable. PLC views culture in all its forms (and as advocated in this book) as a key resource that should be part of the toolkit of community development leaders everywhere.

To learn more about PLC and its many services and publications, visit www.livable.com.

Contents

About the Author iii

    About Partners for Livable Communities iv

Illustrations vii

Foreword ix

Author's Acknowledgments xi

Introduction: Creative Community Building xv

PART ONE   Ideas Behind This Book

  CHAPTER 1   The Role of Culture in Community Building 3

    Community, Culture, Art, Economics, and "Place" 4

    Culture, Social Change, and Community Development 10

  Endnotes for Part One 15

PART TWO   Ten Economic and Social Development Strategies

  CHAPTER 2   Building Strong Economies through Arts and Culture 21

    1. Create Jobs 23

    2. Stimulate Trade through Cultural Tourism 32

    3. Attract Investment by Creating Live/Work Zones for Artists 43

    4. Diversify the Local Economy 53

    5. Improve Property and Enhance Value 62

    Best Practices in Building Strong Economies through
       Arts and Culture 71

  CHAPTER 3   Building Social Connections through Arts and Culture 73

    6. Promote Interaction in Public Space 75

    7. Increase Civic Participation through Cultural Celebrations 84

    8. Engage Youth 94

    9. Promote Stewardship of Place 103

    10. Broaden Participation in the Civic Agenda 113

    Best Practices in Using Arts and Culture to Build
       Social Connections 121

  Endnotes for Part Two 123

  Photographs Illustrating Part Two 127

PART THREE **Steps for Creative Community Builders**

CHAPTER 4 **Step 1: Assess Your Situation and Goals**...................139
TASK 1.1 Define the community...141
TASK 1.2 Identify your strengths and leadership capacity.............143
TASK 1.3 Identify community assets...................................145
TASK 1.4 Clarify values and goals....................................149
TASK 1.5 Write a concept paper.......................................149
TASK 1.6 Review readiness..151
Summary...151

CHAPTER 5 **Step 2: Identify and Recruit Effective Partners**.......153
TASK 2.1 Identify potential partners.................................154
TASK 2.2 Develop expectations for potential partners.................159
TASK 2.3 Recruit partners..164
Summary...165

CHAPTER 6 **Step 3: Map Values, Strengths, Assets, and History**.....167
TASK 3.1 Hold the first meeting to establish commitment..............168
TASK 3.2 Build group cohesion..170
TASK 3.3 Identify assets...172
TASK 3.4 Create a map of community assets............................175
TASK 3.5 Invite contributions from the larger community..............180
Summary...181

CHAPTER 7 **Step 4: Focus on Your Key Asset, Vision, Identity,
and Core Strategies**...183
TASK 4.1 Review data and narrow list of top community assets.........185
TASK 4.2 Choose a key community asset................................187
TASK 4.3 Envision the future...188
TASK 4.4 Develop core strategies based upon your vision..............190
TASK 4.5 Name your identity..193
Summary...194

Chapter 8 **Step 5: Craft a Plan That Brings the Identity to Life**...195
TASK 5.1 Create outcomes...196
TASK 5.2 Set goals...197
TASK 5.3 Attach measures to outcome targets..........................199
TASK 5.4 Generate a list of activities...............................204
TASK 5.5 Organize action steps and resource needs into a plan........205
TASK 5.6 Celebrate your work!..206
Summary...207

CHAPTER 9 **Securing Funding, Policy Support, and Media Coverage**...209
Tips to Secure Funding..210
Tips for Shaping Public Policy..215
Tips for Getting Helpful Media Coverage...............................224
Summary...231

Endnotes for Part Three...232

Afterword...235
Glossary..237
References to Organizations and Agencies..............................249
Bibliography..253
Index...257

Illustrations

PAGE

i   Hope Community Mosaic Dedication (photo by Tom Borrup)

Dance Center at Penn Avenue (photo by Tom Borrup)

Girl participating in HOBT's May Day parade (photo by Tom Borrup)

Glasswork from HandMade in America (photo courtesy of HandMade in America)

iii   Hope Community participants and organizers (photo by Tom Borrup)

v   Intermedia participants playing homemade instruments at a mosaic dedication ceremony (photo by Tom Borrup)

vii   Volunteers stoking fires at a WaterFire event (photo by Thomas Payne, copyright 2005, WaterFire)

ix   Building in Lower Roxbury (photo by Tom Borrup)

xi   Providence, Rhode Island canal (photo by Tom Borrup)

xv   Downtown Lanesboro, Minnesota (photo by Tom Borrup)

The Lanesboro Museum (photo by Tom Borrup)

xvii   Milagro Center youth participants paint an art installation for the Delray Beach Cultural Loop (photo courtesy of Delray Beach Cultural Loop).

1   Potter working in HandMade in America's studio (photo courtesy of HandMade in America)

Yak puppet created by Andrew Kim for HOBT's May Day parade (photo courtesy of HOBT)

Sun puppet created by Sandy Spieler for HOBT (photo by Warwick Faraday Green, courtesy of HOBT)

Lower Roxbury building that has been renovated (photo by Tom Borrup)

3   Dance Center at Penn Avenue (photo by Tom Borrup)

Bench in front of an outdoor mural in Holyoke, MA (photo by Tom Borrup)

7   Artists for Humanity youth participant (photo courtesy of Artists for Humanity)

9   Downtown Lanesboro (photo by Tom Borrup)

13   Mohawk Theater in North Adams, MA (photo by Tom Borrup)

17   The city of Holyoke, MA's sign (photo by Tom Borrup)

Minneapolis group making community asset map (photo by Tom Borrup)

Hope Community participants and organizers (photos by Tom Borrup)

21   In the Heart of the Beast Mask and Puppet Theatre, Minneapolis, MN (photo courtesy of HOBT)

27   Loysen + Kreuthmeier Architects building on Penn Avenue (photo courtesy of Friendship Development Associates)

33   Downtown Lanesboro, MN (photo by Tom Borrup)

41   Commonweal Theatre's production of *The Trouble with Being Earnest* (photo courtesy of Commonweal Theatre)

PAGE

45   Peekskill lamppost banner created by artists Curt Belshe and Lise Prown (photo copyright 2003, Curt Belshe/Lise Prown)

60   MASS MoCA in North Adams, MA (photo by Tom Borrup)

66   Glasswork created by HandMade in America artists (photo courtesy of HandMade in America)

73   Artists for Humanity's painting studio (photo courtesy of AFH)

77   Volunteers lighting basins for WaterFire event (photo by Thomas Payne, copyright 2005, WaterFire)

87   Girl making a mask for HOBT (photo courtesy of HOBT)

91   A map of the Delray Beach Cultural Loop (courtesy of Delray Beach Cultural Loop)

98   Artists for Humanity's EpiCenter (photo courtesy of AFH)

99   Youth Radio student Oliver Rodriguez (photo by Denise Tejada, Youth Radio)

106 Hope Community's Intermedia Arts participants (photo by Tom Borrup)

120 Understanding Neighbors test dialog group (photo by Jay Brause for Out North)

135 Minneapolis group making community asset map (photo by Tom Borrup)
     HOBT's Plaza Verde (photo courtesy of HOBT)
     May Day flower bearers (masks created by Sandy Spieler, photo by Warren Hansen, courtesy of HOBT)
     Artwork created by AFH participant Silvi Naci (photo courtesy of AFH)

139 Music peer teacher Hevanya Gardeen manning the board at Youth Radio (photo by Denise Tejada, Youth Radio)

145 Downtown aerial shot of Providence, RI (photo by Thomas Payne, copyright 2003, WaterFire Providence)

153 Intermedia Arts community asset map project (photo by Tom Borrup)

167 Lanesboro museum (photo by Tom Borrup)

175 Group in Minneapolis working on a community asset map (photo by Tom Borrup)

180 Intermedia Arts community asset map hung outside (photo by Tom Borrup)

183 Hibernian Hall in the Lower Roxbury neighborhood of Boston (photo by Lolita Parker, Jr.)

193 The city of Madison, MN's sign (photo by C. Edwards Studio, Inc., courtesy of Madison Area Chamber of Commerce)

195 Community members painting doors for the Delray Beach Cultural Loop (photo courtesy of Delray Beach Cultural Loop)

197 Plan for Southgate Linear Park (illustration courtesy of James Shermer and the Broward Cultural Division)

209 Mother and daughter decked out for HOBT's May Day parade (photo courtesy of HOBT)

217 Community planning meeting in East Windsor, CT (photo by Tom Borrup)

225 Groundbreaking event for HOBT's Plaza Verde (photo by Tom Borrup)

235 Willmar, Minnesota's downtown redesign project (photo by Tom Borrup)
     Yak puppet created by Andrew Kim for HOBT's May Day parade (photo courtesy of HOBT)

237 Shop in Lanesboro that sells local products (photo by Tom Borrup)

Foreword

TEN YEARS AGO Partners for Livable Communities published its pioneering work *Culture Builds Community,* authored by Kathy Booth. Since then the field of culture and community development has moved considerably. There is strong recognition of asset-based community development, a concept pioneered by Jody Kretzmann and John McKnight that stresses that artists, artisans, and cultural resources are key elements of a community and need to be marshaled and worked with for community improvement.

The work of Bill Strickland at Manchester Craftsman's Guild and Bidwell Training Center, supported in part by the Ford Foundation, showed other community development corporations the importance of having a cultural strategy as part of a group's community mission. The research of Shirley Brice-Heath of the Carnegie Foundation of Education showed the relationship between after-school and out-of-school cultural mentoring programs and entrepreneurial training agendas for young people, with young people ultimately becoming the trainers and mentors themselves. From these examples, it is evident that culture is a building block—be it for improving the lives of at-risk youth, community organizing, or economic development—and a source of pride for diverse communities across the cities, towns, and villages of America.

Partners for Livable Communities is pleased to collaborate with Fieldstone Alliance and with Tom Borrup in preparing not simply an update of *Culture Builds Community*, but a new work based on Tom's long experience and background. We hope *The Creative Community Builder's Handbook* will find an audience among the community development professionals of America; among municipal leaders charged with community improvement; among arts councils; among individual artists who seek credence for their community agenda; among community foundations, United Ways, and service agencies; and among community activists who are looking for new tools for making their communities more satisfying places in which to live. I urge you to not only read this book but also to implement its ideas as you seek to improve your community.

Robert McNulty,
Founder and CEO, Partners for Livable Communities, Washington, DC
May 2006

Author's Acknowledgments

THE INSPIRATION FOR THIS BOOK comes from many sources, most notably the work of artists and community builders, some of whom are included in this book. Ironically, two of the most noteworthy of these artists, Rick Lowe, creator of Project Row Houses in Houston, and Lily Yeh, founder of the Village of Arts and Humanities in Philadelphia, are not included. What they have done is far too wonderful and complex. Their vision, commitment, and skills require and deserve books of their own. More recently, the remarkable work of community organizer Daniel Ross at Nuestras Raices in Holyoke, Massachusetts, and the writing of Britain's Charles Landry have taught me much about the power of culture to leverage economic, physical, spiritual, and political change.

My twenty-two years as executive director of Intermedia Arts in Minneapolis provided many lessons and much insight into building communities around culture and in seeing ways for the arts to catalyze change. Thanks to all the staff and board members there, especially longtime colleagues and collaborators Sandy Agustin (now artistic director), René Ford (former board chair), and Valerie Lee. People who arrived on the scene there in later years and who reinforced my burgeoning interests in community building include Bill Cleveland, Bill Morrish, and Erik Takeshita. Longer-term partners in crime are too numerous to mention, but I do want to acknowledge Ta-coumba Aiken, Cindy Gehrig, Seitu Jones, Marilyn Lindstrom, Beni Matías, Wendy Morris, David Mura, Alexs Pate, Mona Smith, and Sandy Spieler, all of whom showed me multiple ways artists bring about change in lives and communities.

Two incredible opportunities in recent years propelled me to new horizons: a Leadership Initiatives in Neighborhoods grant from St. Paul Travelers and a Knight Fellowship in Community Building at the University of Miami School of Architecture. Both allowed me to travel and meet so many people doing remarkable work. Chuck Bohl, Lizz Plater-Zyberk, and Andrea Gollin, at the School, as well as all the Fellows in the Knight Program provided rigorous exposure to many of the elements that go into making great "places" where communities can flourish.

This book is dedicated to my mother, Audrey C. Borrup-Dunham, and to the memory of my father, Roger Borrup. Much gratitude also goes to my partner, Harry Waters Jr., a theater artist and teacher of renown, who indulged my repeated absences for research and writing.

This book is truly possible thanks to the generous support of Neal Cuthbert and Rip Rapson at the McKnight Foundation, wonderful people and a great institution that has provided two decades of support for my work.

I must thank John McKnight (no relation to the Foundation) and Jody Kretzmann, visionaries in asset-based community development, whose work and workshops influenced me profoundly. It was at a 2003 conference in Chicago that Jody suggested I take my idea for a book to Wilder Publishing (now Fieldstone Alliance). Asset-based work—so central to this book—first came into practical understanding and application for me through the work of VOICE in Phillips, a three-year neighborhood-based project in Minneapolis. Thanks to Deb Rodgers and all my colleagues at VOICE, especially those at Hope Community.

My thanks and praise go to Partners for Livable Communities, whose concurrent idea for a book fit so naturally with mine. Penny Cuff and Bob McNulty provided enormous help in shaping this book's outline and in choosing the case studies. Their phenomenal work over the past thirty years deserves even wider recognition. Staff there were incredibly helpful and guided me to so much useful information.

There are many remarkable colleagues with whom I've traveled this path over the years and from whom I've learned so much. They include amazing pioneers, thinkers, and writers Linda Burham and Steve Durland at Community Arts Network and consultant/writers Arlene Goldbard and Don Adams; also Miguel Garcia at the Ford Foundation for his risktaking, innovative funding, and his trust in me, and Jeremy Liu at Asian Community Development for his out-of-the-box thinking and action. Other colleagues and friends who have added much to my thinking include Maribel Alvarez, Caron Atlas, Phyllis Blyweiss, Claudine Brown, Bill Bulick, Ron Chew, Tim Collins, Dee Davis, Kathie deNobriga, Juanita Espinosa, Maryo Gaard Ewell, Juana Guzmán, Maria-Rosario Jackson, Pam Korza, Brad Lander, Ann Markusen, Libby Maynard, Nick Rabkin, Brendan Rawson, Barbara Schaffer-Bacon, Shirley Sneve, and George Sutton. Although I've never met her, I must pay homage to the legendary urban thinker and fascinating economist, Jane Jacobs.

I also want to acknowledge the wonderful work of Fred Kent and his team at Project for Public Spaces, and Fred's mentor, the late William (Holly) Whyte, whom I saw make a wacky presentation at a conference at Temple University thirty years ago. Whyte repeatedly filmed people crossing busy New York intersections holding newspapers wide open in front of them. The presentation made little sense, but I could never get it out of my mind.

My focus and creative energy were enabled by the place where I did the majority of the writing and editing for this book, and yet, ironically, the community is not profiled here. South Beach, a small and compact part of Florida's Miami Beach, is a walkable, 24/7, cosmopolitan community like no other. It is very much a successful "place" because of culture, the arts, and the utilization of historic and natural assets. It exemplifies nearly all the ideas I've written about.

Thanks to all the gracious people across the United States and United Kingdom who took meetings with me, provided information, and indulged my dropping in, pestering them with questions, and pointing a camera around.

Much thanks to the thoughtful manuscript reviewers for their challenging suggestions and encouragement. They include Kathy Booth, Bill Bulick, Mary Keefe, Brad Lander, Brandee McHale, Wendy Morris, Tracy Taft, Erik Takeshita, and Mike Temali. Thanks to graduate student Sarah Damberger for assistance with case study summaries.

Also thanks to Ron McKinley, formerly with St. Paul Travelers and Wilder Center for Communities, for supporting my work and recommending this project. Finally, thanks to Vince Hyman, editor and publishing director, for his support and hard work from the very first stages of the project, and to everyone at Fieldstone Alliance.

Even though the ink is now dry, please consider this a work in progress and send me your comments and ideas!

Tom Borrup

Creative Community Building

COMMUNITY BUILDING is a creative and interdisciplinary activity. It requires new ways of working across established professions. Some individuals who claim the title of community builder construct roads, houses, and other infrastructure. They make places in which communities exist. People who repair the psychological and physical damage wrought by economic and environmental exploitation, racism, and hopelessness may call their work community building. Other individuals nurture small businesses, nonprofits, and civic institutions or put together networks of mutual support for learning, enrichment, and enjoyment and call those efforts community building.

They are *all* community builders, all contributing essential parts of a whole. Unfortunately, it is unusual for these talented and committed people to sit at the same table, let alone join in a common, coordinated agenda or strategy. This absence of integrated strategies tends to perpetuate or even expand the social and economic inequities that plague our cities and towns.

The term *creative community building* describes efforts to weave multiple endeavors and professions into the never-ending work of building and rebuilding the social, civic, physical, economic, and spiritual fabrics of communities. Creative community building engages the cultural and creative energies inherent in every person and every place.

We are all creative. We each see the world with unique perceptive and interpretive powers. We each possess special skills and professional practices that, in isolation, do not build healthy communities. The most successful community building comes from the synthesis of various fields and their respective best practices. Creative community building brings these practices together around values that lead to equitable and sustainable places, and around respect for human cultures and the creativity in everyone.

Because so many fields of endeavor and study have become increasingly specialized, the urgency for community builders to cross boundaries and re-invent their work is greater than ever. The terms *creative community building* and *creative community builder* describe these cross-disciplinary activities and the visionaries who break the rules to forge new ways to create and repair communities.

Until recently, most professionals involved in different dimensions of community building have not deliberately or systematically looked to the sources of creativity within a community to improve that community's welfare. By applying the practices of asset-based community development,* more and more community builders are beginning to integrate the knowledge and expertise that have evolved in disparate, specialized fields—including community development, arts and culture, planning and design, citizen participation, and the like—into the new practice of creative community building.

This book highlights the innovations and work of creative community builders. It is designed to provide practitioners in the various aspects of policymaking, community planning, housing development, and economic re-revitalization with a more complete understanding of how creative, culturally based projects have played catalytic roles in community change. Finally, it outlines specific steps and practices that individuals or groups can follow to engage in creative community building. By reflecting upon successful efforts and describing a step-by-step planning process, this book helps readers devise and implement strategies to build on the assets and unique qualities of their own communities.

How to Use This Handbook

This book provides community leaders with new tools to bring about economic, social, and physical revitalization of their communities. It will help you identify assets already existing in your community and understand how they can be powerful resources for change.

The first part of the book summarizes emerging ideas behind culturally driven community development, or creative community building. It explains key principles that underlie this work. These principles will help you argue the case for creative community building. Part 1 also reviews research that reinforces long-held convictions that art and culture have great value in community building. These studies reveal ways to understand the impact of culture and the arts on the well-being of communities and ways culture can be a change agent.

Part 2 of the book discusses ten strategies for community revitalization. Each strategy is illustrated by two short case studies. These twenty stories come from a variety of cities, small towns, and neighborhoods across the United States. This section examines how leaders in these places, from all walks of

---

* Asset-based community development is described in Chapter 4.

life, brought about significant improvement in the economic, social, and civic life of their communities.

These examples were chosen to demonstrate how creative community building ideas and strategies work in a variety of geographic regions and communities, how they originate from different kinds of organizations, and how they include a range of activities. The unifying principle is that they are all rooted in the culture(s) of their special place and that they tap the creativity and entrepreneurial nature of artists, businesspeople, municipal officials, community developers, youth, and people of all cultural backgrounds. All these projects are built upon, and have as a central component, cultural and creative energies derived from *within* their communities.

The Milagro Center, a youth arts organization in the Delray Beach community, enlisted the help of some of their students to decorate the "Milagro House," an art installation that was included in the Delray Beach Cultural Loop.

Leaders of the profiled projects were able to see the possibilities and rally *existing* assets or resources. They did not act alone; nor did their efforts represent a panacea for the community's problems. They emboldened the spirit of their respective places, coalesced visions, energies, and resources, and catalyzed real long-term change in ways that often started small and then reverberated outward. This range of examples will provide you, the reader, with a menu of things that are possible and stimulate you to bring positive change to your community. Better yet, it may help you see new opportunities in projects that are already under way.

These examples are followed in Part 3 with a step-by-step guide to assessing, planning, and implementing creative community building projects. Part 3 outlines five major steps, organized one to a chapter:

> Step 1 (Chapter 4): Assess Your Situation and Goals
>
> Step 2 (Chapter 5): Identify and Recruit Effective Partners
>
> Step 3 (Chapter 6): Map Values, Strengths, Assets, and History
>
> Step 4 (Chapter 7): Focus on Your Key Asset, Vision, Identity, and Core Strategies
>
> Step 5 (Chapter 8): Craft a Plan That Brings the Identity to Life

These steps take you through the process of bringing other community builders together around a planning table. You will see how to convert community assets into a community identity and how to develop strategies that build upon the strengths and unique qualities of your place. This handbook includes helpful worksheets to walk you through key steps, and it follows a hypothetical community as it goes through the creative process.

The last chapter of the book includes important tips for securing the funding, public policy support, and media coverage you'll need to make the project a success.

All sections of the book include resources on the topics addressed, as well as footnotes that are rich with information. A list of additional resources—including a glossary, books, web sites, organizations, and research studies—appears at the end of the book.

By understanding the theoretical context (Part 1), learning from case studies (Part 2), and following the five steps (Part 3), the reader will be able to build a more vibrant, creative, and equitable community. The projects or activities highlighted are not meant for replication but as examples of how some creative community builders were able to identify and leverage the unique character and creative capacities of people and of place.

The book is designed for professionals, volunteers, community leaders, and others involved in community planning, architecture, urban and town design, housing, economic and community development, and the fields of art and culture. Because these professions or sectors often speak different "languages," this book attempts to use terminology and approaches that bridge work and interests. The goal is to foster coordinated action and build communities that are more culturally and socially inclusive, economically sustainable and just, and aesthetically welcoming, and that exhibit high levels of civic engagement.

The bottom line of the work described herein is that it builds upon a sense of mutual respect, common purpose, and belief in possibility. From there it propels positive change in very real ways.

PART ONE
Ideas Behind This Book

PART ONE provides a brief overview and analysis of work by researchers, practitioners, and theorists who have addressed one or more dimensions of community building. It explains some of the thinking that motivated this book, and the assumptions used to describe and analyze the community building stories and steps in Parts 2 and 3. The assumptions, interpretations, and assertions come from my thirty years of experience in the practice and observation of community-based social change work. While the research presented in Part 1 reinforces these assumptions, it is through the twenty case studies presented in Part 2 that the case for creative community building is truly made.

As these examples show, important, although often not well understood, relationships exist among the components of communities—including economic drivers, physical infrastructure, health and well-being dimensions, cultural and spiritual activities, and civic engagement. Together they form an "ecosystem" that must be in balance to be sustainable. The creative community builders described have rewoven these elements to make places more balanced and healthy. They have used culture and creativity as a glue to bind together people, ideas, and enterprises and institutions to enable this ecosystem to function.

An increasing number of researchers and writers in fields including economics, social sciences, wellness, and human development have examined the influence of culture and the arts in the formation of healthy individuals, communities, and economies.* Chapter 1 distills some of this research to provide you with a theoretical background and practical information for better comprehending creative community building—and to provide you with a rationale for convincing others to participate in the effort.

---

* There is a large body of work exploring human and educational development and the arts—topics that are related and important. This book focuses on social, civic, and economic thinking and research. For a comprehensive survey of contemporary research in many of these fields, see Kevin F. McCarthy et al., *Gifts of the Muse: Reframing the Debate About the Benefits of the Arts* (Santa Monica, CA: RAND Corporation, 2004).

CHAPTER 1

The Role of Culture in Community Building

BUILDING AND REBUILDING the physical, economic, and social infrastructures of communities large and small has been the object and passion of committed and creative leaders for millennia. In the Americas, anthropologists and historians have documented how the contributions of Native peoples together with those of explorers, colonizers, and immigrants have resulted in what we now consider contemporary civic and political infrastructure.[1] This blending of cultures and traditions brought about exemplary and previously unseen hybrids. The same process continues today with each new immigrant and each new cultural and technological innovation.

By the early nineteenth century, a widespread network of social and civic groups had developed in the United States—a *culture* of mutual aid societies—that demonstrated a remarkable capacity and resilience. French visitor and author Alexis de Tocqueville was profoundly impressed by what he saw. He wrote during his now famous tour of the United States, "Americans of all ages, all stations in life, and all types of disposition are forever forming associations. There are not only commercial and industrial associations in which all take part, but others of a thousand different types—religious, moral, serious, futile, very general and very limited, immensely large and very minute."[2]

In recent decades, others have documented and offered theories about the decline and revival of the social and civic fabric in the United States. While some of their thinking has been used in formulating this book, the most important information comes from the stories of contemporary creative community builders. Their work has served to revive and enrich community life in remarkable ways. They would not only be among de Tocqueville's examples if he were traveling today, they would surpass them. They essentially represent associations of associations—bringing together diverse people and efforts in creative new ways across sectors, professions, and industries to reinvigorate places that had gone stale or were facing complex new challenges.

Community, Culture, Art, Economics, and "Place"

Community is an elusive term. For purposes of this book, the word will refer to the people and the natural and built environments within a geographically defined area. We will look only at "place-based" communities. While this could mean much the same as "neighborhood," "community" is more inclusive of the social, civic, and economic bonds, in addition to the physical bonds, among people who reside, work, or otherwise consider themselves part of a geographic place. It includes their common identity. It may be rural, suburban, small town, or densely urban. It may be one hundred square miles or ten city blocks. What's important is that the place has—or seeks—identity as a community, and has reason to coalesce around common interests.

"Community is something we do together. It's not just a container," said sociologist David Brain.[3] Communities are complex. After all, they're made up of people. The infrastructure, including water, sewer, roads, electricity, and housing, provides an essential shell within which people live. Education, recreation, healthcare, retail business, employment, and other services are some of the things we do together to sustain livelihoods and meet daily needs. However, what makes a community "work," in every respect, is its culture and its governance—the shared understandings and expectations that people have of themselves, each other, and their collective endeavors—the things that make it possible for people to work together.

Culture and art

Culture has been defined as the "values, attitudes, beliefs, orientations, and underlying assumptions" that exist among people.[4] This broad definition is an important place to begin. The assumptions shared by people vary from place to place. As more local communities become global microcosms, it's increasingly crucial to recognize the many and varied assumptions held by people who share a place.

Many people, unfortunately, associate the term *culture* with a sense of refinement—something that's extra or special, above and beyond daily necessities. It is often associated with "art"—the work of highly skilled artists and the institutions that promote it as a commodity. The notion that some people "have" culture and others are "lacking" culture is preposterous. Everyone has, and is part of, a culture, or multiple cultures. As such they carry distinct assumptions, traditions, and behaviors that embody the best and the worst of social practices.

The notion that some people "have" culture and others are "lacking" culture is preposterous. Everyone has, and is part of, a culture, or multiple cultures.

The distinction between "art" and "culture" is important here. This book uses both words and often in tandem. Art refers to the results of one's labor or the outward expressions of people from one of the many cultures on the planet. To some people, art is a more refined form of expression practiced in a milieu of abundance. To others, it is the result of everyday life. In fact, *art* is a word and concept that doesn't even exist in some languages. Art can be both object and act, precious and routine. It is practiced individually and collectively. This book uses *art* inclusively to describe the many manifestations of creativity.

This book also uses *culture* in its broadest meaning: Culture describes the human ability to communicate and to navigate the natural and social environment together. It can be compared to the operating system of a computer.[5] Computers have sophisticated software programs for word processing, accounting, data management, and the like. None of them, however, will work without an operating system, the special, underlying code or common language that enables all the parts and all the functional programs to talk to one another and to flow from chip to chip, and from disk to screen.

Without an operating system there's chaos. In this role, culture provides people and organizations with the capacity to communicate and function. However, we know there are different operating systems, like different cultures, and, while operating systems share many commonalities, they don't always work together without some means of translating their signals. Creative community building tries to bridge the different operating systems or cultures, whether they be rooted in different professions or economic sectors, or in different ethnic or regional backgrounds.

This book does not endeavor to make everyone function on the same operating system, speak the same language, share the same values, or exhibit uniform behaviors. Quite the contrary. Creative community building recognizes that there are many variations, while furthering the ongoing effort to find and build common ground. It's about the flourishing and celebrating of infinite variety, while providing spatial and conceptual ground on which cooperation can germinate. It attempts to help communities work better, and especially to support and connect the work of community builders. Creative community builders employ tools, strategies, and ways of thinking that engage people on the cultural or the operating system level. In so doing, they respect individuality and celebrate what makes each community and each individual within it special.

The central conservative truth is that it is culture, not politics, that determines the success of a society. The central liberal truth is that politics can change a culture and save it from itself.

— Daniel Patrick Moynihan[6]

Culture and economics

Observers of human progress from various disciplines have cited innate behaviors such as "aesthetic curiosity" or "aesthetic appreciation" or the "dynamic tension between different cultural groups" to explain how people bridge differences, innovate, and create goods and ideas that appeal to wider markets. Economist and urbanist Jane Jacobs cites such unique human traits as the fuel that propels some cities and regions over others.[7]

Similarly, anthropologist Jack Weatherford believes dynamic energy or "tension" has fostered innovation in societies across the globe over the past ten thousand years. He asserts that aesthetic curiosity is stimulated in places where cultures "collide," or come into contact, whether through trade, war, exploration, or accident.[8]

More recent and growing research indicates that culture and cultural activities profoundly impact the economic and social vitality of communities. Cultural practices, and institutions that house or sponsor them, have been part of the community building process for centuries. Only recently have they come under serious study as part of the economic *and* social underpinnings of communities. Two of the more well-known authors in the fields of economics and social development since the late 1990s include Richard Florida and Robert Putnam. While these two thinkers disagree on what constitutes a "successful" community, they are on the same page with regard to the overlooked role of culture and art.

Florida, an economist, assesses cities and regions based on their economic output. In today's economy he claims that it is the presence of a critical mass of workers who fit his definition of the "creative class" that fuels economic engines. He asserts that creative-class workers are not attracted to places by jobs but by whether or not a city or town is a cool place to live. The jobs, he says, follow or are created by them. He cites characteristics of tolerance, cultural activity, and social climate as key to attracting and retaining productive, creative workers. In turn, he argues, this results in more competitive industries.[9]

Putnam, a social scientist, argues that the well-being of a city or region pivots on the ability of people to interact constructively around mutual interests. He measures this through a community's level of "social capital." He adds two different labels to this term. The first describes the social connectedness of people across cultures, ages, and other divides (what he calls "bridging social capital"). The second describes the connections between people who are alike and who organize to advance their well-being ("bonding social capital").[10]

Florida makes the case that an active and participatory cultural scene is essential to a strong, creative economy—especially those more "bohemian" in character who offer diverse, edgy arts, music, film, food, and entertainment. Larger, more passive forms of cultural consumption or entertainment are of less interest to the creative class, he says. Putnam makes a similar case but with a different outcome. He says that an active cultural environment, including activities that help people better share their cultures and stories, is one of the best ways people develop their capacity to cooperate and build social and civic connections.[11]

For centuries, cities across the globe have considered the size, quality, and reputation of their major cultural institutions as indicators and symbols of their importance. During the past two decades, architectural design has taken on a seemingly inordinate level of significance. Nonetheless, these edifices have altered not only the image of some places but also their tourist trade, general economy, and world standing. Paris' Eiffel Tower, Sydney's Opera House, Bilbao's Guggenheim, and the proposed and, as of this writing, hotly debated Freedom Tower in Lower Manhattan serve as symbols to elevate those places to international standing. At the beginning of the twenty-first century, cities are fiercely competing to engage world-famous architects to create signature buildings generally for cultural institutions.

Artists for Humanity youth participant, Cassandra Lattimore, working on a painting.

Creative people and iconic institutions may help cities thrive in even more profound ways. Economist Ann Markusen draws a connection between the presence and influences of thriving artist communities with successful industries of all types. She argues that traditional studies of the economic impact of the arts underestimate the full contribution an artistic community makes to a regional economy. She says they fail to trace the many ways in which creative talent contributes to productivity.[12]

Markusen counters the simplistic view of the arts as a consequence of, or even a parasite on, a successful business community. She demonstrates that productivity and earnings in a regional economy rise in correlation to the number of artists within its boundaries, applying the phrase "artistic dividend." She claims that artists are more cause than result of a successful economy. While Florida's creative class is a more broadly defined group, he and Markusen come to similar conclusions about the importance of creative individuals—and environments that attract and stimulate them—to economic growth.

Thinkers in the arena of global economics and governance have also debated the influences of culture—in its broader definition—on the formation and success of large versus small business enterprises and on democratic versus autocratic political institutions. Many attribute the receptivity or resistance to capitalism and democracy to regional culture and patterns of socialization across the globe. Countries with cultures that place family bonds above all other social relations, for instance, have difficulty forming large corporate enterprises. Meanwhile, societies that have high self-expression values are stable democracies, while societies that rank low on such values have authoritarian governments.[13]

Economist Max Weber in 1904 first wrote about the relationship between capitalism and Protestant religious values and is generally credited with founding the line of thinking that connects culture with economics and politics.[14] Social scientist and author Francis Fukuyama more recently points out that cultures in which family and kinship provide the primary orientation to sociability have great difficulty creating large, durable economic organizations, while cultures inclined toward voluntary associations create large economic organizations spontaneously—like those de Tocqueville saw in the United States in the 1830s.[15]

Managers of large business enterprises have appreciated the significance of "organizational culture" for several decades. Corporations, businesses, public agencies, and nonprofits of any size succeed or fail based on the "culture" the leadership is able, or unable, to instill or transform. Business guru Michael E. Porter pushes this thinking beyond the walls of the corporation in his observations of the competitive position of different global regions. "The question is not whether culture has a role but how to understand this role in the context of the broader determinants of prosperity," he writes.[16]

> A culture persists in time only to the degree it is inventing, creating, and dynamically evolving in a way that promotes the production of ideas across all social classes and groups.
>
> —Shalini Venturelli[17]

The creative economy

The term *creative economy* came into more popular use in the 1990s as "creative-sector" industries grew in the so-called postindustrial era. In the for-profit arena, these industries have typically included advertising, media, entertainment, and the design professions, including product, fashion, and packaging design. In the nonprofit sector, they include media producers and performers, as well as entities that preserve and showcase culture, such as art and history museums. These types of industries have grown in size at a faster rate than others since the 1990s, and their importance in shaping and propelling other economic sectors has become clearer.

Since 2000, creative communities, creative workforces, and other dimensions of the creative economy have also come into sharper focus. The New England Council, an association representing major business concerns in that region, issued a report that year examining the nature of this emerging sector and charting the relative size and remarkable growth of this creative economy. The council's report acknowledged the considerable contribution made by the arts industry to "nurturing innovation, developing a skilled workforce, and helping businesses remain competitive."[18]

This heightened awareness of the size and importance of creative industries and creative workers has caused cities, states, philanthropies, and businesses to assess and advocate strengthening this sector and its support systems.

Key elements of this support system include networks of small, medium, and large cultural organizations, bohemian neighborhoods, active artist communities, and the cultural and social values that appeal to diverse, talented entrepreneurs and workers. Educational opportunities that stress the use of the imagination are also critical to equip, train, and stimulate creative workers and thinkers.

Creative community building is more than installing or building a creative economy. It includes and recognizes value in creative "industries" but goes beyond that, finding the broader identity of place and connecting people across sectors.

Culture creates "place"

Some professionals involved in the design of community infrastructure—from streets and sidewalks to residential and commercial buildings, plazas, and the like—stress the often-overlooked impact of architecture and design on the ability of people to interact and function efficiently in social and civic settings. "We shape our cities and then our cities shape us," assert the authors of *Suburban Nation*.[19]

In his groundbreaking work, *The Organization Man*, William H. Whyte observed and documented a virtual encyclopedia of behaviors brought on by the structure and expectations (or culture) of business organizations during the 1950s.[20] Whyte then turned his attention for the remainder of his life to observing human behaviors in urban settings and how design and policies that regulate spaces affect social behaviors. Whyte asserted that crowded, pedestrian-friendly spaces are safer and more economically productive and contribute more to healthy civic communities.[21] Cities or other places that are unwelcoming and have only scattered human activity, are less so.

Root River State Trail, in southeastern Minnesota, is forty-two miles of trail for bicyclists, hikers, and cross-country skiers. It connects six communities including Lanesboro, MN.

Design professionals have a big impact on the spaces that shape communities. Some observers credit design methods popular since World War II, and under the influence of automobiles, for the decay in social capital. "The average American, when placed behind the wheel of a car, ceases to be a citizen and becomes instead a *motorist*," write Elizabeth Plater-Zyberk and her colleagues. "As a motorist, you cannot get to know your neighbor, because the prevailing relationship is competitive."[22]

Close-knit and smaller-scale towns and cities of the past may have provided more potential for collective action and connections among people of different economic and social classes. However, the United States is now more typified by suburban sprawl and economic segregation than by walkable town centers with a wide mix of people.

Aesthetic preferences, fear of others, and concentration of single uses such as housing, retail, work, and recreation, along with dependence on automobiles, have created a new culture and new social structures and behaviors. Because design, placemaking, and human cultures are so intertwined, they can be difficult to unravel—and it is therefore difficult to know where to begin to make change.

Culture, Social Change, and Community Development

Social relationships and networks are built and evolve in a variety of ways. And, they are complex. Communities large and small are increasingly made up of a mixture of immigrants from around the world, long-term residents, and people of different faiths, lifestyles, and economic classes. Initial connections are often made through economic transactions in marketplaces in pursuit of basic goods and services. But relationships that are meaningful and sustainable require relating on a level that is cultural—acknowledging and respecting the other person's values, beliefs, aspirations, and ways of understanding the world. Such connection does not require giving up one's own identity and values, nor asking anyone else to do so. Instead, connection means learning to live and work side by side as partners in the civic enterprise.

Finding new norms and cooperative ways of working across cultural boundaries is difficult, but success results in a society that is more innovative, productive, and just. Some professionals in the community development and social change fields have come to address culture head on.

"As community builders, understanding culture is our business. Whether you live in central Kansas or New York City, whether you live in Miami, Nevada, or the Pacific Northwest, you are working with and establishing relationships with people—people who *all* have cultures," states *The Community Tool Box*, a resource designed to assist organizers and community development professionals.*

Some of the most successful strategies for establishing understanding and connection are through the medium of cultural and artistic activities. Experiencing and appreciating the expressions of another's culture, and being able to communicate on a deeper level, is the most profound way to understand and participate in substantive dialog.**

---

* *The Community Tool Box* (www.ctb.ku.edu) is a project of the Work Group on Health Promotion and Community Development at the University of Kansas at Lawrence. It provides a detailed curriculum for enhancing cultural competence—nurturing the tools to respectfully approach, enter, and develop an understanding of other cultures.

** For an extensive body of practice in civic dialogue stimulated by art and cultural practices, see Animating Democracy, a project of Americans for the Arts. www.animatingdemocracy.org.

Economic developers, social change activists, and community builders of all kinds cannot hope for much lasting success without cultural understanding and cultural strategies. This includes the most difficult culture to observe and comprehend—your own! Understanding and having a vocabulary to talk critically and nondefensively about your own cultural makeup is essential in order to meet others on equal ground.

Members of extended families, tribes, or tight-knit communities typically take common values, vocabularies, and levels of trust for granted. Anglo Americans, who comprise a robustly empowered (albeit shrinking) group in the United States, have tended to take for granted their way of communicating, understanding, and organizing the world. Given a rapidly changing population in most urban, suburban, and rural settings, culturally based interactions and planning are increasingly important. The exclusion of diverse ideas (or lack of opportunities to express them) blocks real progress. The exchange of ideas and the creative expressions of cultures propel innovation and forward movement in all fields.

How culture and the arts impact communities

In the late 1990s, the Urban Institute in Washington, DC, began an extensive project to measure the variety of impacts of culture and the arts in community building. The Arts and Culture Indicators in Community Building Project (ACIP) has developed a wide body of evidence from which to create a methodology for measuring these impacts.[23] Its purpose is to gain a better understanding of how arts and cultural activities affect many dimensions of communities. Heretofore, the absence of such measuring tools has made it difficult to build a strong case for investment in arts and culture in community building.

Other studies in several U.S. cities consistently conclude that cultural organizations, particularly small, community-based cultural groups, have far greater impact than their size would suggest—and that this impact is felt in areas not typically associated with the arts.

A University of Pennsylvania study found that small arts groups in neighborhoods had multiple positive effects.* Areas with higher levels of cultural activity—in both poor and middle-class neighborhoods—experienced a positive impact on school truancy, youth delinquency, civic engagement, teen pregnancy, and a host of other factors associated with community well-being. These same researchers also cited positive relationships between arts participation and population stability and real estate values. They assert that small cultural groups are typically more important to communities and to revitalization of neighborhoods than major institutions.[24]

---

* Mark J. Stern, professor of social welfare and history at the University of Pennsylvania, and urban planner Susan Siefert have studied community-based arts groups for more than ten years through the Social Impact of the Arts Project (SIAP). www.sp2.upenn.edu/SIAP.

The activities of small cultural groups stimulate community revitalization less through direct economic impact and more through building the social connections between people. They motivate neighbors and help them visualize and make changes in their community. They increase connections among neighborhoods of different ethnic and economic groups. Community arts organizations stimulate broader civic engagement, expand residents' sense of efficacy, and strengthen the bridges between neighborhoods.

A Chicago-based study in 2003 also examined the social and economic activity that goes on around cultural organizations. It found that community-based arts organizations leveraged a variety of relationships, capacities, and activities in unusually effective ways. The study found that cultural organizations had three overarching results: they build social relationships, enable problem solving, and provide access to resources.[25]

This Chicago study concluded that the presence and work of small cultural groups promote neighborhood stability, enable a sense of belonging, create productive uses of underutilized spaces, create links to nonlocal resources, provide space for cross-cultural dialogue, and provide a safe haven and opportunities to learn new skills. It also found that these arts programs engage neighbors in creative problem solving, engage youth as citizens, develop leadership and decision-making skills, build cultural identities and positive relationships among neighborhood groups, build knowledge across cultural boundaries, and build understanding and engagement in democratic processes.

In a 2003 survey of activities that contribute to building social capital, Robert Putnam and Lewis Feldstein arrived at similar conclusions. "We believe that the arts represent perhaps the most significant underutilized forum for rebuilding community in America." They assert that America's cultural institutions and the people who work in them have much potential to "create opportunities for political expression, community dialogue, shared cultural experiences and civic work—all with an eye toward making citizen participation fun."[26]

Smaller-scale community arts organizations and the inclusion of artists in community planning and development stimulate participatory group practices and new ways of thinking. Putnam and Feldstein contend that these kinds of cultural activities create "safe" space around potentially hot issues and provide "practice" in the experience of citizenship.

The intersection of culture and community development

The economic, social, physical, and civic dimensions of community building are equally important and interrelated—in fact, inseparable. This interrelationship is increasingly being recognized by professionals in community and economic development. Over the past thirty-five years, the field of community development has focused on construction and management of low- and mixed-income housing, job training or workforce development, commercial real estate development, and small business startup and incubation. Community development organizations sometimes operate youth development, health, sports and recreation, family counseling, human services, and—in rare instances—cultural programs.

The field typically includes planners and trainers, housing, real estate, and economic development specialists, and community organizers and advocates. They generally function through community development corporations (CDCs). These organizations depend largely on government, philanthropic, and corporate support, and they have become successful in building and managing housing and commercial real estate and in replicating other economic development models. Many CDCs accrue significant portfolios of real estate assets and are expert at property and small-business development.

In North Adams, the Massachusetts Museum of Contemporary Art was created through dynamic relationships built between many organizations. These relationships have stimulated the launch of creative economy enterprises.

Creative community building borrows from these and other areas of professional endeavor at the places where they intersect and share values. A 2002 report by New York's Center for an Urban Future saw potential in this effort. It called for integrating cultural and business development, asserting that the two had the greatest impact when they worked side by side. However, the researchers also reported rarely finding such coordination. They wrote, "In our survey of over 150 [New York City–based] economic and community development organizations, only six were involved in efforts that directly linked the arts with business."[27]

The Ford Foundation, together with a team of leaders in the culture and community development fields, looked at innovative community development strategies during 2002 and 2003 and both years came up with the same findings.[28] They observed that art and culture organizations support community involvement and participation, increase the potential for people to understand themselves and change how they see the world, and bolster community pride and identity. They also saw that the arts serve to improve derelict buildings, preserve cultural heritage, transmit values and history, bridge cultural, ethnic, and racial boundaries, and stimulate economic development.

The foundation study found that practitioners in distressed communities have successfully used arts and culture as part of community development strategies—but that community development and arts organizations most often were disparate and isolated from one another. The study identified an important "synergistic relationship" but that it is rarely acknowledged or exploited.

The stories in Part 2 and planning method in Part 3 show how some organizations have created this synergy and bridged these worlds—and how you might do the same. Only in doing so can you bring all the assets available to your community to the task of community building—including the many assets that are evident and those previously excluded or unseen.

Endnotes for Part One

[1] Jack Weatherford, *Indian Givers: How the Indians of the Americas Transformed the World* (New York: Ballantine Books, 1988) and *Native Roots: How the Indians Enriched America* (New York: Ballantine Books, 1991).

[2] Alexis de Tocqueville, *Democracy in America* (New York: Bantam Dell, 1835).

[3] David Brain, "Placemaking and Community Building," *Presentation at the University of Miami School of Architecture* (Coral Gables, FL: March 2004).

[4] Samuel P. Huntington and Lawrence E. Harrison, eds., *Culture Matters: How Values Shape Human Progress* (New York: Basic Books, 2000), xv.

[5] Don Adams and Arlene Goldbard, *Community, Culture and Globalization* (New York: The Rockefeller Foundation, 2002).

[6] As quoted by Huntington and Harrison, *Culture Matters*, xiv.

[7] Jane Jacobs, *Cities and the Wealth of Nations* (New York: Vintage Books, 1984), 222.

[8] Jack Weatherford, *Savages and Civilization* (New York: Fawcett Columbine, 1994), 11.

[9] Richard Florida, *The Rise of the Creative Class and How It's Transforming Work, Leisure, Community and Everyday Life* (New York: Basic Books, 2002).

[10] Robert D. Putnam, *Bowling Alone: The Collapse and Revival of American Community* (New York: Touchstone, 2000), 22–24.

[11] Robert D. Putnam and Lewis M. Feldstein, *Better Together: Restoring the American Community* (New York: Simon & Schuster, 2003), 10.

[12] Ann Markusen and David King, "The Artistic Dividend: The Arts' Hidden Contribution to Regional Development," University of Minnesota, 2003. www.hhh.umn.edu/img/assets/6158/artistic_dividend.pdf

[13] Ronald Inglehart, "Culture and Democracy," *Culture Matters*, 94.

[14] Max Weber, *The Protestant Ethic and the Spirit of Capitalism*, trans. Talcott Parsons (New York: Charles Scribner's Sons, 1958).

[15] Francis Fukuyama, *Trust: The Social Virtues and the Creation of Prosperity* (New York: Free Press Paperbacks, 1995).

[16] Michael E. Porter, "Attitudes, Values, Beliefs and the Mircoeconomics of Prosperity," *Culture Matters*, 14.

[17] Shalini Venturelli, *From the Information Economy to the Creative Economy* (Washington, DC: Center for Arts and Culture, 2001), 10.

[18] New England Council, "The Creative Economy Initiative: The Role of the Arts and Culture in New England's Economic Competitiveness," June 2000. www.newenglandcouncil.com/initiatives

[19] Elizabeth Plater-Zyberk, Andres Duany, and Jeff Speck, *Suburban Nation: The Rise of Sprawl and the Decline of the American Dream* (New York: North Point Press, 2000).

[20] William H. Whyte, *The Organization Man* (New York: Simon & Schuster, 1956).

[21] William H. Whyte, *The Social Life of Small Urban Places* (New York: Project for Public Spaces, 2001).

[22] Plater-Zyberk et al., *Suburban Nation*, 60–61.

[23] Maria-Rosario Jackson and Joaquin Herranz, *Culture Counts in Communities: A Framework for Measurement* (Washington, DC: Urban Institute, 2002. www.urban.org/nnip/acip.htm

[24] Mark J. Stern, "Performing Miracles," Center for an Urban Future, 2002. www.nycfuture.org/content/reports/report_view.cfm?repkey=86

[25] Diane Grams and Michael Warr, "Leveraging Assets: How Small Budget Arts Activities Benefit Neighborhoods," a study commissioned by the John D. and Catherine T. MacArthur and Richard H. Driehaus foundations, 2003. www.macfound.org/speeches/special_reports/index.htm

[26] Robert D. Putnam and Lewis M. Feldstein, *Better Together: The Report* (Saguaro Seminar, Kennedy School of Government, Harvard University, 2003) 34. www.bettertogether.org/pdfs/FullReportText.pdf

[27] Neil Scott Kleiman, "The Creative Engine," Center for an Urban Future, 2002. www.nycfuture.org/content/reports/report_view.cfm?repkey=90

[28] Ford Foundation, *Downside Up: The Listening Tour Project, Asset Building and Community Development Program*, 2003.

PART TWO
Ten Economic and Social Development Strategies

PART TWO of the book describes twenty culturally based, or creative community building, projects that had numerous and complex impacts on their communities. It is divided into two chapters—one focusing on economic strategies and one focusing on social strategies. Chapter 2 looks at five creative community building strategies employing local cultural assets that had direct impact on the economic development of the communities profiled. Chapter 3 looks at five strategies contributing to social, civic, and physical development.

For each of the ten strategies, two case studies are offered from communities that are generally quite dissimilar from one another. They include rural, urban, and suburban communities across the United States. They are old and new, rich and poor, dominated by one ethnic population and very mixed. They also represent projects of differing scales relative to their communities. An important point in this book is that each creative community builder and each place should employ approaches such as these in a way that fits the community's capacity, size, and needs.

It's artificial to view these projects as impacting their communities in only economic terms or social terms. *All* of them contribute to their communities in more holistic ways, building both economic and social capital. For the purposes of this book, however, we'll look at one key area of impact per example, and indicate other significant outcomes, where appropriate.

The case studies do not provide a complete analysis of the pitfalls and challenges that each of these communities faced, nor do the studies trace the variety of unique paths these communities followed—or invented. The studies *do* give the reader a taste of community accomplishments and a context within which the community builders brought their work to fruition—and upon which they continue to build.

The paradox of economic development is that economic values are not enough to ensure it. Economic development is too important to be entrusted solely to economic values. The values accepted or neglected by a nation fall within the cultural field. We may thus say that economic development is a cultural process.

— Mariano Grondona [29]

As mentioned earlier, these examples are *not* offered as models to be replicated—quite the opposite. Each evolved in its unique setting, led by visionary individuals, and each employed indigenous assets in response to local challenges. They should be examined for how each of the communities identified their assets—especially artistic and cultural assets—and mined them to generate an economic turnaround and broad-based civic involvement. They can provide lessons and inspire your community to draw and build upon its distinct assets and meet its unique needs and aspirations. The solutions your community uncovers will be quite different.

Figure 1, Economic and Social Capital Development Strategies, on page 19, shows these strategies and the examples that illustrate them.

The specific efforts within the communities profiled have been generated from various types of organizations, including community development corporations, municipal agencies, arts organizations, and other kinds of organizations, and from partnerships among them. Some were spearheaded by a unique leader, while others arose through joint efforts.

The variety of starting points and diversity of communities are intentional. The goal is to help you understand how any community can leverage its unique assets, identity, and creative powers and to show that wherever you're at, you can launch, formalize, or complete a process to build your own community.

Figure 1. Economic and Social Capital Development Strategies

Economic Development Strategies

1. **Create Jobs**
   Nurture artists and small cultural organizations as businesses and microenterprises to increase employment
   - Penn Avenue Arts Initiative, Pittsburgh, PA
   - San José Arts Incubator, San José, CA

2. **Stimulate Trade through Cultural Tourism**
   Create the right conditions for, and engage in, cultural tourism to bring new resources to the community
   - Pilsen/Little Village Information Center, Chicago, IL
   - Lanesboro Art Council, Town of Lanesboro, MN

3. **Attract Investment by Creating Live/Work Zones for Artists**
   Support artists and artist live/work spaces as anchors around which to build local economies
   - Artist Loft Program and Arts District, Department of Planning and Development, City of Peekskill, NY
   - Torpedo Factory Artists' Association, Alexandria, VA

4. **Diversify the Local Economy**
   Cluster arts organizations as retail anchors and activity generators to attract and support other enterprises
   - ACT Roxbury and Madison Park Development Corporation, Boston, MA
   - Massachusetts Museum of Contemporary Art, North Adams, MA

5. **Improve Property and Enhance Value**
   Leverage the proximity of cultural amenities and the artists' touch to improve property and increase its value
   - West End/Clingman Revitalization, Asheville, NC
   - Paducah Artist Relocation Program, Paducah, KY

Social Development Strategies

6. **Promote Interaction in Public Space**
   Engage people in public spaces through public art and collective cultural experience
   - WaterFire Providence, Providence, RI
   - Voice of the River Project and Leo Adler Memorial Parkway, Baker City, OR

7. **Increase Civic Participation through Cultural Celebrations**
   Strengthen connections between neighbors through cultural celebrations and festivals
   - May Day Parade and Festival, Minneapolis, MN
   - Delray Beach Cultural Loop, City of Delray Beach, FL

8. **Engage Youth**
   Include young people in civic affairs and enterprises through meaningful work and activity
   - Artists for Humanity, Boston, MA
   - Youth Radio, Berkeley, CA

9. **Promote Stewardship of Place**
   Develop civic pride and responsibility through good "place making" and design practices
   - Hope Community, Minneapolis, MN
   - Southgate Linear Park, City of Tamarac, FL

10. **Broaden Participation in the Civic Agenda**
    Expand involvement in civic issues and governance through community-centered arts and cultural practices
    - Danville Transportation Enhancement Project, Danville, VT
    - Understanding Neighbors, Anchorage, AK

Building Strong Economies through Arts and Culture

MANY COMMUNITY BUILDERS now believe that developing a network or cluster of locally owned businesses that serves the immediate community and attracts customers from outside is more desirable than recruiting a major employer to fill an old factory or clearing large tracts of real estate for a developer who will concentrate a single use there.

Such "big-box" solutions to community economic or social problems tend to be the opposite of long-term solutions.* They have fewer equitable, balanced, and sustainable impacts, whether they are a manufacturing plant, giant retail outlet, sports or convention center, or even a giant performing arts complex. A diversified economy that is rooted in a community's assets and in tune with its identity provides a more stable base and returns more to the local economy. A large number and diverse mix of such enterprises, and an environment that supports their startup and growth, are ideal.

Likewise, a cultural "ecology" that includes a wide mix of ethnic groups and a balance of producers, presenters, and preservers of culture is more stable, healthy, and productive. Big-box developments alone do not tap into or nurture the unique and sustainable assets of their communities. They import and depend upon outside capital, labor, goods, cultures, and consumers. Often they remove profit, damage the natural environment, overshadow the identity of place, and diminish the integrity and value of the people and cultures of the community.

Chapter 2 presents five economic strategies that build upon a community's artistic and cultural strengths. Each is illustrated by two case studies. The five strategies are to

1. Create Jobs: Nurture artists and small cultural organizations as businesses and microenterprises to increase employment

2. Stimulate Trade through Cultural Tourism: Create the right conditions for, and engage in, cultural tourism to bring new resources to the community

Human cleverness, desires, motivations, imagination, and creativity are replacing location, natural resources, and market access as urban resources. The creativity of those who live in and run cities will determine future success.

— Charles Landry [30]

---

* The Institute for Local Self-Reliance makes available more than twenty research studies that examine the impact of large retail chains on city and state costs, local businesses, jobs, wages, benefits, and consumers. www.hometownadvantage.org.

3. Attract Investment by Creating Live/Work Zones for Artists: Support artists and artist live/work spaces as anchors around which to build local economies

4. Diversify the Local Economy: Cluster arts organizations as retail anchors and activity generators to attract and support other enterprises

5. Improve Property and Enhance Value: Leverage the proximity of cultural amenities and the artists' touch to improve property and increase its value

The projects and organizations are described in a way that is designed to help the reader see how the special qualities and assets of each community leveraged change. While the challenges and problems addressed are familiar, the response is unique to that place.

The work accomplished by these communities also exemplifies the best practices described on page 71.

Create Jobs

STRATEGY 1 IS ABOUT CREATING JOBS via the development of arts and culture as a productive economic sector and as one that stimulates other enterprises. Successful programs treat artists and small cultural organizations as businesses and microenterprises that increase employment.

The arts and culture sector—most often associated with nonprofit organizations large and small, and a wide range of individual practicing artists—has not generally been considered a major contributor to the U.S. economy. However, this sector makes up a significant industry and a larger and far more influential portion of most communities' workforce than previously understood. When recognized and nurtured as small business enterprises, individual artists and nonprofit cultural organizations provide significant employment in our communities.

The small business sector in the United States accounts for more than half of all private sector employees. Small businesses are growing faster than large firms, creating three-quarters of the new jobs. They're also more innovative, producing thirteen to fourteen times more patents per employee than large firms.*

The number of artists drawing all or part of their living from their artistic work is virtually impossible to ascertain. In 1970, the Bureau of Labor Statistics estimated that there were 730,000 artists in the United States; by 2001, that estimate had risen to more than two million.[32] Since many working artists operate "under the radar" and are not counted by either the Small Business Administration or the Bureau of Labor Statistics, these figures are likely even higher.

In a 2002 study by Americans for the Arts, it was estimated that the country's nonprofit arts industry generates $134 billion in annual economic activity.[33] This places nonprofit arts among the top ranks of national industries, drawing more audience participation and expenditures than professional sports, among others. Significantly this study covers only formal nonprofit organizations, not individual artists or related fields such as design, media production, or any "informal arts" activities that take place outside institutional settings.**

Small businesses play a number of important roles in the economy, serving local and niche markets for products and services, employing half of private sector workers, including many young, old, female, and minority workers, and creating most of the net new jobs.

— U.S. Small Business Administration[31]

---

* According to the Small Business Administration, Office of Advocacy, 2.5 million of the 3.4 million jobs created in 1999 and 2000 were among small businesses. An estimated 16.5 million sole proprietorships were active in 2000. Of all small businesses, 53 percent are home-based, while only 3 percent are franchises. www.sba.gov/advo/stats/sbfaq.html.

** For a detailed study of the high degree of participation in "informal arts" taking place outside nonprofit or formal organizations, see Alaka Wali, *The Informal Arts in Chicago: Finding Cohesion, Capacity and Other Cultural Benefits in Unexpected Places* (Chicago: The Center for Arts Policy, Columbia College, 2003).

Artists are pure entrepreneurs, creating unique products and services that have value well beyond the raw materials used. They work in all corners of the country, yet they rarely rely on business plans, investors, operating policies, or marketing campaigns.

Whether artists and their work are the cause or effect of robust economies, as economists have argued, is a less important distinction. It's not an either-or scenario. The potential of artists and arts organizations to create jobs and an environment supportive of innovation is evident in both arguments.

The examples that follow are but two of many. The first resulted from a strategy devised by two Pittsburgh community development corporations that set out to revitalize a nearly abandoned commercial corridor. As legendary urbanist Jane Jacobs said, "New ideas must use old buildings."[34] And old buildings were something this neighborhood had in abundance. These CDCs also found that creative entrepreneurs were in no short supply, and they went about matching the two.

The second example is an effort launched by a city agency in San José, California, to professionalize and stabilize nascent arts activities for the purpose of serving, engaging, and motivating the city's culturally diverse and talented workforce.

STRATEGY ❶
Create Jobs

Nurturing Artist Enterprises

The Penn Avenue Arts Initiative, Pittsburgh, Pennsylvania

www.pennavenuearts.org

The Setting

Penn Avenue transects the residential neighborhoods of Friendship and Garfield about four miles east of downtown Pittsburgh. For decades it was a bustling connection between two of the busiest shopping districts in western Pennsylvania: Downtown Pittsburgh and East Liberty. Both centers lost their edge to outer developments during the 1960s and '70s. As jobs in the mills and foundries disappeared, household purchasing power diminished and the number of retail businesses that once lined Penn Avenue drastically decreased. The avenue was also a boundary between African American and White residential neighborhoods—less of a main street or meeting ground than a service area for passersby.

By 1980, population flight to other cities and suburban neighborhoods further weakened the viability of the businesses that remained. More than fifty small retail shops and services gradually closed their doors. Corner bars gave way to open-air drug trafficking and other illicit activity. The strip of two- and three-story mixed residential and business properties was nearly vacant when two CDCs turned their attention to the area.

Organization Type/Description

The Penn Avenue Arts Initiative (PAAI) is a partnership between two non-profit community development corporations—the Bloomfield-Garfield Corporation and Friendship Development Associates, Inc. Launched in 1998, PAAI expresses a development strategy that intertwines neighborhoods, commercial areas, and cultural projects. It is driving the redevelopment of a culturally diverse district and creating an economic engine working with two distinct neighborhoods and a largely vacant commercial corridor.

Mission or Statement of Purpose

After surveying the corridor during the late 1990s, the two partnering CDCs discovered the area was already home to a surprising number of artists and fledgling arts organizations, most of whom had moved in unheralded. PAAI was designed to build on these assets and transform a twelve-block strip of Penn Avenue into a quirky, thriving multicultural street with artists, arts organizations, arts-related businesses, ethnic restaurants, and neighborhood-serving businesses.

Goals and Strategies

The organization enhances public perception of the district, instills pride in the neighborhood, fosters inter- and intracommunity ties, and establishes an artists' niche. It helps artists and nonprofits create viable enterprises that, in turn, support a variety of other businesses and result in an economically vibrant commercial and residential corridor. Key strategies include the following:

• Increase the number of artists who own live/work spaces

• Support the purchase and renovation of properties to make them more accessible to artists

• Attract and support artists, cultural groups, and arts-related activities

• Empower local youth by encouraging artists to engage them in arts-related projects

• Make decision makers and investors aware of the burgeoning activity by hosting tours

• Encourage civic engagement by mobilizing neighborhood volunteers for PAAI committees and other civic activities

• Attract and support new midsize "anchor" arts organizations

Snapshot

The Penn Avenue Arts Initiative
Pittsburgh, Pennsylvania

Setting
A commercial and service corridor lined by vacant mixed-use properties

Community Assets
• Two established community development corporations
• Existing artist population
• Several small arts organizations

Strategies
• Form a partnership between community development corporations and artists and arts groups
• Develop financial products and incentives to encourage investment in artist live/work spaces and community arts groups
• Develop cultural activities to show off artwork and attract visitors

Outcomes
• Seventy-three new arts-related jobs
• Eighteen new arts businesses
• $6.5 million in arts-related private investment
• New property, sales, and income tax revenues
• Percentage of local artists rose from 2 percent to 16 percent

• Develop public arts projects to distinguish the district and leverage artist involvement in infrastructure reconstruction

General Description of Activities

Using multiple financing tools, PAAI first stabilized existing artist live/work spaces and helped develop and upgrade facilities for nonprofit arts groups. Such tools are generally as alien to artists and small nonprofit arts groups as performance art is to mortgage brokers. Versed in both areas, Jeffrey Dorsey, arts district manager, has "translated" or acted as an intermediary to provide business and financial help to artists.

Recognizing that Penn Avenue has to be more than a place where artists come to create, PAAI both promotes existing activities and develops a variety of festivals and events throughout the year. These not only attract residents from across the city and region but also provide incentive for artists, residents, and businesses to work together. PAAI draws from the strengths of Penn Avenue's anchor arts businesses—Pittsburgh Glass Center, Dance Alloy, and Garfield Artworks—as well as from the many small arts studios on or adjacent to Penn Avenue. The area's emerging vitality is not just in the creative work taking place there but in the interactions of individuals of diverse social, racial, and economic backgrounds. Among the activities developed are

• An artist loan and grant fund

• A weekly e-mail news listing of available buildings, cultural events, classes, jobs, calls for volunteers, and community meetings

• Micro-grants to pay artists to engage neighborhood youth in meaningful activities

• A studio/gallery opening event on the first Friday of each month to highlight artists, arts studios, galleries, and activities on the avenue

• An annual community arts festival with hands-on activities for children, live performances, vendors, displays, and other activities that attract art buyers and families from a wider area

Among PAAI's proudest accomplishments are the spectacular studio, rehearsal, and office spaces for the Dance Alloy Company, and the stunning 16,000-square-foot facility for the Pittsburgh Glass Center. By 2004, more than thirty artist-owned studios, twenty artist-rented studios, and several small performance and exhibition spaces had sprung up along the avenue. It is emerging as the kind of bohemian environment that Richard Florida, guru of creative communities, points to as essential to a city's ability to be economically competitive. In the chicken-or-egg conundrum of whether the artist or the bohemian environment came first, PAAI is building upon the existing artist population while attracting more residents and visitors who spend money locally at the increasing number of cafes, restaurants, and shops.

Complementing this renaissance has been the emergence of ethnic restaurants and a coffee-house, which feed off of the energy that a younger audience wants in its urban culture. Also, a National City Bank branch office returned to Penn after an eight-year hiatus.

— Shop Mainstreets Pittsburgh[35]

A once largely depopulated commercial corridor is now thriving as a desirable destination and place to live and work.

Assets Employed

• Presence of artists and small and midsize arts groups

• Vacant mixed-use building stock suitable for retail, light industry, and housing

• Expertise of two established CDCs

• Growing public interest in edgy artistic and culturally active neighborhoods

• A variety of financing and small business development tools

• Increasing need among artists for inexpensive and versatile live/work space

Direct Outcomes

Between 1998 and mid-2004, PAAI recorded

• Forty-nine artists relocated to the area

• Seventy-three new arts-related jobs created in small nonprofits, sole proprietorships, small fabrication shops and others

• Stabilization of several nonprofits through property ownership

• Five arts organizations started in or relocated to the avenue

• Eighteen new arts businesses established

• Space totaling 127,991 square feet put to use for arts activities

• Forty-seven new studio spaces created, used by 278 artists

• More than $6.5 million in private investment leveraged in arts enterprises

• A growing number of new retail and services businesses

• Physical rejuvenation of declining mixed-use area

• Nearly $5 million in additional investments scheduled

Indirect and Potential Impacts

• Development of a more socially active commercial corridor

• Expanded regional trade and tourism stimulated by ongoing arts events and annual festivals

• Increased property, sales, and income tax revenues

• Interaction between neighborhoods with mixed cultural, racial, and socio-economic backgrounds

• Development of a more stable and civically engaged community with increased local property ownership

• Enhanced neighborhood safety as a result of increased activity and upgraded property condition

After working on PAAI renovation projects, Loysen + Kreuthmeier Architects purchased this building and will move their business to Penn Avenue. PAAI works with businesses and potential building owners to obtain a sales agreement, renovate the property, and encourage visitors to the area.

The Business of Startups in Silicon Valley

The San José Arts Incubator, San José, California

www.sanjoseculture.org

The Setting

California's Silicon Valley, located in the south Bay Area, is home to innovative global high-technology enterprises. The city of San José, with a population of just under 900,000, considers itself the capital of Silicon Valley. The city includes an older urban downtown with sprawling outlying areas. Real estate values are among the highest nationally, with an average household income of $93,570. Its economy grew rapidly during the last quarter of the twentieth century, as did its population, which is 36 percent Caucasian, 30 percent Latino, 27 percent Asian, 4 percent Other, and 3 percent African American. San José is the third-largest city in California and the eleventh largest in the United States. Between 1990 and 2000, the White population continued to decline, dropping by 14 percent, while fast-growing Asian and Latino populations grew by 8 percent and 4 percent, respectively. The community includes a number of large older cultural institutions primarily presenting European-based cultural forms, and a growing mix of newer and smaller arts organizations representing the ethnic mix indicated above.

Organization Type/Description

In 1991, San José's Office of Cultural Affairs launched the San José Arts Incubator (SJAI). The organization functioned like a small business incubator offering selected fledgling cultural groups space in its downtown office, resources, expertise, and connections to funders and suppliers. SJAI also provided services to other nonprofit clients. Its budget hovered around $300,000, three-quarters of which was provided by city and state grants. The remainder came through service fees and private sources. A transition in 2004 dissolved the incubator space and placed the fledgling groups that had been "in-residence" into city-operated community centers. In addition to reducing costs, the goal was to better meet each group's needs by connecting them to specific neighborhoods and facilities such as dance and theater space. This action also allowed the arts incubator programs to serve more parts of the city.

Mission or Statement of Purpose

The mission of the Office of Cultural Affairs is to promote the development of San José as a regional arts center that nurtures the artistic expression of its diverse people. The incubator program was established to foster startup programs, especially those representing growing immigrant communities tied to the rapidly expanding and well-educated workforce. In 2004, in response to its successes and changing conditions, the incubator program repositioned itself. It became a coordinated set of initiatives designed to develop and sustain maturing arts organizations that more closely reflect the city's diversity. For example, in one pilot project, three dance organizations representing Indian, Filipino, and Latino cultures were provided office, rehearsal, and performance space in an underutilized school facility on the city's west side. The project gave people a place to celebrate and share their cultures, volunteer their time, and become connected to a new place through familiar activities.

Goals and Strategies

- Provide emerging cultural organizations with direct technical assistance, workshops, and fully equipped office space

- Stabilize and grow emerging groups by developing ongoing professional staff positions

- Help emerging groups gain experience in audience development, generate earned income, and produce public presentations

- Provide experience in nonprofit structure and management by involving clients in committees and governance

- Foster cross-fertilization and peer network development among groups

- Provide support in accounting, grantwriting, marketing, personnel, board and volunteer development, pricing, ticketing, business planning, and contracting

- Expand audience and supporter base by engaging a more diverse range of artists and immigrant communities in professional and participatory arts activities

General Description of Activities

The San José Arts Incubator served about twenty-five organizations annually and until 2004 operated a 3,700-square-foot facility on the ground floor of a downtown office building. Known as the Arts Development Center, it housed eight resident organizations with private offices, meeting space, shared equipment, computer workstations, and technical support. The incubator program also provided workspace and equipment for nonresident groups. Programs included the following:

- Multicultural Arts Incubation Program (MAIP) to assist multicultural arts groups with administrative, organizational, and leadership development. Principal components included an annual $5,000 technical assistance grant, workshops, and direct staff assistance. In 2002, the program accommodated six groups in three-year cycles. Most groups entering the program were volunteer run.

Snapshot

The San José Arts Incubator
San José, California

Setting
- Center of growing Silicon Valley, population 900,000
- Rapidly growing Asian and Latino populations
- Established cultural institutions that are primarily European-based

Community Assets
- A dynamic economy attracting a highly skilled global workforce
- An active City Office of Cultural Affairs

Strategies
- Establish an arts incubator to provide office space, management assistance, technology, and access to funding opportunities
- Develop a community of arts organizations more representative and engaging of the area's cultural diversity

Outcomes
- Participating arts groups built a professional staff and grew by over 600 percent in budget size during the first ten years
- Dozens of full-time and part-time jobs created
- More than thirty multicultural arts events offered annually downtown
- Increased visibility of arts representing a diverse population
- Welcoming, supportive, and stimulating environment for newly arrived high-tech workers

• Arts Development Program (ADP) supported organizations at a development stage beyond the MAIP groups. ADP participants had paid administrative staff. They received consulting services and assistance from Office of Cultural Affairs staff, along with individual office space, computers, and shared office resources, such as meeting space, a photocopier and fax machine, and a graphics workstation.

• Downtown Arts Series (DAS) provided emerging multicultural groups with production support and entry-level professional performance space at the two-hundred-seat San José Stage. Support included facility and rehearsal subsidies, box office coordination, group marketing, and printed promotional materials. The Office of Cultural Affairs contracted production and management to the San José Stage Company. In the spring of 2002, eleven groups participated in DAS, drawing almost 2,000 audience members.

• Performing Arts Series (PAS) served more established multicultural arts organizations at the five-hundred-seat Montgomery Theater. PAS offered workshops and training, performance facility subsidies, and marketing assistance, all of which culminated in a one-month performance series. The Office of Cultural Affairs contracted out production, marketing, and management. Typically ten groups participated in PAS, drawing 4,000 attendees during its season.

Assets Employed

• Nonprofit management expertise

• City agency stature as a major supporter and adjudicator of cultural programs

• Rapidly changing demographics within a highly skilled workforce seeking connection to its cultural heritage and contemporary forms

• Grassroots energy for formal recognition of cultural production

• Group buying power

• Collective presence and multiple connections in multiple communities

Direct Outcomes

• Between 1992 and 2001, the number of multicultural groups (participants in the incubator) competing for Office of Cultural Affairs grants increased by 125 percent (from twelve to twenty-seven), in comparison to a 45 percent increase in the overall number of Office of Cultural Affairs grantees.

• Overall income for multicultural groups grew 141 percent, three times the rate of growth for all Office of Cultural Affairs grantees.

• Organizations participating in the Multicultural Arts Incubation Program experienced tremendous growth in income, especially in their early years. The first twelve organizations participating from 1991 to 1994 increased their income by 155 percent during that time, and by 2001 their income

A rts incubators today are defining themselves more as community development tools, and moving away from the business model approach more popular in the early 1990s. The goals are more about enlivening buildings, neighborhoods, schools, and specific communities through the arts.

—Laurel Jones,
Bay Consulting
Group[36]

had grown by more than 600 percent. Of all groups entering the San José Arts Incubator between 1991 and 1997, their average income growth by 2001 was 311 percent.

Indirect and Potential Impacts

• Heightened visibility of diverse cultural arts forms and artists

• Strengthened fabric of emerging ethnic communities

• More than thirty multicultural arts programs drawing nearly 6,000 audience members to events downtown each year

• Stronger cross-cultural understanding and working relationships

• Enhanced and more meaningful cultural environment for creative-class workforce

• Stimulation of downtown cultural and related business activity

Summary of Examples in Strategy 1: Create Jobs

Both the Penn Avenue Arts Initiative and the San José Arts Incubator resulted in many new and prosperous enterprises providing direct and indirect employment opportunities. While relatively small, the programs produced a variety of benefits in addition to jobs. They brought residents of differing cultures and age groups closer together and created vibrancy in the social and civic environments, and they brought comfort to people in changing circumstances.

The two programs developed in conditions and places that could hardly be more different—and that is good evidence that Strategy 1 has broad application. The population contraction in Pittsburgh and loss of manufacturing jobs contrast starkly with Silicon Valley's rapid growth and importing of high-tech, international workers. The value of real estate is sky-high in San José, while Pittsburgh is rife with abandoned and near-giveaway property. Steel and high tech, however, are similar in this way: both are high-demand products but in different centuries. Ultimately, these cities' longer-term prosperity depends upon their ability to develop new and varied enterprises.

Both the Penn Avenue Arts Initiative and the San José Arts Incubator thoughtfully examined and employed their assets, values, and aspirations in ways that engaged the entrepreneurial drive. They both built "ownership." Pittsburgh helped artists invest and build equity in the neighborhood. San José helped immigrants build a sense of belonging.

The next strategy uses culture as a platform to stimulate trade.

Traditional arts celebrate the heritage, history, landscape, and even politics of places in ways that emphasize the unique features of a community. "Exporting" the traditional products that are ties to the unique features of local cultural communities fits squarely within the widely accepted theories of economic development.

— Chris Walker et al.[37]

Stimulate Trade through Cultural Tourism

STRATEGY 2 IS ABOUT CREATING THE RIGHT CONDITIONS for—and engaging in—cultural tourism to bring new resources to the community. Sometimes a community's greatest assets are "invisible in plain sight." This section looks at some of the thinking and trends in the growing industry of cultural tourism. As importantly, it looks at how communities positioning themselves for tourism are strengthened in a multitude of ways.

The travel and tourism industry is one of the largest in the United States, accounting for estimated economic activity in 2004 of over $600 billion. And there is increased interest among travelers, especially among the growing numbers of people of color who travel, to experience cultural, arts, historic, and heritage activities. Some 81 percent of U.S. adults who traveled in 2002 included historic/cultural sites and activities as part of their travel, an increase of 13 percent from a similar study in 1996. In contrast, about 9 percent of travelers included a visit to a theme or amusement park in that same year.*

Travelers visiting historic or cultural sites spent significantly more money than travelers visiting other destinations ($623 per traveler per trip versus $457, excluding the cost of transportation), and four in ten travelers added extra time to their trip specifically to participate in a historic/cultural activity. Most travelers indicated that trips where they learn something new are more memorable.

Travel to historic and cultural sites has been termed cultural heritage tourism and defined as: "Travel based on interaction with both human-built and natural environment as a means to learn about and experience the arts, heritage, and the special character of a place."[38]

Mobilizing local assets to participate in cultural heritage tourism requires taking a new look at one's own community, a difficult thing for community insiders to do. It requires ongoing and interdisciplinary planning. When done successfully, cultural tourism can strengthen the ability of community members to work together in many ways. Successful projects transform local residents from being grudging hosts to eager advocates for their communities. Cultural heritage tourism is generally based upon multiple small-scale

---

* Travel Industry Association of America, www.tia.org/Travel/EconImpact.asp. The travel industry generated more than 7.2 million jobs, $158 billion in payroll income taxes, and $95 billion in local, state, and federal tax revenue in 2003. Tourist travel by African Americans grew at a rate of 4 percent in 2003, double the growth rate of all tourists. Asian American travel grew by 10 percent and Latino travel was up 20 percent between 2000 and 2002. www.tia.org/Travel/traveltrends.asp.

enterprises that come from community-based entrepreneurial spirit and that create a ripple effect within the regional economy.

While tourism is a proven way to bring outside resources into a community, its side benefits can be of equal importance. These include building a more unified identity and increasing the degree of cross-sector, cross-business collaborations. Cultural tourism tends to increase real estate values, attract investment, and bring new ideas into the community.

Cultural tourism advocates stress the value of authenticity over slick marketing strategies, but it takes both to be successful. When the attraction is genuine, people will seek it out, and those who do tend to have a higher level of respect for the place they're visiting. "Although crafts and regional music may be sold in some form to passing tourists, the principal value of local culture is in personal and community expression. Through such expression, culture reaffirms community values, reinforces identity, undergirds resistance, and satisfies the soul," writes Dee Davis, founder and director of the Center for Rural Strategies in Whitesburg, Kentucky.[39]

Visitors to Lanesboro, Minnesota, population 788, can enjoy theater, art, music, fine cuisine, and charming accommodations. The area also offers scenic biking, horseback riding, canoeing, golf, tennis, and hiking.

Other cultural tourism consultants stress the importance of being sure that what the community has is of value to the outside. They cite among the field's best practices the testing of local assets and plans with target visitors, ensuring that visitors' basic needs are accommodated and incorporating ongoing marketing strategies.[40]

According to Partners for Livable Communities, a national, nonprofit organization working to restore and renew communities, cultural heritage tourism is a unique and essential form of community development because it

• Encourages residents to view their own condition in a positive light; to believe they have something of value to cherish and care for

• Empowers residents to craft a vision and, if properly executed, provides a vehicle that brings residents, leaders, and outside funders together in a mutual cause

• Strengthens existing social groups and support networks

• Awakens a spirit of community connections and creates networks of collaboration

• Nurtures the revival of traditional building techniques, crafts, and skills[41]

The examples in Strategy 2 represent cultural tourism efforts in a major inner-city immigrant neighborhood and in a small town in a rural region—locations that at first appear very dissimilar. However, they are very much alike in that the programming and activities they developed are rooted in the history and values of the people in the community. In both cases, success was brought on by unprecedented cooperation across local government, business, and nonprofit sectors.

The Pilsen/Little Village Information Center on Chicago's south side works with small businesses and the Mexican Fine Arts Center Museum to build those cross-sector, cross-business collaborations and to invite tourists to enjoy the neighborhood's Mexican culture, food, and products. The Lanesboro Art Council, located in a picturesque small Minnesota town, brings together natural resource attractions, creative talents, and a tradition of hospitality to create a cultural and recreational mecca that attracts thousands.

STRATEGY ❷
Stimulate Trade through Cultural Tourism

Connected by Culture

The Pilsen/Little Village Information Center (now Latino Information Center) and Mexican Fine Arts Center Museum, Chicago, Illinois

www.pilsenlittlevillage.org
www.mfacmchicago.org

The Setting

The Pilsen and Little Village neighborhoods are located west of Chicago's downtown and the Chicago River and extend to the western border of the city. The two neighborhoods are home to 127,000 people. Active commercial corridors connect them. The neighborhoods are served by elevated public transit and city buses.

Pilsen/Little Village has served as a port of entry, welcoming countless immigrants to the United States. In the early nineteenth century, workers arrived to build the Southwestern Plank Road, the Illinois and Michigan Canal, and the Chicago, Burlington, and Quincy Railroad. Many of these workers continued to live in the neighborhoods.

By the late nineteenth century, rapid industrialization had transformed the largely Czech and German working-class neighborhoods into a national center of labor activism. Today the area is peppered with mostly abandoned industrial sites. Now one of the largest Mexican communities in the United States, Pilsen/Little Village and their residents have, for more than three decades, engaged in a struggle for political representation, educational reform, social justice, and workers' rights.

Currently, the two neighborhoods house 29 percent of the city's total Mexican population. Little Village is 95 percent Mexican, and its eastern neighbor Pilsen is 85 percent Mexican, together representing the highest concentration of Mexicans in Chicago. Forty-two percent of these residents are twenty years old or younger, compared with 30 percent of the general city population.

Organization Type/Description

The Pilsen/Little Village Information Center was founded as a nonprofit civic improvement organization in 2000 by Juana Guzmán, a specialist in organizing economic development in the arts, with a consortium of business and nonprofit groups. The Pilsen/Little Village Information Center strives to facilitate community development and increase social and economic opportunity by acting as a resource and by promoting local businesses, organizations, and individuals. It coordinates and builds on the skills, capacities, and activities of local partners and promotes a positive image of Pilsen/Little Village and the Chicago Latino community by encouraging engagement in cultural activities.

One of the key partners is the nonprofit Mexican Fine Arts Center Museum (MFACM), a young institution founded by Carlos Tortolero in 1987 in the Pilsen neighborhood. The museum grew rapidly, and in 2005 it was the nation's largest Latino arts organization and the only Latino museum accredited by the American Association of Museums. It has attracted a growing international and local mix of artists and audiences and has become an important economic and social force in the community.

Mission or Statement of Purpose

The information center's mission is to empower the Pilsen/Little Village community and the Chicago area's Latino community by providing information and coordinating community efforts. The information center recognizes that many of the central issues facing its population are interconnected and require solutions that involve collaboration across sectors and industries. As the information center provides information and coordinates community efforts, it creates the right conditions for cultural tourism. As it fosters collaboration and coordination among groups and sectors, it strengthens the collaborators' capacity to work together.

Goals and Strategies

The Pilsen/Little Village Information Center stimulates greater visitor traffic to the neighborhoods, businesses, and organizations, and helps businesses grow. The information center provides increased access to social programs, cultural community events, and other opportunities, and it coordinates community and business cooperation around projects that advance

Snapshot

The Pilsen/Little Village Information Center *and* Mexican Fine Arts Center Museum
Chicago, Illinois

Setting
- Older south side neighborhood, population 127,000
- Primarily Mexican American and relatively young

Community Assets
- Cohesive ethnic identity with strong leadership
- Well-known museum reflecting local interests
- Large number of small business entrepreneurs

Strategies
- Encourage civic engagement
- Facilitate business and community collaboration
- Provide small business support services
- Foster cultural tourism

Outcomes
- Improved community image
- Significant growth in local business sales
- Growing economic and political power in the Mexican-American community

common interest. Its central strategy is to build the cross-sector collaborations necessary for the neighborhoods to become successful host communities. It works to make the communities assets visible and to mobilize those assets through production of cultural events and community tours.

The Mexican Fine Arts Center Museum presents major art exhibitions, many of which have traveled across the United States and Mexico; two annual performing arts festivals; regular literary events, concerts, dance productions, film and video screenings, and theater and performance arts presentations; and special performances for schools. It also sponsors a noncommercial, youth-run, bilingual radio station that trains young people, ages fifteen to twenty-one, in broadcasting, while encouraging them to have a greater commitment to their community. Radio Arté gives the neighborhood and the Mexican community a voice to audiences across the city. The museum's gift shop, Tienda Tzintzuntzan, features beautiful crafts born of the hands of Mexican artisans and generates considerable income.

General Description of Activities

The information center serves daily as a referral agency for residents, businesses, organizations, and visitors through its storefront, a web site, workshops, community meetings, information fairs, resource guides, and monthly newsletters. Information on community social and educational resources, services, and businesses is provided in Spanish and English. The storefront visitor center is located on West 18th Street, the major commercial artery in Pilsen, and is open to the public Monday through Friday from 9:00 a.m. to 5:00 p.m.

Through the activities of the information center, the neighborhoods have been able to coordinate several seasonal and cultural events. For example, the Cultural Engagement Summer Program began as the Chinatown/Pilsen Free Trolley Program. The program operates free trolley buses on weekends and holidays from Memorial Day to Labor Day in cooperation with adjacent Chinatown. It hosts Chinese and Mexican musical performances in both Chinatown and Pilsen as part of the city's Music Everywhere program. Trolley stops include the Mexican Fine Arts Center Museum and businesses featuring Mexican-style clothing, foods, and crafts. Riders receive a schedule of events, maps, listings, coupons, and sponsorship information. During 2002 and 2003, the program served more than 50,000 people.

An annual Day of the Dead celebration, led by the Mexican Fine Arts Center Museum, is a major event for the information center. It sponsors a tour of *ofrendas* (commemorative altars) at community businesses and helps organize a community-wide Dia de los Muertos celebration and parade. Thousands of visitors come from across the city and from outside the region. Through the efforts of the museum, the information center, and the city's tourism office, this event in particular has become widely known within the Mexican community and more broadly.

The information center serves as an anchor for stimulating trade and tourism by first helping to strengthen local business and connect entrepreneurs to each other and to resources from the broader community. In 2004, the group began a series of economic empowerment workshops held at a local library and at the museum. Topics included legalities for startup businesses, first-time home buying, and investing in property.

Assets Employed

- Emerging commercial centers serving largely Mexican communities
- A highly visible museum attracting visitors interested in Mexican culture
- Federal Empowerment Zone incentives to help nurture the local economy
- A sense of ethnic focus and connectedness
- Visionary leadership with expertise in culturally driven tourism
- Expertise in international trade and importing, supplying products to a rapidly growing immigrant population
- Emerging identity as a regional and national center for Mexican culture, products, and services

Direct Outcomes

- Pilsen/Little Village now the city's second-largest generator of sales tax
- Growth in local business sales
- Expanded public transportation to serve neighborhoods
- Improved image of the neighborhood and Mexican community through the Mexican Fine Arts Center Museum's success with over fifty-two exhibitions since its beginnings
- In 2003, more than 220,000 visitors to the museum, half from surrounding neighborhoods
- The museum's main meeting room, one of the few public gathering places in the area, used daily by a wide variety of community groups

Indirect and Potential Impacts

- Growing economic and political power of the Mexican-American community
- New bridges crossing the city's multiple ethnic and geographic lines
- New economic and intellectual resources moving into and through the community

When we're looking at how to strengthen cities, often we overlook the economic viability of a neighborhood. In a global economy, we first need to look within our home, look at our backyards, and see how we can strengthen our neighborhoods.

—Juana Guzmán, Vice-President, Mexican Fine Arts Center Museum[42]

Brand Identity in a Rural Town

Lanesboro Art Council and the Town of Lanesboro, Minnesota

www.lanesboroartcouncil.org
www.lanesboro.com

The Setting

Lanesboro, population 788, is nestled in the Root River Valley of southeastern Minnesota. It lies at the foot of dramatic river bluffs and among tree-covered rolling hills uncharacteristic of the Midwest. Lanesboro is an hour southeast of Rochester (home of the Mayo Clinic), over two hours south of Minneapolis–Saint Paul, and three hours from Madison, Wisconsin. In 1886, it was the end of the line for the Southeastern Minnesota Railroad Company, connecting the area's farms with urban markets and a destination for tourists seeking a rural retreat. According to town historian Don Ward, Buffalo Bill Cody, a frequent visitor to the town, produced his first Wild West Show in Lanesboro. The town's early efforts at tourism had a short life, but other industries did well. It once boasted four flour mills and a canning factory, the last of which closed in 1920. The town's population peaked then at around 1,500 but reached a low of 600 after World War II. Agriculture declined, beginning in the 1960s, and the last train left in 1979. Arriving in Lanesboro feels like stepping back in time.

Organization Type/Description

Lanesboro Art Council is a nonprofit membership organization founded in 1981 to sponsor Art in the Park and other music and arts events. It owns the St. Mane Theater, which has housed the Commonweal Theatre Company since 1989.

The Town of Lanesboro was organized in 1868. A five-member city council, including the mayor, governs affairs for the town. Lanesboro also has a full-time city clerk/administrator.

Lanesboro has a compact and well-defined downtown, much of which has been designated a National Historic District, and there is an active Heritage Preservation Commission.

Mission or Statement of Purpose

A comprehensive city plan, adopted in 1998, calls for "The City of Lanesboro [to be] a place that should be a walking and biking friendly town." In addition to preserving its historic feel and pedestrian qualities, the community diligently maintains exemplary parks, playgrounds, softball fields, a skateboard park, a bass fishing pond, a historic footbridge, and a community center with a 4,300-square-foot auditorium/gymnasium and 1,500-square-foot meeting and function room. These and other amenities both improve the quality of life for local residents and welcome visitors.

Goals and Strategies

Long in decline, the community saw new prospects for itself in the 1980s. Local leaders, aware that change would come, examined the assets that could attract people to Lanesboro, and devised a strategy to build upon the town's historic charm and natural beauty and its friendly small-town feeling. The Lanesboro Art Council and Town of Lanesboro, together with the Lanesboro Area Chamber of Commerce, continue to work closely with business, cultural, and civic groups. The chamber's widely shared goals include the following:

- Advance the civic, commercial, industrial, cultural, environmental, and recreational interests of Lanesboro and its residents

- Ensure cooperation among Lanesboro area businesses and community organizations

- Retain, expand, and develop beneficial area businesses

- Promote Lanesboro as the best place to live, learn, work, visit, and operate a business

General Description of Activities

While locals and a few adventuresome tourists knew of Lanesboro's remote charm, the transformation of the abandoned rail line to a bicycling and walking trail in the 1980s set off the town's revival. The Root River State Trail System—more than sixty miles of paved surface through spectacular bluffs and countryside—quickly became one of the Upper Midwest's most popular recreational trails. The opening of the first bed-and-breakfast, "Mrs. B's," which boasted a five-star chef, was followed by another bed-and-breakfast in a Victorian house with a restaurant serving French cuisine.

The Lanesboro Art Council bought the St. Mane, an old theater space on the virtually abandoned main street, for $5,000 in the 1980s. At first, the council produced community events there on a voluntary basis. When the trail system began attracting more tourists, the council convinced Eric Bunge, a native of the community who had gone to graduate school in Denver, to return and start a theater company. This company, the nonprofit, professional Commonweal Theatre Company, describes itself as a collective of artists and administrators who value community, diversity, learning, and artistic integrity.

Snapshot

Town of Lanesboro and Lanesboro Art Council

Setting
- Small rural town, with 800 residents
- Population and commercial decline since the 1940s

Community Assets
- Natural beauty and outdoor recreation opportunities
- Vacant but unblemished historic downtown
- Active artist groups
- Friendly people, culinary talents

Strategies
- Reinforce and validate community identity
- Advertise community assets to increase tourism
- Cultivate growing artistic community
- Actively recruit creative workforce

Outcomes
- Increased tourism trade
- Restoration and re-occupation of downtown storefronts
- Expansion of theater and art center
- Increased investment in real estate and business improvement

The theater, together with other arts groups, added to Lanesboro's revival. Commonweal began in 1989 with an eleven-week summer season. Word-of-mouth and hard work built a widespread audience, and, by 2004, it operated an eleven-month season with a full-time staff and eight hundred subscribers—more than the entire population of the town. One-third of the audience is local, one-third from within a sixty-mile radius, and the final third from cities two and three hours away. For visitors, a trip to the theater is accompanied by a wonderful dining experience and perhaps a bike ride or walk along the scenic Root River.

Cornucopia Art Center opened in 1994 as a nonprofit to "serve as a catalyst for artistic and educational development in southeastern Minnesota and the Upper Midwest, provide meaningful opportunities for people of all ages, and contribute to the cultural vitality of the community where art nourishes both body and soul." From its prominent location on the town's main street, the art center offers exhibits and gallery sales of some of the area's best-known artists. Its National Artist in Residence Program brings four to six artists to Lanesboro annually to make new work and engage the community in the creative process. Top-notch, visionary artists and arts administrators live and work in this lovely corner of Minnesota where they are warmly embraced.

By 2000, Lanesboro leaders—key among them the Lanesboro Art Council—had arrived at a strategy and "brand identity" for their community, realizing it was the aesthetics of the natural environment coupled with hospitality and a panoply of arts activities that would be ingredients for success. They began advertising the rich amenities of a city in a rural town. Along with scenic biking, canoeing, horseback riding, golf, tennis, and hiking, visitors can enjoy theater, art, music, fine cuisine, and accommodations. In 2004, Lanesboro was home to *seven* five-star chefs, making it as much a destination for the culinary arts as the theater and visual arts. In addition, the historic downtown had never been disturbed or updated, which allowed gradual and careful restoration to maintain its nineteenth-century charm.

Lanesboro leaders, aware of the town's assets, became sophisticated in leveraging them, supporting a music festival, summer concerts, a farmers market, and an art-in-the-park program. They brought high-speed Internet access to town and began advertising for visual and performing artists, musicians, writers, and other self-employed creative people who would enjoy living and working in a beautiful small town.

The current leadership of Lanesboro knows the value in a visitor's experience of the town. The town recognizes that the strongest marketing tool by far is word-of-mouth.

— Hal Cropp,
Commonweal Theatre[43]

Assets Employed

- Tradition of hospitality and entrepreneurship
- Infrastructure for small inns and restaurants
- Natural beauty and remote feel of the valley
- Untouched historic town center and homes
- Options for outdoor recreation
- A view of the arts as partners in economic development
- Small arts organizations with visionary and persistent leadership
- Community leadership receptive to change, yet clear on aesthetic and community values
- Resident artists and craftspeople seeking broader markets
- Clarity and unity of community self-image

Commonweal Theatre's production of *The Importance of Being Earnest.*

Direct Outcomes

- More than $1.2 million spent in the community by tourists attending Commonweal Theatre since 1989
- Sales of area artists work through Cornucopia generating $12,000 per month
- Increase in the number of tourist beds from 20 in 1989 to 176 in 2004
- Summer camping facilities accommodating bicyclists and canoeists
- More than $200,000 in annual box office revenue for the theater company
- Thirty-eight of forty downtown storefronts in full use by 2004 compared with thirty-eight of forty downtown storefronts vacant in the mid-1980s

Indirect and Potential Impacts

- Burgeoning investment in real estate and business improvements
- A $3.5 million facility planned for Commonweal Theatre, increasing capacity from 126 to 178 seats (a sizeable increase for a small theater).
- A proposed expansion for Cornucopia, including artist housing, retail and exhibition space, and education facilities

Summary of Examples in Strategy 2: Stimulate Trade through Cultural Tourism

Communities can be overrun and torn apart by tourism. Insensitive outsiders or predatory franchise businesses can take away a community's identity and sense of self—the unique qualities that made it an attraction in the first place. The two examples provided here are among those where local identity and assets not only remain intact but also are enhanced.

The ambitious Mexican Fine Art Center Museum rapidly built an international reputation and facilitated exchange of both culture and products from Mexico, the place of origin for the majority of residents. Together with the Pilsen/Little Village Information Center, it built cross-sector partnerships that created a sense of pride and belonging and stimulated local businesses to cater to both residents and visitors.

Lanesboro may seem worlds apart from Pilsen/Little Village. But Lanesboro similarly built upon the culture and sensibility of its people. An unprecedented level of collaboration among the cultural, recreational, business, and government sectors welcomed outsiders to feast on the community's wide range of activities. In both cases, artists and entrepreneurs found that they have much in common and can work together.

For a summary of the best practices exemplified in this and other strategies, see page 71.

In the next section, we will see examples of communities that have leveraged their artistic and cultural assets to attract investment.

Attract Investment by Creating Live/Work Zones for Artists

STRATEGY 3 IS ABOUT CREATING LIVE/WORK SPACES for artists. Such spaces have served as anchors around which local economies are rebuilt. This strategy illuminates ways in which artists form a core that, in turn, attracts business and helps shape a favorable environment for investment and renewal.

Older urban neighborhoods and smaller communities have a great deal in common when it comes to suffering disinvestment and population loss. The creative community builders profiled in this section began with existing community assets and rebuilt viable, sustainable, and flexible local economies that have attracted considerable investment. They've enlisted creative entrepreneurs, chiefly artists, and made use of vacant real estate to jumpstart broader efforts to rebuild local economies. They've turned around their community's image and established climates of creativity.

Many areas of the United States have endured depleted natural resources and economic maladies in a changing global economy. Disinvestment, poisoned industrial sites, a deteriorating tax base, and crumbling infrastructure plague once-thriving areas whose economies were based around agriculture, manufacturing, and mining. Great damage has resulted where communities have abandoned core values and cultural identities that kept them together through good times and bad.[45]

Population shifts and the dispersal of investment in infrastructure, housing, and jobs have resulted. "For too long, creative enterprises have been overlooked by economic developers and public services that have consistently cast their nets for the big fish, rather than the more abundant—and ultimately more self-sustaining—schools of small fish," writes Stuart Rosenfeld, a researcher on rural economies. Communities, he says, can "increase their competitiveness and reach growing numbers of people who are searching for authenticity and meaning in what they own."[46]

Local entrepreneurs and microenterprises are vastly underappreciated as revenue and job generators.* "Where they cluster, they can become a major economic force. Even where concentrations of these enterprises are lower, those that choose to network and aggregate their output through co-ops, guilds, and nonprofits achieve significant impact," Rosenfeld writes.

These arts facilities have distinguished themselves as extremely stable and highly desirable additions to the urban landscape . . . generating an immediate and significant positive impact on the surrounding neighborhoods, providing the momentum necessary to further revitalize distressed urban areas.

—John Villani[44]

---

* For more on the general use of local microenterprise as a community economic development strategy, see Mihailo Temali, *The Community Economic Development Handbook* (Saint Paul, MN: Fieldstone Alliance, 2002).

One of the ways these microenterprises have been clustered and nurtured is through development of artist live/work spaces. Typically these are conceived in tandem with the reuse of historic, commercial, or industrial structures. The artists themselves, living and working in the community, stimulate development of more active street-level environments. Economist Ann Markusen, studying the impact of artists on local economies, says, "The thing about artists in these live-and-work spaces, they're around 24 hours a day. They're not like your residents who live in a condo and go off to work. They have unusual hours; they're around, coming and going. They have families. These kinds of patterns are really great for reducing crime and stabilizing a community."[47]

Some cities looking for a silver bullet have been convinced to underwrite bond issues to finance construction of major arts facilities in much the same way they've turned to sports arenas, convention centers, aquariums, and other "big-box" solutions. Meanwhile, evidence suggests there is *far greater impact* from the mix of less glamorous small galleries, theaters, artist studios, and live/work spaces for artists and their families.

"Being able to foster a local arts scene, provide low- and moderate-income housing, preserve historic buildings, and promote downtown and neighborhood economic revitalization—all at the same time—makes these types of projects rewarding far beyond their bottom line," writes John Villani, author of *The 100 Best Small Art Towns in America*.[48]

Minneapolis-based Artspace Projects is the country's largest developer of artist live/work spaces. During the past twenty years, the nonprofit has completed more than twenty projects in eleven states and has a dozen more at various stages of development.*

The two examples in this section illustrate how artists and arts organizations have worked in tandem with community leaders to bring about enormous economic benefits to their communities. The town of Peekskill, New York, on the Hudson River in rural Westchester County, used its Artist Loft Program to seed a remarkable renaissance. Abandoned by a major employer and suffering from deterioration of its once-lively downtown, Peekskill devised a visionary strategy to attract creative residents, galleries, and creative-sector businesses. By combining its Artist Loft Program with a variety of celebrations that emphasized its local character, the town rebuilt its retail and business economies and repopulated its core.

Alexandria, Virginia, one of the nation's oldest port cities, wrestled with a mammoth, abandoned munitions factory on its historic Potomac River waterfront. Turning the factory into artist studios was a risky venture in 1976, but it turned out to be the lynchpin in a revitalization of the historic district, turning the city's image and economy around.

---

* For information on Artspace Projects, Inc., visit www.artspaceprojects.org.

Contemporary Artists Revitalize a Historic Downtown

Artist Loft Program and Arts District, Department of Planning and Development, City of Peekskill, New York

www.ci.peekskill.ny.us
www.peekskillartscouncil.org

The Setting

A historic Hudson River city of 20,000, Peekskill, New York, dates from the 1600s. It sits just forty-five miles north of New York City. Like so many older small cities, Peekskill suffered the multiple impact of out-migration and proliferation of suburban shopping malls, beginning in the 1950s. In 1977, the closing of a major manufacturing plant sent the city's economy into a tailspin. By the early 1990s, the downtown was nearly abandoned.

By 2004, however, Mayor John G. Testa was upbeat in his state of the city address. He cited the community's newfound successes, describing its "beautiful location on a prime Hudson River site, both old and new homes, historic downtown, excellent train service [to New York City and Albany], advanced education opportunities, burgeoning artists district, quality cultural center, and the opportunity to 'belong' by engaging in many community activities."

Organization Type/Description

As a municipal agency, Peekskill's Department of Planning and Development is charged with policy and administrative responsibility for land use, economic development, and historic preservation. It encourages the development of new businesses and the expansion and relocation of existing businesses, all of which lead to the creation or retention of jobs for Peekskill residents. The department administers a mix of programs and federal, state, and local funds. It also manages the city's Artist Loft Program. It focuses historic preservation work on the Downtown Historic District and the overlapping, city-designated Artist District. The latter was created to revitalize a failing central business district by developing live/work spaces on the upper floors of historic commercial buildings and by promoting arts-related retail business on the street level.

Mission or Statement of Purpose

The Department of Planning and Development is responsible for advising the city manager, mayor, and common council on current and long-term land use, development, and historic preservation issues. Professional staff from the department act as liaisons between the public and various boards and commissions and provide technical information on land-use matters.

FABRICATIONS: An Outdoor Installation. Local artists Curt Belshe and Lise Prown created eight large banners that are hung on Peekskill city lampposts. The brightly colored banners depict iron stoves, once manufactured in Peekskill, and the faces of local ironworkers from that period.

Snapshot

Artist Loft Program and Arts District, Peekskill Department of Planning and Development
City of Peekskill, New York

Setting
- Hudson River Valley town, forty-five miles from New York City
- Population 20,000
- Economic decline since 1970s
- Underused downtown

Community Assets
- Vacant mixed-use properties
- Existing theater and artist population
- Scenic riverfront and historic architecture

Strategies
- Create a downtown artist and historic district with live/work space
- Establish partnerships between government agencies and community groups
- Provide incentives for property improvement and business and educational program relocation
- Attract new business and tourism by promoting cultural events

Outcomes
- Concentration of new residents in live/work units
- Re-activation of retail space and construction of significant new space
- Increased tourism
- New public and private investment in the downtown area

Goals and Strategies

The city's goals are to revitalize its downtown economy and historic building stock and to uplift community spirit. Its collaborative efforts center on attracting artists to live and work in vacant historic downtown commercial buildings and supporting light retail, galleries, and other amenities. These developments, in turn, attract shoppers and tourists, which restores pedestrian street life, and protect and restore historic architecture. As part of these efforts, Peekskill also attracts, develops, and supports nonprofit arts centers, educational programs, and creative industries. Strategies include the following:

- Create a welcoming and supportive environment for artists and support the Peekskill Artists Council

- Build partnerships with the Peekskill Chamber of Commerce, Business Improvement District, arts groups, and education groups

- Designate and maintain both historic and artists districts

- Leverage public funds for renovation and new construction

- Provide building owners with tax incentives, grants, and loans to renovate buildings that can be used as live/work spaces by artists

- Provide space and incentives to relocate strategic educational programs and related creative-sector businesses

- Coordinate monthly gallery tours and other annual events and festivals to include and highlight the city's new creative image

- Connect cultural and historical assets with the scenic riverfront to promote tourism

General Description of Activities

During the 1990s, the city hired Ralph DiBart, son of a former mayor, as a downtown consultant. DiBart understood that artists could attract visitors and businesses and be a catalyst to revitalize the downtown. At first, many observers were skeptical. Building on the existence of the Paramount Center of the Arts, the city created the Artists District.

The vintage 1930s Paramount, a one-thousand-seat movie palace, is now a county landmark. It was acquired by the city in 1977 in tax default, opened briefly in 1979 as a performing arts venue for local groups, and mounted its first performance season in 1982. A subsequent grassroots campaign in 1996 to save the building leveraged the formation of an arts center. The Paramount Center of the Arts now houses live performances, arts-in-education programs, films, and visual arts and serves more than 50,000 people annually.

Using a variety of available funding, Peekskill created an affordable cooperative loft project that opened in 2002, providing twenty-eight live/work spaces. The New York State Department of Housing and Community Renewal chose the loft cooperative as a demonstration project to show how housing can be rethought to include workspace. The Artist Certification

Committee reviews prospective residents. It defines an artist as "an individual who practices one of the fine design, graphic, musical, literary, computer, or performing arts; or an individual whose profession relies on the application of the above-mentioned skills to produce creative product; i.e., architect, craftsperson, photographer, etc."

By 2004, the Peekskill Business Improvement District boasted more than one hundred artists maintaining studio or live/work spaces in the storefronts, lofts, and studio buildings that are scattered throughout Peekskill's downtown. The district lists twelve galleries and related businesses such as graphics, framing, music, photography, and piano rebuilding. On the third Saturday of each month, the district sponsors tours of artists' studios.

Each August since 1997, a multifaceted festival called the Peekskill Celebration brings the community together with tourists to the Riverfront Green and now revitalized historic downtown. The Hudson River's rich heritage and the new cultural vitality are showcased by more than forty events, including concerts, arts and crafts sales, environmental and educational exhibits, kayaking, a farmers market, Underground Railroad tours, river excursions, a road race, a sailing regatta, and more.

Westchester Community College located a branch campus in the Artists District and now offers full academic programs in addition to high-tech digital photography, graphics, music, and video courses. Other new businesses opened in 2003—a grocery co-op, coffeehouse, beauty supply store, deli, gallery and espresso bar, West Indian restaurant, clothing store, day spa, and full-service restaurant.

Retail stores have returned to downtown Peekskill. Restaurants stay open evenings. The local weekly and daily newspapers have expanded in size and circulation. Summer 2004 saw the opening of the Hudson Valley Center for Contemporary Art in a 12,500-square-foot former home-improvement store on Main Street. It houses its founders' private collection and is the launch point for arts education, programs fostering emerging artists, an artist-in-residence program, and a lecture series.

> Our hard work will continue to improve Peekskill's reputation and image in the eyes of others but it's equally important to enhance community pride and identity.
>
> — Mayor John G. Testa[49]

Assets Employed
- Vacant, historic, mixed-use downtown building stock
- An existing nucleus of downtown resident artists
- Scenic placement on the Hudson River and proximity to New York City and Catskill Mountain resorts
- Visionary leadership
- Historic downtown theater
- Long-standing community support for a performing arts center
- Cooperative relationships among city agencies, artists, businesses, and nonprofits

Direct Outcomes

- Revitalization of historic, largely vacant downtown

- Investment of $8 million in housing, retail, and cultural facilities since 2000 with additional investment slated

- Relocation and expansion of education programs focusing on creative industries and skill development

- Increased tourist traffic

- Recognition that artists are contributors to economic vitality

- Construction of 23,000 square feet of new retail space and twenty-eight new live/work units

- Formation by the city of the "Grow Peekskill Fund" to provide loans, finance job creation, eliminate blight, and leverage local investment

- Opening of a new pharmacy and 65,000-square-foot supermarket

Indirect and Potential Impacts

- Revitalization of civic life through pedestrian activity, social events, and re-invigorated civic organizations

- Increase in tax assessments for the first time in a decade

STRATEGY ❸
Attract Investment by Creating Live/Work Zones for Artists

A Historic Waterfront Comes Alive

Torpedo Factory Artists' Association and the City of Alexandria, Virginia

www.torpedofactory.org
http://alexandriava.gov/city/about-alexandria

The Setting

Situated on the west bank of the Potomac River between Washington, DC, and Mount Vernon, Alexandria, Virginia, was established as an active port for nearby plantations in 1749. In the nineteenth century, it served as a rail transit hub for a booming manufacturing and commercial center. During the past half century, it became a growing suburb of Washington, DC. Its population grew to over 135,000, of which 54 percent is White, 22 percent African American, 15 percent Latino, and about 6 percent Asian American.

The Torpedo Factory was built on the historic waterfront in 1918 to manufacture and store armaments. During World War II, ten additional buildings were added to the complex; but, at the conclusion of the war, it became a warehouse for the military, U.S. Congress, and Smithsonian. It was then sold to the City of Alexandria in 1969. During the 1960s, the city took an interest in its historic structures and district and began to preserve and restore key elements. However, vigorous debate continued through the 1970s about what to do with the hulking factory.

Organization Type/Description

The City of Alexandria was incorporated in 1779. It operates with a mayor, council, and city-manager form of government. The city purchased the Torpedo Factory from the federal government and remains the building owner, leasing the property to the Torpedo Factory Artists' Association (TFAA). It managed and maintained the building until 1998, when it began to transfer responsibility to the artists' group.

The Torpedo Factory Artists' Association was formed in 1976 as a non-stock C-corporation under the leadership of Marian Van Landingham, then director of programs for the Alexandria Bicentennial Commission and president of the Art League. The TFAA operates the Torpedo Factory Art Center and derives its income from studio and gallery lease payments, gallery sales commissions, and event rentals. It works with a parallel nonprofit tax-exempt organization, the Friends of the Torpedo Factory Art Center, to raise funds to promote tours, educational programs, and artist services.*

Mission or Statement of Purpose

The TFAA is dedicated to creating and exhibiting fine arts and fine crafts in open studio settings and galleries where the public and the cultural community can meet, learn, and interact in the promotion and appreciation of the visual arts. While supporting the development of artists and their enterprises, the Torpedo Factory Art Center has served as the cornerstone of a revival of the waterfront and historic districts.

Goals and Strategies

Using the former weapons facility as an art center was conceived as a three-year Bicentennial project to attract attention and visitors to Alexandria's deteriorated waterfront area. It wasn't considered a permanent use. However, an enormous positive response from the public and artists assured continuation of the project. By providing suitable space for working artists with ample opportunities for public tours and sales, the project coincided with increasing interest in adjacent historic neighborhoods along the waterfront. The combination generated investment in retail, restaurant, and other cultural activities in the district, leading to a $4-million renovation of the Torpedo Factory in 1983. Strategies included the following:

• Promote high-quality artistic work through jury selection of artists for the eighty-three studios

Snapshot

Torpedo Factory Artists' Association
Alexandria, Virginia

Setting
• Historic port city outside Washington, DC, population 135,000
• Deteriorated industrial waterfront and historic area

Community Assets
• 71,000-square-foot unused munitions factory
• Strong leadership and active city government
• Scenic riverfront setting adjacent to historic area

Strategies
• Convert factory to artist studio, gallery, and museum space
• Develop and promote cultural activities
• Maintain high-quality artistic product
• Jointly promote historic district and artists

Outcomes
• More than 500,000 tourists each year
• Millions spent annually by art center visitors
• New perception as creative community
• Widely known cultural activities and educational programming

* A complete copy of the Governing Documents and Economic Impact Reports may be purchased through the Torpedo Factory Artist's Association. For more information, please visit www.torpedofactory.org.

- Require that the 160 resident artists maintain public hours and interact with and provide demonstrations for visitors
- Amplify activity levels through co-location of artists, galleries, the Art League, and the archeology museum, all of which work with large numbers of volunteers and students
- Encourage tourism by maintaining well-lit, clean, and welcoming circulation areas
- Coordinate activities with nearby food, commercial, and historical entities to promote circulation of visitors in adjacent neighborhoods
- Operate a sales gallery (the Target Gallery), and lease space for private and cooperative galleries
- Maintain a high level of public activity through rental of space for events and sponsorship of annual and periodic cultural activities and festivals
- Operate with a high level of involvement of artists in governance

General Description of Activities

The Torpedo Factory Art Center serves as the hub for 160 active artists. These artists create their work, engage with visitors, and sell directly from their studios or through one of several galleries in the facility. They work in a wide range of visual arts forms, including painting, pottery, photography, jewelry, stained glass, fiber, printing, sculpture, and digital arts.

As an entity, the Torpedo Factory Art Center sponsors a variety of regular and special cultural events, attracting an estimated 500,000 visitors each year including Arts Safari, Second Thursday Arts Nights, Holiday Open House, and other events.

The Torpedo Factory Artists' Association leases space to the fifty-year-old Art League for its instructional programs, which host more than 2,000 students each term with four terms per year. The nonprofit Friends of the Torpedo Factory Art Center sponsors exhibits, lectures, seasonal events, programs for children, and services for artists working in the Torpedo Factory. Events within the facility include the annual embassy reception and exhibition in the Target Gallery, Second Thursday Art Night lectures, and Friends mentoring program. The Target Gallery curates and hosts ongoing artist exhibits. Five other galleries lease space and promote the openings of regular exhibitions. Alexandria Archeology, housed within the center, is recognized as the most comprehensive city archeology program in the United States. It holds a collection of two million artifacts associated with eight thousand years of human history in Alexandria and works with up to 200 volunteers annually who actively uncover local history. It receives more than 30,000 visitors of all ages each year.

With the Torpedo Factory Art Center as the centerpiece, the historic district, along with a marina and promenade, regularly attracts residents and visitors alike. Since 1988 Alexandria has experienced an unprecedented revival known for its artists, galleries, museums, architecture, special events, restaurants, and hotels.

Assets Employed

- Heavily built industrial space on prominent waterfront location
- Competition among artists for suitable, accessible, prominent space
- Visionary leadership with experience in both the arts and civic affairs
- Willingness of city council to try artist-led venture
- Synergy created through emerging historic district, waterfront revival, and cooperation among key groups
- Growing interest among public to purchase quality arts-and-crafts objects and to see the creative process in action

Direct Outcomes

- Key position on the historic waterfront revitalized
- Conversion of a hulking abandoned factory into a hub of creativity and tourism

  According to a study prepared for the Torpedo Factory Artist Association by the International Institute of Tourism Studies at George Washington University in 1994 (Note: While the most recent formal study was conducted in 1994, all indications demonstrate that the economic impact has steadily grown during the past decade):

  – Visitors spent $2.3 million at the Torpedo Factory Art Center

  – The art center generated more than $1.8 million in local tax revenue

  – Art center visitors accounted for 12 percent of citywide purchases of lodging and 10 percent of food service purchases

  – Of about 500,000 visitors to the Torpedo Factory, 163,000 were motivated to visit Alexandria solely by the art center and spent more than $3 million in the city

  – Artists working at the art center spent more than $389,000 in the city for supplies and other expenses related directly to their business

- Transformation of image of Alexandria from an old industrial and shipping hub to a vibrant and creative retail and historic destination
- Shift to creative-service-based economy and desirable residential area

Most people like to watch others work, particularly if the work is skilled. Curiosity over how things are made is a basic human emotion. Open studios where visitors could watch painters, sculptors and print-makers as well as potters, jewelers, stained-glass workers and makers of musical instruments would be a great attraction.

— Marian Van Landingham, founder and first director of Torpedo Factory Art Center [50]

Indirect and Potential Impacts

- Nearly $150 million in new commercial and public construction in 2003

- Site of 460 technology companies, employing 12,000 people—an increase of 300 percent between 1997 and 2003

- Growth in employed residents through 2003, in reverse of national trends

- Continuing expansion of the existing 15 million square feet of office space in the central business district, with more than 3 million under construction in 2003

- Growth in local retail sales between 1997 and 2003 of 30 percent to more than $2 billion

Summary of Examples in Strategy 3: Attract Investment by Creating Live/Work Zones for Artists

Economists have advanced different theories as to the role and impact of artists and contemporary cultural expression. Whatever the theory, creative work has a gravitational pull of its own. Both the Peekskill Artists Loft Program and Alexandria's Torpedo Factory nurtured small, "creative solar systems," orbited by galleries, festivals, restaurants, small shops, and a variety of other enterprises. Ultimately, the gravitational spin drew in people and investment that brought these places new economic vitality.

It is unlikely that a more traditional industrial or commercial tenant of these seemingly obsolescent spaces would have attracted such a dynamic mix of human and economic activity. Communities abandoned by large-scale manufacturing companies were transformed by creative projects that synergized artists' creative work, local pride, new tourist attractions, and small business investment. Where there was emptiness, vibrant, hopeful communities came to life.

In the next section, we'll look at how arts and culture helped to diversify local economies.

Diversify the Local Economy

STRATEGY 4 IS AN ARTISTIC TWIST on the standard economic practice of diversification. The more legs, or sectors, an economy has to stand on, the more resistant it is to a downturn in any one sector. The creative community builders highlighted in this section tapped existing assets in their communities and applied creative strategies to support a variety of businesses and activities. They employed both imagination and art to build multiple legs for their economies. Building the connections between those sectors was perhaps their most creative act.

Cultural organizations and activities are able to attract people and investment to business districts, encourage growth in entertainment venues, and stimulate retail, restaurant, and office development in residential areas. They tend to increase commercial rental rates, decrease vacancy rates, and increase tax revenues, jobs, and incomes, according to Bill Hudnut, former Indianapolis Mayor and Senior Fellow at the Urban Land Institute.[52] Of course, not all the impacts of arts centers or arts districts are positive or sustainable. Much has to do with scale and with the nature of that enterprise as it relates to the cultures of the people and the place.

Roberta Brandes Gratz, an urban and historic preservation activist and writer, warns against the "big fix" and the "grand plan." She has chronicled dozens of successful urban redevelopment projects where the key was "thinking small in a big way."* Not only did these projects have more equitably distributed economic benefits but also they retained and built upon threads of existing social fabric. They served to strengthen communities first, a sharp contrast to more typical big-fix projects that demolish or dislocate the old to make way for investors, large chain stores, or transient manufacturers.

In this section, we'll look at examples of communities where the cultural, business, and civic sectors have come together to create interdependent economic networks. Lower Roxbury, a Boston neighborhood, and North Adams, in rural western Massachusetts, both used the unique assets of their residents, natural environment, proximity to other attractions, and local cultural assets to diversify their economies.

The arts, increased tourism and community participation, and regional economic redevelopment are mutually reinforcing and inextricably linked. The arts create and bestow community identity. Identity rallies hope, productivity and pride and economic vibrancy. These are the base conditions for a healthy community; they cannot be created, however, without risk, creativity, adventure, and the willingness to embrace the new.

— Massachusetts Museum of Contemporary Art (MASS MoCA)[51]

---

* Gratz has observed community redevelopment strategies for several decades, first in the United States and more recently in decimated Eastern European countries. In her two books, *The Living City* (1994) and *Cities Back from the Edge* (1998), she is critical of "urban removal" projects prominent in the 1960s and 1970s—but still practiced today—as well as mega-projects that destroy urban fabric. She advocates building from within, employing grassroots and bottom-up strategies.

Once a thriving section of Boston, and long an African American community, Lower Roxbury fell into deep distress forty years ago. A thirty-five-year-old community development corporation there is making painstaking, long-term efforts to restore Lower Roxbury's bustle and sense of pride. The CDC has drawn on the culture and creative abilities of residents as the catalyst.

In the historic rural milling center of North Adams, the Massachusetts Museum of Contemporary Art was created through dynamic relationships built between the city, state, nearby institutions, local businesses, and private funders. These relationships have resulted in a dramatic turnaround for businesses and residents alike. North Adams has drawn tourists, stimulated the launch of creative economy enterprises, and constructively interacted with all parts of the community.

STRATEGY ❹
Diversify the Local Economy

Trading on Local Talent

ACT Roxbury and Madison Park Development Corporation, Boston, Massachusetts

www.actroxbury.org
www.madison-park.org

The Setting
Once the second-largest shopping district in Boston, the Lower Roxbury/Dudley Square area is home to 41,000 people, numerous vibrant but lesser-known cultural organizations, many artists, and the city's largest bus transfer hub. In its 1940s and '50s heyday, the neighborhood boasted ballrooms, theaters, jazz clubs, and an ice cream parlor as important parts of community life. Since then, the area has experienced massive decay, loss of local businesses and retail shops, and an increase in crime and poverty. Commercial arteries retain the classic look of a nineteenth-century urban neighborhood, albeit with a few "missing teeth," that is, empty lots and boarded retail spaces. During the neighborhood's worst times, the businesses that survived were a few culturally based food, art, and music enterprises. And they remain today as key assets of a revitalization strategy.

Organization Type/Description
Arts, Culture, and Trade Roxbury (ACT Roxbury) is a program of forty-year-old Madison Park Development Corporation. This community development

corporation boasts a highly successful history of developing housing and business real estate, dating to its 1966 origins as the Lower Roxbury Community Corporation. One of the nation's first community-based development corporations, it was an outgrowth of community opposition to highway construction through the heart of Boston's most vibrant African American neighborhood. The community lost wide swaths of housing, businesses, and jobs to demolition for the highway, but it mounted a formidable political campaign that stopped the road construction. However, destruction of parts of the community, along with economic and social forces ravaging Black communities nationwide, took a toll on Roxbury. Throughout its first thirty years, Madison Park Development was highly successful at rebuilding housing for low- and mixed-income residents. However, it then had to seek strategies for bringing back businesses and jobs.

Today, Madison Park Development Corporation operates job training, community organizing, small business development, and youth programs, along with ACT Roxbury. Madison Park formalized ACT Roxbury in the late 1990s. Building on cultural assets became the cornerstone of its strategy to bring retail and service businesses to the neighborhood and to help them succeed. Addressing the business development and marketing needs of artists was also a key piece of that puzzle.

Mission or Statement of Purpose

ACT Roxbury's mission is to use arts and culture to enrich and strengthen the physical, economic, and social revitalization of the Dudley Square Business District and Lower Roxbury community. It engages and cultivates cultural businesses, artists, and institutions as economic resources and community assets.

Goals and Strategies

- Increase the economic viability of Roxbury artists, cultural institutions, and arts-related businesses by broadening their entrepreneurial savvy and their audience and customer base

- Actively partner with retail and service businesses to capture more economic activity in the neighborhood

- Rehabilitate the former Hibernian Hall into the Roxbury Center for Arts to host year-round events

- Transform the image of Roxbury from a community filled with violence and poverty to a community rich in creative talent and cultural heritage

- Develop a more diverse and interactive economy by attracting creative-sector businesses and generating local employment

- Assist artists and small organizations with creating events and programs

- Foster collaboration with multiple institutions and organizations

Snapshot

ACT Roxbury and Madison Park Development Corporation
Boston, Massachusetts

Setting
- Dudley Square and Lower Roxbury neighborhood, population 41,000
- Deteriorated business district
- High rates of crime and poverty

Community Assets
- Resident artist population
- African American businesses and cultural organizations
- Vacant lots and commercial properties
- Established multifaceted CDC

Strategies
- Create Roxbury Center for Arts at Hibernian Hall
- Reposition area as a creative and distinct community
- Create annual arts events to attract visitors and engage community
- Coordinate retail businesses and arts activities to increase impact
- Expand role of artists through business development support

Outcomes
- Community and visitor involvement in cultural activities
- Positive image and media attention resulting in re-investment
- Increased sales for artists and galleries, restaurants, and retail

Housing and traditional retail wasn't going to do it alone. We wanted to develop some "legal" nightlife activities.

— Candelaria Silva, director of ACT Roxbury[53]

General Description of Activities

ACT Roxbury forms multiple partnerships to create annual events and invests in the support structure for artists in the neighborhood. It developed a cultural center in Hibernian Hall, a four-story former Irish social club. The acclaimed annual Roxbury Film Festival celebrates the vision and the voice of New England filmmakers of color. Roxbury Open Studios showcases the work of visual artists and craftspeople in group shows, individual studios, and galleries and encourages cultural tourism that brings locals and outsiders to visit the many talented artists residing and working in Roxbury. Visitors also patronize local food and retail businesses.

To help artists develop the business side of their work, ACT Roxbury launched the "Roxbury Is Rich Holiday Shopping Guide," a colorful mini-catalog promoting creations of local artists as holiday gifts. Workshops are offered to strengthen artists' entrepreneurial skills.

The annual Roxbury in Motion performing arts event features area play-wrights and actors. The Roxbury Literary Annual, which includes a publication and series of readings at various sites, is a valuable vehicle for Roxbury writers to share their work. In 2004, the Roxbury Literary Annual began publishing a youth edition, featuring the work of high school students from Greater Roxbury.

Ultimately, Madison Park and ACT Roxbury have been the architects of a new identity and a revitalized economy for Roxbury—an identity as a vibrant African American cultural hub and a mixed economy including growing creative-sector businesses. This, in turn, is the catalyst to rebuild the community's sense of self and attract visitors, new residents, and investment. Madison Park and ACT Roxbury are building their community's cultural assets, identity, and skills while building its economy, housing, and infrastructure.

Assets Employed

- Existing Afro-centric businesses serving local residents
- WILD, a radio station serving the Black community for more than fifty years (WILD has since been sold and moved.)
- An African art gallery and the Museum of the National Center of Afro-American Artists, which bring visitors and buyers from near and far
- Northeastern University, Roxbury Community College, and other major institutions in walking distance of the commercial district
- The community's central commercial streets
- Artists who maintain residences and studios in the neighborhood
- Abandoned commercial building stock and vacant lots
- Visionary leadership that values the connections between community history, identity, and the work of artists

• Leadership with the skills to serve as intermediaries between artists, marketing, and small business development

Direct Outcomes

• Arts and cultural programs involving locals and visitors

• Positive media attention to Roxbury

• Renewed sense of community pride and identity

• Reinforced cohesion and entrepreneurial energy

• Increased business investment and new local jobs

• Strengthened for-profit and nonprofit cultural and service enterprises

• Increased sales for galleries and artists

• More invitations to Roxbury artists to participate in craft shows and art fairs and to teach

• Rejuvenated restaurant and retail sales

• Redevelopment of long-abandoned Hibernian social hall

Indirect and Potential Impacts

• Expanded tourism and trade

• Increased sense of connection among existing residents

• Greater population stability

STRATEGY ❹
Diversify the
Local Economy

Postindustrial Yankee Ingenuity

MASS MoCA (Massachusetts Museum of Contemporary Art), North Adams, Massachusetts

www.massmoca.org

The Setting

North Adams in northwestern Massachusetts sits at the confluence of two branches of the Hoosic River, a fertile area for the Mohawk Indians for centuries and the site of colonial-era manufacturing in the late 1700s. Industries included makers of shoes, bricks, cabinets, hats, wagons, and sleighs, as well as sawmills, machine shops, marble works, and ironworks. In 1860, Arnold Printworks set up as a textile printer. This manufacturer grew rapidly and, by the 1890s, twenty-five of its twenty-six now-standing mill structures were built. Arnold employed 3,200 workers but closed in 1942. Shortly thereafter, Sprague Electric Company moved in, eventually

MASS MoCA (Massachusetts Museum of Contemporary Art)

North Adams, Massachusetts

Setting

- Rural mill town, population 14,700
- Population decline since 1900
- High unemployment, especially since major mill closing in 1980s

Community Assets

- 700,000-square-foot mill on thirteen acres in town center
- Access to state and private funding
- Low-cost housing and commercial space
- Near major performing arts and visual arts venues and Williams College

Strategies

- Invest MASS MoCA in the economic success of the community and the economic success of the community in the museum
- Diversify the economy by promoting and housing creative businesses
- Create an attractive environment for creative-economy entrepreneurs

Outcomes

- At least 230 new jobs in first five years
- Major new business investment and spending
- Improved community image and civic engagement

employing over 4,000 workers—out of a total population at the time of 18,000. North Adams hit an economic low in the 1980s when the electronic components plant closed.

North Adams was once the largest city in the Berkshire Hills and one of the most prosperous, but by 1990 it ranked as the poorest. The economic boom of the 1980s, touted as the "Massachusetts Miracle," boasted a statewide 2.8 percent unemployment rate. Meanwhile, North Adams lagged far behind with a 19 percent unemployment rate. Negative self-image, youth flight, deterioration, and the usual panoply of ills plagued the scenic valley. Well-to-do summer tourists, while not far away, rarely ventured to North Adams.

Organization Type/Description

The Massachusetts Museum of Contemporary Art (MASS MoCA) is a nonprofit cultural institution launched by a partnership that included the City of North Adams, the State of Massachusetts, and nearby Williams College. The museum occupies the thirteen-acre site and 700,000 square feet of mill space once occupied by Sprague Electric. The site, which is adjacent to the city's downtown, is owned by a public commission of the City of North Adams. Just after the closing of Sprague Electric, the director of the Williams College Museum of Art, Tom Krens, envisioned using the space to exhibit large and unconventional works of contemporary art. As plans evolved, and when Krens became director of the Guggenheim, the site was briefly considered as a satellite for the famous New York museum.

Under the direction of Joseph Thompson, also from Williams College, the institution took on a more complex form. It now includes contemporary performing and interdisciplinary arts, artist residencies, and stronger ties to the history and culture of the local community. At its formal opening in 1999, MASS MoCA was the largest contemporary arts center in the United States. It was brought about by $18.6 million in state funding and approximately $8 million in private support. Since opening, it has attracted an additional $25 million in state, federal, and private funds for capital investments.

Mission or Statement of Purpose

The mission of MASS MoCA is to foster and present exciting new work of the highest quality in all media—and in all phases of production—and to position the arts as a vibrant catalyst for community revitalization. Founding Director Joseph Thompson sees MASS MoCA as "a place for innovation and fabrication using the most advanced knowledge and technology of the day." He eloquently compares this purpose to that of the previous users of the site, Arnold Printworks and Sprague Electric, drawing a link to the changing economy. The museum is integral to the creation of new markets, good jobs, and the long-term enrichment of the region. More than an art center, it's a nucleus of production for a new and growing creative economy, building on the history of its site.

Goals and Strategies

The museum had a long and difficult on-again off-again gestation period. The silver lining, according to Thompson, was the necessity to repeatedly re-conceptualize and re-articulate the goals of the museum in the context of the benefits it would bring the community and the region. Persistence paid off, and the museum is now more tied to the fortunes of North Adams than if it had been an outpost of the Guggenheim or if it had relied solely on tourist traffic. MASS MoCA describes itself as "an open platform where some of the best artists alive today come and work across media, making, showing, and teaching." It engages with local schools, audiences, and businesses, all of whom have a stake in it. Thompson and the staff frequently draw inspiration for exhibits from the history and culture of the community, the kind of "Yankee ingenuity" that drove its economy for so many years.

General Description of Activities

About 100,000 square feet of renovated exhibition space exhibits well-known and lesser-known contemporary American and international visual artists. Some 50,000 square feet is dedicated to performing arts—dance, theater, music, and multimedia presentations by nationally renowned artists and many indigenous and global cultures. A similar amount of outdoor space hosts summer performing arts events.

It is perhaps the 90,000 square feet of space leased to businesses that contributes to a diversified local economy in untold ways. Leasing is a significant part of the institution's income, and the closest thing it has to an endowment. But business leasing means more than that to North Adams. In 2004, MASS MoCA had nine tenants employing 300 people in intellectual-property-based businesses. They generated almost $1 million in lease income, and many millions more in employee income and taxes for the community. Tenants include a provider of online subscription publishing services, two regional law firms, a national book publisher, a software firm, an accounting firm, and a heating and air conditioning controls company. In addition, the Northern Berkshire District Court has leased 21,000 square feet for its new courthouse on adjacent property owned by the museum—an institutional neighbor the museum sees as putting it more at the center of civic activity.

One new enterprise is the Center for Creative Community Development (C3D). This center arose as a partnership among MASS MoCA, Williams College, and economics professor Stephen Sheppard. C3D leases space on the museum's "campus." With startup support from the Ford Foundation, C3D has set out to devise and test methodologies for assessing the impact of arts organizations on neighborhoods and cities, expanding on research Sheppard conducted in North Adams. The center also offers training, fellowships, and conferences.

We are entering another . . . new century and this city is doing a great job of diversifying its economic base by getting involved in MASS MoCA and high-technology businesses, with all of those being built on the traditional strengths of North Adams. We're changing with the times without letting go of those things which made the community great.

— State Senator Jane M. Swift [54]

The museum and enterprises leasing space there are following in the region's footsteps of "manufacturing" goods to meet contemporary needs—which happen to be a bit less tangible than the shoes, cabinets, textiles, or electronics historically made there, but which are no less important in today's economy. In choosing as its home a vacant postindustrial icon, now a symbol of artist lofts and creativity, MASS MoCA has become the community's most significant nexus of economic development activity.

Assets Employed

• Vacant, viable industrial space

• Vision and risk taking among local civic and business leaders

• State and regional economic developers with investment resources in search of exciting and viable strategies

• Intellectual resources at nearby Williams College, especially known for its arts and museum programs, as well as at a state college in North Adams

• Connections with high-net-worth individuals through Williams College and Berkshire area summer residents

• Persistence

• Proximity to seasonal cultural attractions such as Jacob's Pillow, Tanglewood, and Williamstown Theatre Festival

• Collaboration with tourism industries

• Spectacular valley setting amidst Berkshire Hills

• Low-cost quality housing and commercial space to attract workers

Direct Outcomes

• At least 230 new jobs created

• More than $14 million in annual new business spending

• More than $11 million in capital investments in hotel properties

• Downtown retail vacancies significantly reduced

• Estimated total increase in residential property value, or community wealth, of $14.3 million in 2003 dollars.

• Increased property values for homes near the museum of more than $10,000 in 2004 dollars

• No increase in residential turnover, with a constant or reduced percentage of households moving as compared to the previous decade

• New artist housing developed in other former mill properties, attracting scores of new residents from outside the area

MASS MoCA (Massachusettes Museum of Contemporary Art) in North Adams. The museum's 700,000 square feet of space once occupied an electronic components plant.

Indirect and Potential Impacts

• Turnaround in population loss, beginning with fewer young people leaving and new arrivals staying

• Dramatic turnaround in the community's self-image, pride, and civic engagement

• Increases in student test scores in subjects associated with programs conducted by the museum

Summary of Examples in Strategy 4: Diversify the Local Economy

Roxbury's ongoing revival is built equally upon physical infrastructure, cultural heart, creative spirit, history, and the entrepreneurial drive of artists and local small business owners. The long-term work of community developers and political advocates laid the groundwork. The arts and cultural activity generated through ACT Roxbury and its many partners stimulated ongoing neighborhood business activity and changed the image of the community. A variety of small "manufacturers" grew and retail and service businesses returned. Arts events and promotions, and now the renovated Hibernian Hall, feed the emerging local economy and bring people and business to a once-devastated part of Boston.

Although the setting and story differ (scenic rural community; industrial abandonment), North Adams leaned on a similar strategy. Seemingly out of place in small town America, the contemporary art museum both represents and stimulates the ingenuity and creative spirit of the people and the place. It renewed hope while creating a radically different image for a place once seen as a remnant of a bygone age. The success of MASS MoCA ignited the belief in possibility and motivated townspeople and others to become entrepreneurs. The museum provided business incubation space and an environment attractive to creative-class, or creative-economy, workers. Most of the investment and employment subsequent to the museum's opening have come through the other enterprises on the museum's campus, as well as in the adjacent downtown and surrounding neighborhoods.

ACT Roxbury and MASS MoCA are but two examples of groups that have leveraged the arts to diversify their local economies.

In the next section, we'll see how the arts can be used to improve property and enhance its value.

As a neighborhood attempts to re-form itself (or is re-formed by external forces) it must be proactive in working to prevent the displacement of its poorer residents and to encourage positive social and economic integration and identity building.

—Stephen Sheppard, Director of the Center for Creative Community Development [55]

Improve Property and Enhance Value

STRATEGY 5 IS ABOUT WAYS TO IMPROVE HOUSING and small business property by putting artists and the arts to work. Artists involved in restoring and building new housing can help stabilize communities in surprising ways and raise the value of place.

Bringing abandoned or underused real estate back onto tax rolls is a typical economic development strategy among cities and small towns across the United States. They are constantly looking for ways to revitalize downtrodden areas and improve the general prosperity of their citizens. Increasingly, some are courting creative industries, creative-class workers, and even artists, but a few have seen artists as investors and hands-on workers to revitalize property. The creative community builders highlighted in this strategy involved artists directly in investing their talent and resources to rebuild neighborhoods. In different ways, these two programs put artists to work to improve real estate while returning financial benefit to the artists and helping them build artistic careers.

Putting artists and craftspeople to work in neighborhood redevelopment is a strategy employed by HandMade in America and the West End/Clingman Avenue Revitalization Project in Asheville, North Carolina. Artists there are at work creating and enhancing affordable housing and animating nearby recreational environments. HandMade has successfully created a "brand name" for the region's treasure trove of craftspeople, calling it the center of the handmade object in America. In Asheville, HandMade has set to work to engage artists to improve a neighborhood's housing stock.

Paducah, Kentucky, suffering from long-term disinvestment and a sagging economy, made national headlines in 2001 with its Artist Relocation Program. The community offers a significant package of incentives to artists who move there, purchase and restore one of its many vacant and neglected historic homes, and set up shop. The town's quaint setting and architecture, combined with a low cost of living, have attracted many new artist homeowners who have become invested community members.

These examples illustrate how bold and creative ideas that build upon local assets and talents can make a difference in a community's short-term economic fortunes while creating long-term value in the place.

The Downside of Increasing Property Values

Bringing artists into a community to improve property and enhance value can have unintended consequences. It can set off a process of gentrification that results in dislocation of poor and/or longtime residents. For example, some New York City real estate values increased so rapidly when artists moved in that the sight of them literally set off protests.[56] A 2002 study by the Center for an Urban Future confirmed that such concerns were justified. "In five of the seven neighborhoods we assessed, concerns about displacement were plainly laid at the feet of cultural development," the report stated. In another study, the same group examined commercial rents and found a clear correlation between areas where artists and cultural development were present and escalation in rents far in excess of city averages.[57]

Of course, while artists or small arts groups are often blamed for bringing about gentrification, they are as often its victims. "Cultural development that drives away longtime residents and artists might benefit property owners in the short term but cannot be considered successful for the community and in the long-term interests of local business."[58]

Gentrification or "condominiumization" often results in dislocation of poor, working-class, and elderly residents. It does seem to follow on the heels of transient artists as demonstrated in some New York neighborhoods. Some creative community builders are trying to address this unintended consequence.* Finding ways to increase prosperity and build equity for all is the challenge.**

* For information on gentrification and equitable development practices, PolicyLink provides a variety of resources, including the handbook *Advocating for Equitable Development*, 2004. www.policylink.org.

** Two remarkable arts organizations in two major cities have rehabbed abandoned houses and provided housing for low-income residents. Project Row Houses renovated and built over fifty residential units in one of Houston's poorest areas. (www.projectrowhouses.org) Likewise, the Village of Arts and Humanities in Philadelphia restored many units and brought hope and an emerging economy and vitality to a devastated area of that city. (www.villagearts.org)

STRATEGY **5**

Improve Property and Enhance Value

Adding That Handmade Touch

West End/Clingman Avenue Revitalization Project and HandMade in America, Asheville, North Carolina

www.handmadeinamerica.org
www.mtnhousing.org

The Setting

Asheville sits at the heart of North Carolina's picturesque Blue Mountains. One of its oldest neighborhoods, the West End/Clingman Avenue area, steadily declined over much of the past century as the area was carved up by city, state, and federal governments. Road projects and city maintenance facilities were located there with disregard for the existing community. Streets, churches, schools, homes, and meeting places were removed, and the area became a pass-through for people going elsewhere.

Snapshot •

West End/Clingman Avenue Revitalization Project and HandMade in America
Asheville, North Carolina

Setting
- Historically defined neighborhood near the downtown of a regional rural center
- Population of 2,900 in decline
- Poorly planned highways cutting off the neighborhood

Community Assets
- Large population of crafts artists in the region
- Active neighborhood association and nonprofit housing developer
- Historic architecture and natural amenities

Strategies
- Integrate handmade crafts in housing rehab and construction
- Involve community members in renewal of neighborhood
- Develop public spaces and cultural events to enhance neighborhood identity

Outcomes
- Improved property and more positive perception of area
- Increased market and appreciation for crafts
- More active public spaces

With a growing community of artists and nearby natural resources (French Broad River to the west and a ten-acre one-hundred-year-old riparian forest to the east), the West End neighborhood was a microcosm of the region's attractive qualities. Its nineteenth-century mill cottages and early-twentieth-century bungalows located on narrow and steep winding streets and fronted by hedge-enclosed gardens added to the ingredients for a walkable, mixed-use community.

The West End had 2,914 residents in 2000, a 15 percent decrease from ten years earlier, with a 5 percent loss of African Americans and a 4 percent increase in Asians and Latinos. It was a transitional area of mostly renters, yet with 30 percent of residents reporting they had lived in the same house for more than twenty years and several for more than fifty.

Organization Type/Description

HandMade in America, a nonprofit community development corporation, was founded in 1994 by a group of western North Carolinians struggling to find new approaches to economic development. They were committed to finding strategies rooted in the strengths and identity of the region—as opposed to recruiting new industry. In less than ten years they succeeded at coalescing a major "new" industry—one that had been there all along—and developing new local and tourist markets. HandMade in America is well on its way to making the region "the center of the handmade object in America."

The West End/Clingman Avenue Neighborhood Revitalization Project is a partnership of Mountain Housing Opportunities, the WECAN Residents' Association, and the Odyssey Center for Ceramic Arts. HandMade in America saw an opportunity in this housing development project to bring the craftsman's touch and joined forces with these groups.

Mission or Statement of Purpose

HandMade in America's mission is "to celebrate the hand and the handmade, to nurture the creation of traditional and contemporary craft, to revere and protect our resources, and to preserve and enrich the spiritual, cultural, and community life of our region." The organization's work centers on nurturing indigenous crafts and developing both a local and a broader market for handmade objects. Working primarily through partnerships, HandMade in America pursues economic, cultural, and social development in Asheville and the region.

One of its most successful partnerships has been with the West End/Clingman Avenue Revitalization Project. This project uses arts-based strategies to change the perception of the West End neighborhood from that of a pass-through area to that of a strong, vibrant community in which all the disparate parts are connected and engaged in issues that affect the community. In working together with HandMade in America, the project brings handmade objects and high-quality craftsmanship into the building and renovation process to both stimulate the crafts economy and add value to the homes and distinctiveness to the neighborhood.

Goals and Strategies

The West End/Clingman Avenue Revitalization Project came about as the partners discovered the characteristics of the neighborhood and the importance of a responsible reaction to changing housing trends. With a surge in national attention as one of the best places to live, Asheville's housing market began to heat up in the mid-1990s. Organizational partners ascertained that housing design and construction was the third-fastest growing economic sector in the region. HandMade saw the simultaneous need to protect artist and low-income housing in the West End neighborhood, less than a half mile from downtown, while creating a vibrant, livable community.

Guiding objectives established for the West End/Clingman project are

- To support the development of new economies in the neighborhood born of the work of local artists and craftspeople

- To recognize and celebrate the unique spirit and history of the locale

- To create and revitalize active and meaningful public space

Key strategies include the following

- New affordable housing construction and rehabbing historic homes

- Incorporation of artist-made elements in housing construction

- Inclusion of landscaping, environmental restoration, and gardens

- Development of public spaces that have strong aesthetic qualities and that bring people together

General Description of Activities

The West End/Clingman Avenue Revitalization Project set out to build and rehab affordable housing in a racially mixed neighborhood while simultaneously developing new markets for the region's artists and craftspeople. By combining resources, the partners were in a unique position to build model homes to demonstrate the incorporation of handmade objects in home construction. Included were artists working in architectural glass, fiber, metal, ceramics, and stone, as well as in liturgical and public art. Those model homes provided the basis for development of a catalog and showroom of crafts features. These features have included kitchen and bathroom tile, cabinetry, woodwork, and windows, as well as optional furniture and landscaping elements.

To attract further attention to the West End neighborhood, the groups, together with others, created a festival to both showcase local architecture and crafts and promote the considerable presence of artists and craftspeople living or working in the neighborhood. This is in addition to monthly tours of artists studios (there were more than forty in 2003) and neighborhood gardens.

> **M**uch of heritage development had been focused on historic preservation or recreation, such as rivers, mountains, and old houses. [HandMade] broke that wide open and brought attention to the fact that the region's living culture is perhaps one of its most important assets.
>
> — Lynda McDaniel, *Appalachian Magazine* [59]

Glass and ceramic work done at HandMade in America's EnergyXChange Incubator program that supports entrepreneurs.

Working with the neighborhood and city, the West End/Clingman Avenue Revitalization Project planned a new streetscape for Clingman Avenue, which included new trees, sidewalks, and front gardens and hedges, emulating the historically vibrant public realm. Further improvements included commissioning public arts projects that embody the spirit of the neighborhood, and involving artists and residents in developing pocket parks in and around in-fill development sites. Restoration of a ten-acre riparian forest parallel to Clingman Avenue with walking trails, signage, and public art was also begun.

The partners launched an oral history and photo documentation project to integrate stories from the past with those of the present. The project is inclusive of the neighborhood's diverse voices and has resulted in an exhibit and performance piece connecting old and new residents, along with securing permanent documentation of the community's transformation.

The involvement of artists in the design of new affordable housing and rehabbing of historic homes, along with public art and public amenities, creates a community with far greater meaning—a place that will have greater value to residents well into the future.

Assets Employed

- Relationships with a wide range of quality crafts artists
- A high-potential urban neighborhood with an active residents' association
- Strong partnership between a creative and flexible nonprofit housing developer, advocates for artists, and a neighborhood
- Marketing savvy based on the perceived and real value of handmade crafts

Direct Outcomes

- Elevated desirability of West End/Clingman as a residential and commercial destination
- Long-term, sustainable home values
- Increased market for handmade crafts
- Stronger social integration and understanding across ethnic groups
- Visibility and positive perception of the neighborhood
- Greater appreciation of artists, crafts, and creativity in a community setting
- More active public spaces

Indirect and Potential Impacts

- Elevated home and urban design values
- Increased city tax base
- Vast market potential for handmade crafts
- A more civically engaged community

No Down Payment Required

The Paducah Artist Relocation Program, City of Paducah, Kentucky

www.paducaharts.com
www.ci.paducah.ky.us

STRATEGY ❺
Improve Property
and Enhance
Value

The Setting

The Southern river town of Paducah, Kentucky, is located at the junction of the Tennessee and Ohio rivers, halfway between Saint Louis and Nashville. Like many such towns, its historic downtown was slowly drained when shopping malls opened on the outskirts during the 1960s. The population is about 75 percent White with 22 percent African American and a small Latino community. The Port of Paducah is a regular stop for riverboats, averaging thirty-five stops a year by the *Mississippi Queen, Delta Queen, American Queen,* and several others. These stops bring about 11,000 visitors to the downtown area each year.

Lowertown, directly adjacent to the downtown, is Paducah's oldest residential neighborhood. It is now zoned for both residential and business uses. Once home to the town's more well-to-do, Lowertown contains many large houses in Victorian, Italianate, Queen Anne, and Romanesque styles. Most of these houses had been left to deteriorate or been divided into boarding houses since the 1950s.

The community sees its distinguishing character as its love for the arts. Home of several arts organizations, including the world's largest quilt museum, Paducah is becoming a regional and national cultural destination. Paducah also boasts: Four Rivers Performing Arts Center, a new $44 million presenting venue; Market House Theatre, named one of the top ten community theaters in the United States; Maiden Alley Cinema, showing independent, foreign, and first-run feature films; Paducah Symphony Orchestra; River Heritage Museum; and Yeiser Art Center, home to a permanent collection of nineteenth and twentieth century art and ongoing exhibitions of regional and national artists.

Organization Type/Description

The City of Paducah, Kentucky, serves a community of just over 26,000 people in McCracken County, population 65,500. It operates with a city manager/mayor/commissioner form of government. Together with locally owned Paducah Bank, the town launched its Artist Relocation Program in August 2000. Through this high-risk venture led by artist and resident Mark Barone, the city advertised nationally for artists to relocate, purchase, and renovate homes and studios in the distressed Lowertown neighborhood. An

The Paducah Artist Relocation Program
Paducah, Kentucky

Setting
- Older Mississippi River town, population 26,000
- Sagging economy, deteriorating commercial and residential properties

Community Assets
- Low real estate costs
- Vacant retail and commercial properties
- Abandoned and underused historic residential properties
- Active regional arts organizations

Strategies
- Offer relocation incentives to attract artists
- Promote collaboration between arts, business, and city government
- Support and promote community and cultural activities
- Invest in infrastructure and cultural institutions

Outcomes
- Seventy new resident artists and property owners since 2000
- An increase of 300 percent in residential property values in five years
- Community branding reinforced by awards and media attention
- Increased civic involvement and pride

extensive package of incentives was offered and, combined with extremely low real estate costs, the effort resulted in an astounding revival.

Mission or Statement of Purpose

The Artist Relocation Program was conceived to transform a down-and-out residential area into an up-and-coming community of artists, galleries, and other businesses and to become a self-sufficient creative neighborhood designed by and for artists. Mark Barone, a painter and seventeen-year resident of Lowertown, first proposed the idea to city leaders and gained their support along with that of Paducah Bank. Barone made the audacious suggestion that just as the presence of artists helped transform New York City's SoHo, TriBeCa, and Chelsea neighborhoods, they could revitalize Lowertown, restore neglected buildings, add cultural diversity, bring new life and business, and increase the town's tax base.

Goals and Strategies

The program's strategy of combining investment by artists, the city, and private lenders focuses on expanding ownership in live/work spaces and motivating creative new residents to take an active role in their neighborhood. It also relies on collaborative efforts across the arts, business, and all parts of city government, including planning, inspections, police, and the city council, as well as the major involvement of the Paducah Bank. The effort is built around the availability of low-cost real estate as well as vacant lots available to artists who agree to a building plan and loan package.

Key strategies include the following

- An aggressive package of financial incentives for artists
- Promotion of the walkable downtown and the adjacent arts/historic district
- Support and promotion of activities such as Downtown After Dinner, which coordinates six blocks of live entertainment on Saturday nights, gallery walks, and other outdoor public events May through September
- City investment of more than $2 million in infrastructure and streetscaping in Lowertown and major upgrades to a downtown cinema
- Coordination of the multiple cultural assets with other services and resources
- Combination and coordination of development of galleries, coffee shops, restaurants, visitor accommodations, and other services for the growing central district population and for visitors and tourists

General Description of Activities

Aided by Tom Barnett, the city's director of planning, and other partners, the Paducah Artist Relocation Program has drawn national attention. Its success is credited to the fact that the city and its major private lender made the program a front-burner priority.

Artists are actively recruited through national advertising, follow-up calls, and visits. Low interest rates on real estate loans are available with discounts on closing costs as much as 100 percent. Loans are often approved at up to 300 percent of the appraised property value to finance renovations. The city pays up to $2,500 for architectural services or other professional fees in the renovation or building process.

Artists acquiring historic properties are eligible for a preservation tax credit of up to 20 percent for rehabilitation of historic structures. Federal Enterprise Zone incentives are also available, making all renovation materials tax free. The program offers artists free web pages and joint marketing and promotion by the city. Perhaps as important for the artists is that they are warmly welcomed and quickly made to feel like contributing members of an active and engaged community.

Local visits and tourism traffic are generated through a mix of citywide events, other special events, advertising of artists, and regular gallery walks. Seasonal riverboat passengers stopping at the Port of Paducah are encouraged to stroll and shop in local art galleries and stores. A city floodwall has been the site of a long-term mural project by artist Robert Dafford, now with over twenty mural panels that reflect the city's history. They provide the backdrop for an annual celebration, the Arts in Action Festival, where actors portray the characters in the murals and during which a Taste of Paducah, an artist fair, and other community and cultural events take place.

In late 2004, thirty properties were still available for purchase, including old Victorian homes, bungalows, historic office buildings, storefronts, and studio/gallery apartments. Properties were advertised on the relocation program web site for as low as $27,500.

Assets Employed

- Low-priced, architecturally significant housing stock
- Compact, walkable downtown and adjacent historic residential area
- Visionary artist leadership able to advocate and dedicate time
- City leaders open to bold risk-taking venture
- Location on major river and tourist stop for riverboat cruises
- Locally owned bank willing to take a risk on artists as owners and restorers of historic homes
- Existing arts organizations to both help promote new resident-artists and draw visitor traffic
- City zoning and code flexibility allowing mixed uses in the historic district

I decided instead of going where the "cool" is, we should bring the "cool" to us—and that is exactly what this program is doing. The benefits we are giving the city are almost as important to me as the satisfaction I get from making art. It's nice to be able to walk home to a house that I love in a neighborhood that I love and work on my art.

— Nathan Brown, Paducah artist [60]

Direct Outcomes

- As of fall 2005, seventy artists relocated to Paducah from all regions of the United States, becoming property owners and engaged citizens
- Abandoned properties brought back to productive use
- Growing tax rolls (houses purchased for $20,000 to $45,000 were appraised three to four years later at up to three times that value)
- Private investment in real estate of more than $11.5 million
- $1.2 million in city funds committed to infrastructure upgrades, including 144 historic-designed lights enhancing the gallery district
- Feature articles in eighteen national publications and a public television documentary
- Awards from the Kentucky Governors Office, Kentucky Chapter of the American Planning Association, American Planning Association, Kentucky League of Cities, Kentucky Bankers Association, and National Recreation and Parks Association

Indirect and Potential Impacts

- A $44 million performing arts center built downtown with public and private money
- Growing momentum for sustainable economic development based on entrepreneurship, wider sales of locally made products, and tourism
- Reversal of the "brain drain" from this small city
- Dramatic increases in civic pride and civic participation

Summary of Examples in Strategy 5: Improve Property and Enhance Value

In taking raw materials and creatively altering or adapting them, artists enhance value and change meaning. These transformations may or may not seem complex, but they are not simple to evaluate in economic terms. HandMade in America and Paducah have shown that, when artists are involved in home construction, rehabilitation, or restoration, they can bring properties into productive use while increasing their value in multiple ways.

HandMade's dual purposes of providing a livelihood for regional artisans and regenerating an Asheville neighborhood benefited from a thriving community of artists and craftspeople. New and historic homes with unique features and quality, handmade amenities retain value—and tell stories. These homes will be places to live that also have greater meaning. In turn, they will move their inhabitants to have a stronger feeling of investment in the place they call home.

Many of the houses in the river town of Paducah were originally built with great artistry and craftsmanship. It may well be those features that attracted artists to these period properties. Seeking inexpensive live/work space and a supportive, small-town environment, artists drawn to Paducah, in turn, bring value back to these houses through painstaking labor. In bringing vibrant enterprises, economic activity, and a high quality of neighborhood life, these artists represent a new generation of creative community builders and leaders.

Best Practices in Building Strong Economies through Arts and Culture

Chapter 2 examined these five strategies to build strong economies through arts and culture:

Strategy 1: Create Jobs

Strategy 2: Stimulate Trade through Cultural Tourism

Strategy 3: Attract Investment by Creating Live/Work Zones for Artists

Strategy 4: Diversify the Local Economy

Strategy 5: Improve Property and Enhance Value

Ten examples illustrated these community revitalization approaches. Each, multifaceted in its own right, represents a number of best practices, all of which are important to consider in developing strategies for your community.

1. Build on existing assets and capacities and begin on a scale appropriate to the means and needs of the community and the initiators

2. Renew hope, engage the imagination, and create a sense of positive momentum that is both real and symbolic

3. Project and build upon a distinct identity that focuses the community's cultural and natural amenities and taps artists and entrepreneurs who reflect that identity and contribute to it

4. Build and rely upon mutually beneficial relationships and exchanges across sectors and among artists, trades, developers, local businesses, cultural groups, policy makers, and public agencies

5. Engage diverse populations, especially youth, in design and realization of projects, activities, and programs; include learning experiences for everyone

6. Utilize familiar public and private spaces that foster social interaction among neighbors, artists, visitors, and community partners

7. Include in leadership roles intermediaries who understand and can "translate" ideas and skills from one sector or culture to others

8. Help artists and entrepreneurs establish ownership, especially in under-utilized spaces that have capacity for living, work, and mixed-used development

9. Incorporate multiple activities and policies that promote artists, cultural products, and community events based upon long-term impacts and benefits

Chapter 3 presents five more strategies. These strategies emphasize the non-economic side of community building—actions that increase the sense of connectedness between people and thus create the kinds of neighborhoods people want to live in.

CHAPTER 3
Building Social Connections through Arts and Culture

THE LINKS BETWEEN the economic health of a community and the quality of its social bonds are becoming increasingly clear. A growing school of economists see a cause-and-effect relationship between social capital and economic development. Robert Putnam and other sociologists have supplied convincing evidence that strong social connections—and the ability to form them across differences—are necessary ingredients of economic success.

In looking for the ingredients that affect the physical well-being of people in different kinds of places, Dr. Felton Earls, a Harvard professor of public health, conducted an extensive, fifteen-year study in neighborhoods across Chicago. His research found that the single-most important factor differentiating levels of health from one neighborhood to the next was what he called "collective efficacy." He was surprised to find that it wasn't wealth, access to healthcare, crime, or some more tangible factor that topped the list. A more elusive ingredient—the capacity of people to act together on matters of common interest—made a greater difference in the health and well-being of individuals and neighborhoods.[62] In addition, Earls found that children were the most universal common ground around which people act—a source of common interest and agreement through which a community's level of collective efficacy is demonstrated.

Is it any surprise that material, physical, and social well-being are interrelated? They manifest differently, but they all depend on the connections people have with each other. The "glue" that holds communities together and allows them to function is based in relationships that transcend family structures, race, class, religion, ethnicity, and other definers. Regardless of what we call it—"social capital" (Putnam), "trust" (Fukuyama), or "collective efficacy" (Earls)—without this glue, communities and their business and civic enterprises would grind to a halt. What is less well known is how it gets produced or where it comes from.

Chapter 3 looks at ways social capital is both generated and exercised. We'll study examples where public agencies, arts organizations, and community development corporations have successfully built or rebuilt heightened levels

Over the past generation, America's communities have undergone profound social and cultural changes, which meant that as the new millennium dawned, we were no longer building the dense webs of encounter and participation so vital to the health of ourselves, our families, and our polities.... Reweaving social webs will depend in part on the efforts of dedicated local leaders who choose to pursue their goals through the slow, frequently fractious, and profoundly transformative route of social capital building.

— Robert D. Putnam and Lewis M. Feldstein[61]

of social capital or civic engagement by creatively harnessing art, culture, and design as community building tools.

Finding greater common ground and ways of working together that address other types of concerns—for example, public infrastructure and civil rights—is challenging. The communities profiled here found opportunities for people to come together in creation and celebration of culture. They developed their social capital by cooperating, sharing, and seeking and finding shared goals, and by developing ties on a cultural level. These connections serve these communities well in their other endeavors—from economic development to civic participation to healthy living.

This chapter surveys five specific strategies for building social and physical infrastructure.

6. Promote Interaction in Public Space: Engage people in public spaces through public art and collective cultural experience

7. Increase Civic Participation through Cultural Celebrations: Strengthen connections between neighbors through cultural celebrations and festivals

8. Engage Youth: Include young people in civic affairs and enterprises through meaningful work and activity

9. Promote Stewardship of Place: Develop civic pride and responsibility through good "place making" and design practices

10. Broaden Participation in the Civic Agenda: Expand involvement in civic issues and governance through community-centered arts and cultural practices

Each strategy is illustrated with two examples from different parts of the United States and from communities large and small. These selections reflect the unique qualities, strengths, and interests of their communities. They also spring from different kinds of organizations—arts groups, community development organizations, municipal agencies, and others.

While each is described under one of the five strategic headings, it is truly artificial to categorize them by one type of outcome. To discuss WaterFire Providence, for example, as promoting social interaction in public space, is not to ignore its enormous economic impacts. Or, to cite Artists for Humanity for building cross-cultural working relationships among youth is not to ignore its long-term contribution to a creative economy. These efforts are successful because they "fire on many cylinders" as engines of social, civic, and economic development.

The solutions you find for your community may resemble some of the examples, but to succeed, they must be created from homegrown assets. The following also exemplify a number of best practices that are described on page 121.

(1) (2) (3) (4) (5) **(6)** (7) (8) (9) (10)

Promote Interaction in Public Space

STRATEGY 6 IS ABOUT ENGAGING PEOPLE in public spaces through public art and collective cultural experience. Bringing people together this way can build social capital. This strategy uses cultural activities and the process by which they are created to increase civic involvement and enhance social networks.

Public space and marketplaces are essential ingredients in every community. Public space provides opportunities for people to meet and be exposed to a variety of neighbors. These meetings often take place by chance, but they also can come through active organizing. Public spaces include streets, sidewalks, parks, waterfronts, and civic buildings. Other important, often privately operated, spaces include places for the exchange of goods, such as farmers markets, grocery stores, coffee shops, and restaurants. Public markets are an age-old forum for the exchange of cultural products and forms of expression. There are many wonderful ones across the country, and they seem to be on an upswing.

The art of promoting constructive interaction among people in public spaces has been nearly forgotten. Planners, architects, and public administrators have focused more on creating aesthetic places and on providing for the unimpeded movement and storage of automobiles than on creating places that encourage social interaction.[64] More recently, public officials have been even more concerned with security and maximizing their ability to observe and control people in public spaces.

As mentioned in Chapter 1 of this book, William H. Whyte asserted that crowded, pedestrian-friendly, active spaces are safer, more economically productive, and more conducive to healthy civic communities. "What attracts people most, it would appear, is other people," he wrote.[65] Since the 1950s, city planners, developers, policy makers, and transportation engineers have built and modified communities in just the opposite vein.

While the design of public space influences its use, leaders in the field claim that 80 percent of the success of a public space is the result of its "management,"[66] referring to how the space is maintained and activities programmed. In other words, even in the best-designed spaces for public interaction, activities need to be planned, and the space needs to be clean, secure, and well maintained, or it is unlikely to serve people well.

Equally for urban planners and policymakers, there is recognition that artistic works can enable dialogue between diverse people and groups; that cultural heritage can become a focal point for regenerating derelict neighborhoods or, indeed, for reinventing a whole city's "sense of place"; and that by valuing self-expression, the arts and culture contribute to active citizenship.

— Neil Bradford [63]

The term place in creative community building refers to a location within a community that has achieved deep and widespread meaning and value to locals and visitors alike. Taking mere "space" and turning it into "place" (what some observers call "place making") means creating something collectively valued and used as a key building block to a vital community. This is what the groups highlighted in Strategy 6 have done—engaged people, their creativity, their cultures, and their civic instincts in both making and using good places that, in turn, result in a stronger civic culture.

Research on civic engagement also points to the importance of places in which people feel comfortable and cross paths. In such spaces, important informal community interaction occurs. These include neighborhood stores, laundromats, schools, playgrounds, churches, and sidewalks. In such spaces, interpersonal communication occurs by chance as neighbors encounter one another.[67]

Public art administrators and cultural planners of all kinds can be significant players in designing, managing, and programming public space. Increasingly, artists are being tapped to collaborate with architects, landscape architects, engineers, and city planners in the design and creation of public spaces, buildings, roads, highways, and public transit facilities.

"Public art goes far beyond sculptures plopped in plazas or murals painted on walls," writes Jack Becker, a national leader in this field.[68] Becker goes on, "It now includes pyrotechnic performances, sound installations, light projections, puppet parades, and playful plastic animals."

As important as the space, piece of art, or event is the process by which it is created. A puppet parade may simply be a group of artists marching in the street, or it may be the result of a lengthy, community-wide process involving hundreds of residents who brainstorm themes, construct and paint the puppets, plan the activities, and march together with their families and neighbors.

Creating and bringing activity to meaningful public spaces in ways that generate collective efficacy, trust, and social capital is the focus of Strategy 6. Following are two examples of programs that not only bring people into public spaces but also instill pride, belonging, interaction, and human connection.

Created by a public artist, WaterFire, a public art event in Providence, Rhode Island, brings unprecedented numbers of people together on a regular basis to share a profound experience. Equally important to this old New England city, WaterFire involves hundreds of volunteers and supporters, and it has become part of the community's collective identity. On the opposite side of the country, the residents of the small town of Baker City, Oregon, responded to a benefactor's affinity to the banks of the Powder River and came together to build public spaces that connect the community to its past and future.

Igniting a New Urban Spirit

WaterFire Providence, Providence, Rhode Island

www.waterfire.org

The Setting

Providence, the capital of Rhode Island, is a New England transportation and manufacturing center of 173,000 people. Founded in colonial times, it began a gradual decline at the start of the twentieth century. The city faced abandonment, deterioration of business and physical infrastructure, and a sharp drop in civic self-esteem. Providence was known as the "armpit" of New England. Population stagnated and schools and other public institutions were in tough shape.

Built at the convergence of two rivers, Providence covered its polluted downtown waterways in the 1950s with roads, rail yards, and expanded parking lots. In the early 1990s, the city uncovered, or "daylighted," the rivers and lined them with public promenades and pedestrian-friendly parks. Along with preserving its colonial-era architecture, Providence promoted an event known as First Night, a family-friendly, alcohol-free New Year's Eve celebration to attract downtown visitors. But the once-a-year event wasn't enough to trigger a downtown renewal or entice residents to use the new promenades.

Organization Type/Description

WaterFire, a public art event that takes place on the downtown waterways, became the needed catalyst for revitalization. The event involves music, performances, ceremonial bonfires, boats, and ritual and, when it is staged, transforms nearly one mile of Providence's downtown. Artist Barnaby Evans conceived Water-Fire as a one-time event in 1994 as part of First Night, but he was persuaded to reprise it two years later for a national public art conference. Private citizens immediately recognized the power of Evans' spectacle, in which fire evoked a ritual feel and the flames symbolized the renaissance of the city. Their support, seconded by the city's mayor, led to the institutionalization of WaterFire as a community ritual in 1997.

Evans created WaterFire Providence in 1997 as a nonprofit organization to carry on the public art event. Today, twenty-five events, or "lightings," are held each year, spring through fall. Each event attracts as many as 100,000 people to downtown Providence's public spaces. The organization has a full-time staff of twelve, a seasonal crew of five additional workers, a dozen subcontractors, and hundreds of volunteers. Over $1.4 million in annual

Volunteers lighting fire basins for a WaterFire event. The events engage hundreds of community volunteers and attracts thousands of visitors each year.

funding comes from local sponsorships, grants, and individual contributions. Multiple partnerships with social service, education, arts, and civic groups help promote other causes through the event and provide a steady stream of volunteers, weaving a fabric of community through multiple levels of participation.

Mission or Statement of Purpose

WaterFire Providence was established to continue the WaterFire event and to foster and promote the creation, exhibition, and performance of other works of art by Rhode Island artists. The presence of large crowds during WaterFire provides opportunities to feature presentations of other visual and performing artists. In addition, the public's enthusiasm has allowed other partnerships to sponsor permanent public art installations, such as a memorial wall dedicated to victims of the September 11 tragedy in New York City.

Goals and Strategies

WaterFire is a key element in the remarkable revitalization of downtown Providence's community spirit as well as its economic fortunes, and it has been called the crown jewel of the Providence renaissance. The event involves diverse elements of the community in a ritual that brings international recognition and tourism to a once-sleepy, old New England city. The strategies of WaterFire Providence are to

- Produce a recurring event with evocative underlying symbolism
- Transform the public perception of the rivers and downtown area
- Use visual metaphors and references to Greek mythology, great rivers of the world, and Providence's heritage as a historic harbor
- Induce ritual-like responses through engagement of all the senses
- Employ indigenous skills of woodcutting, fire tending, and boating
- Engage a large number of volunteers in functionally and symbolically meaningful tasks
- Maintain high-environmental standards in acquiring and burning wood, and in cleaning the river and public spaces

General Description of Activities

WaterFire creator and director Barnaby Evans, a graduate of Providence-based Brown University, explained in 1997, "Fire and water are both seen as living entities. They're both seen as powerful forces of both good and evil in many traditions. So you've got purifying fires, you've got purifying rivers, you've got all-destroying fires and all-destroying floods."[69]

WaterFire is both ritual and spectacle. One hundred fire baskets, or braziers, are placed at regular intervals in waterways that wind through the center of downtown. Filled with fragrant local firewood and set ablaze at dusk, they're

Snapshot

WaterFire Providence
Providence, Rhode Island

Setting
- Nearly 400-year-old colonial city, population 173,000
- Seaport city built on intersection of two rivers

Community Assets
- Well-designed public areas
- Risk-taking city leadership
- Growing downtown artist community

Strategies
- Support public art project utilizing downtown rivers
- Celebrate creativity and cultural identity through public events
- Partner with social service, education, and civic groups to promote community volunteerism

Outcomes
- Renewed civic pride and cultural identity
- Improved perception of downtown area
- $25 million in new revenue each season
- 100,000 participants in each event; more than 1 million participants annually

fed late into the night by black-garbed "fire tenders" who make their way from fire to fire in small boats. Powerful and mesmerizing music, conducted through an elaborate speaker system, seems to emanate from the flames. WaterFire music programs feature unusual music from all around the world, reflecting the diverse culture of the city.

While WaterFire has had a strong economic impact, its most important outcome is renewing the community's sense of pride. Just as the Mardis Gras is associated with New Orleans and the Gateway Arch with Saint Louis, WaterFire has spearheaded Providence's emerging identity. Now internationally recognized, it draws more than one million people per year, two-thirds from outside the area.

An observer remarked, "It can be very moving, and you can become introspective when you hear some of the music and you smell the smoke and you hear the crackling of the wood and you just watch the flames. And then it seems to bring about a bonding experience. People turn and talk to people in a way they wouldn't ordinarily. Everyone is sharing a special moment."[70]

Assets Employed

• Creative vision and organizational capacities of lead artist

• Symbolism of fire and water in most cultural traditions

• City leadership willing to take a risk

• Rivers running through the center of downtown

• Well-designed public plazas and promenades

• Ambiance created by the contrasting architectural styles, scale, and eras represented by buildings that overlook the rivers

• Volunteers attracted to participate in a moving public ritual

• Civic and business leadership recognizing the potential of this spectacle

• Human desire to "take over" streets and public space for celebration, ritual, and protest

Direct Outcomes

• Renewed sense of civic pride

• Restorative experience of art and beauty in the heart of the city

• Inclusive, free festival

• Renewed awareness of Providence as a waterway-laced port city

• Hundreds of volunteers working together on a moving and internationally recognized public event

• More than $25 million spent per season by one million tourists and observers

In participating together in the ritual, and entering the special psychological state induced by the sounds, the sights, the smells, and the presence of so many others, we come to feel a sense of solidarity with one another. Lines of social division that otherwise structure our lives and divide us—by age, gender, social class, or ethnicity—melt away.

—David I. Kertzer, professor of anthropology and Italian studies, Brown University[71]

- Nearly 100,000 participants in each lighting event, nearly three-fourths of whom are tourists who plan their travels to coincide with the lightings
- Public and private interests, businesses, artists, philanthropists, and city leaders working together
- Reinvigorated downtown public space, businesses, and cultural organizations

Indirect and Potential Impacts

- Positive reception of city funding needs in state legislative arena
- Reinvestment in downtown residential and commercial buildings
- Restored support for the state's capital city by surrounding communities whose residents now come downtown again

STRATEGY ⑥

Promote Interaction in Public Space

Creating Place Together

Voice of the River Project and Leo Adler Memorial Parkway, Baker City, Oregon

The Setting

Baker City, population 10,000, sits just west of northeastern Oregon's Blue Mountains. In the early 1800s, it was a stagecoach stop on the Oregon Trail and half a century later a station on the Transcontinental Railroad. The town, which was incorporated in 1874, grew as a center for gold and limestone mining. By 1900, it was a thriving regional center with milling and agriculture as its mainstay. A nearby ski area began operation in the 1930s, and Hell's Canyon National Recreation Area was added in 1975.

At 3,471 feet above sea level, Baker City prides itself on the "history, hospitality, and breathtaking grandeur of our high-desert community." The Powder River, which winds through the community, originates in spectacular mountains to the west. The colorful history of stagecoaches, railroads, mining, lumber milling, and agriculture is ever present, although the town has struggled economically in recent decades.

Baker City is the largest municipality in northeastern Baker County, population 16,743. The population of Baker County grew 9 percent between 1990 and 2000. However, in 2003, the county reported three consecutive years of job losses with an unemployment rate of more than 12 percent. The region's economy has been in transition for decades, shifting from a natural resource base to one that includes small business, services, light industry, and tourism. The county continues as the Pacific Northwest's second-largest producer of portland cement. Social problems include out-migration of young people and abuse of alcohol and other drugs. The population is 96 percent White with smaller numbers of Latinos, Asians, and Native Americans.

Organization Type/Description

The Voice of the River Project originated in an effort to plan and develop the Leo Adler Memorial Parkway, a paved trail for walking and biking along the Powder River. The parkway honors Leo Adler, a Baker City entrepreneur who died in 1993, bequeathing his estate, estimated at more than $20 million, to support scholarships and community improvements. Adler had lived his entire life two blocks from the river's edge.

Crossroads Center for the Creative and Performing Arts, founded in 1963 as a nonprofit, is eastern Oregon's oldest community arts organization. Located adjacent to the Adler Parkway, it took a leadership role in the Voice of the River Project, engaging the community in planning the parkway and creating public art projects for it. Crossroads Center received funding to administer the Voice of the River Project from the Oregon Arts Commission.

Mission or Statement of Purpose

Crossroads Center was founded with the vision that anyone, regardless of financial resources or artistic potential, should have the opportunity to participate in classes and cultural events. The center showcases the many talented artists in Northeast Oregon and taps them to share their skills with children and the community at large.

Goals and Strategies

Planning for the Leo Adler Memorial Parkway, through the Voice of the River Project, linked the many assets, lifestyles, and interests of the community's residents. The parkway's development allowed the community to honor history while creating a vision of the future.

Accommodating travelers has always been a central activity and key part of Baker City's economy. The Voice of the River Project strengthened the social fabric of the community while providing an attraction for reviving tourist traffic. Voice of the River is a vehicle through which the story of the Powder River and the town's history could be told, but it is also a way for people in the community to tell and share their own stories.

General Description of Activities

Work on the Leo Adler Memorial Parkway began in 1997, drawing on funds from the bequest of the Adler estate. In three working design sessions, residents, artists, designers, and city officials came together to develop parkway plans. Neighbors created an interpretive design that included installation of public art showcasing the history and natural and cultural landscapes through which the Powder River flows.

Snapshot

Voice of the River Project and Leo Adler Memorial Parkway
Baker City, Oregon

Setting
- Eastern Oregon foothills community, population 10,000
- Once a key stop on the transcontinental Oregon Trail
- Transient economy with high unemployment

Community Assets
- Scenic location on the Powder River
- Active local cultural and historic organizations
- Large bequest from a local resident

Strategies
- Create a recreational parkway to provide a link between local institutions
- Use public art and storytelling to celebrate history and natural assets
- Restore and cultivate natural elements with community help

Outcomes
- Strengthened community relationships
- Strong sense of community identity and ownership
- Increased understanding of community history
- Improved civic infrastructure

They decided to begin the project with a highly visible bridge that calls attention to Baker City's natural assets and heritage. The bridge serves as a key connection from the downtown and county library to the parkway, history museum, and restored Adler home. A community process selected artists who created murals for the bridge, wrought-iron lampposts, and a stone column with plaques recounting the story of the river and of Leo Adler. Other local artists contributed painting, poetry, ironwork, and stonemasonry. Young people and volunteers from local schools worked with the artists.

Meanwhile, pathway construction progressed. In addition, high school students cultivated indigenous plants for the river's banks. A fish habitat was restored. The path was also designed to connect important infrastructure, including the library, Crossroads Center, historic downtown, sports complex, history museum, and historic Adler home.

In future phases of the plan, pathways will connect more amenities and thematic parks and gardens honoring historic contributions to the development of Baker City. These will include the Miner's Garden, Timberland Playground, Chinese Gardens, Oral History Garden, community celebration space, Native River Garden, and the Leo Adler Walk of Scholars. The last mentioned recognizes another part of Adler's bequest, a scholarship fund for local high school graduates.

Assets Employed
- Civic leadership and philanthropy
- Scenic river, which has served the local economy throughout history
- Deeply rooted connections to nature and outdoor lifestyles
- Strong connection with local history
- Transportation infrastructure
- Tradition of hospitality
- Cultural and historic organizations and institutions
- Historic architecture
- Oregon Trail Interpretive Center and Regional Museum
- Diversified (albeit struggling) economy
- Tradition of participatory planning and civic improvement

Direct Outcomes
- Intergenerational connections through participation in the parkway and public art development and river improvement projects
- Reweaving community infrastructure and physical connections from roots along the river
- Reinvigorated awareness of community history, heritage, and pride
- Elevation of artists and creative work as key to community improvement

W e heard from many residents, who obviously had been waiting for an opportunity to share ideas about possibilities for our community. The excitement conveyed as they uncork their visions is very encouraging . . . but if nothing else is accomplished, the experience of providing a forum for residents of the county to express and share their visions, values and passion about their home has been well worth the effort.

— Baker County Cultural Plan [72]

- New and strengthened cooperation among cultural, environmental, economic, and civic leaders, sectors, and institutions
- Emergence of new community leaders
- Increased contact among community members in new public spaces and in organization of new or expanded activities taking place

Indirect and Potential Impacts

- Enhanced tourism
- Greater cooperation and planning among diverse economic sectors
- Reinvigoration of local economy
- New sense of ownership in community, helping to retain youth

Summary of Examples in Strategy 6: Promote Interaction in Public Space

Providence and Baker City may be a continent apart, but both have experienced a revival of their public spaces and of citizen involvement through the process of bringing those spaces to life. They creatively built on their histories and unique qualities.

Visionary Providence leaders set the stage by uncovering the city's downtown rivers and creating well-designed public walkways. However, it required a spark—quite literally—to ignite public interest in and use of those spaces. The creation of WaterFire touched the human psyche and imagination in a primal way. Recognizing this, city leaders formed a broad partnership led by WaterFire's artist. Visitors now come from around the world, and local residents volunteer for and attend the event again and again. By working across public, business, and nonprofit sectors, the city revived its economy. Perhaps more importantly, WaterFire boosted the community's spirit and self-image beyond what anyone could have imagined.

At his death, a native son left Baker City a legacy that provided resources for a public space project. It was the living residents who rallied to create a splendid plan and to work together to make a place for all. Artists were called upon and the art center played a key role, but the design and realization of Adler Memorial Parkway belong to many leaders, especially the youth. Their parkway honors the ethnic groups and natural resources that built this small Oregon community. It also creates connections, both real and symbolic, between parts of the town and its different people, as do the best of public spaces.

In the next strategy, you will learn about ways that civic participation can be strengthened through cultural activities.

Culture stimulates revitalization not through direct economic impact, but by building the social connections between people . . . it increases the inclination and ability of residents to make positive changes in their community, and it increases the connections between neighborhoods of different ethnic and economic compositions.

— Mark J. Stern[73]

Increase Civic Participation through Cultural Celebrations

CREATING THE KIND OF CONNECTIONS between people that lead to collective civic action is a challenge for any planner, organizer, or community builder. It's a lot of hard work and there's no secret formula, but it's an essential ingredient in a democratic society. The creative community builders profiled in Strategy 7 found ways to build bridges across ethnic and geographic divides—some long-standing, some new. And they did it in ways through which neighbors work together, make decisions, solve problems, and share in the celebration of success.

Management or programming of public spaces can include large-scale or ongoing events to intentionally build connections and facilitate cooperation. Such events develop collaborative problem-solving skills that can be used to address other issues, and they increase people's comfort with group activity in the public or civic arena.

Annual or seasonal events such as festivals or farmers markets can be especially effective in communities with great social, ethnic, and economic diversity. As in the earlier discussion about public space and public art, the processes used to plan and carry out these events are at least as important as the events themselves.

Eighty percent of participants in community cultural activities travel outside their own neighborhoods to attend these events. This is one way in which participation in cultural events differs from other forms of civic engagement. By attracting people of all types and from all communities, cultural events reduce social isolation and build connections across divides of ethnicity and social class.[74]

While it's estimated that 77 percent of United States residents participate in structured or formal arts activities,[75] those numbers increase when informal activities are included. Recent research into participatory and informal arts activities indicate that significant cultural activities take place in home, neighborhood, marketplace, and social settings that escape most participation surveys. These activities are especially effective at creating trust and opportunities for collaboration, behaviors that contribute positively to involvement on other civic and economic levels.[76]

Research also points to the important role for culturally specific arts and celebrations, especially in immigrant communities. Such participation reinforces community social fabric and helps build relationships with people of other cultures.[77]

The capacity to create social, civic, and economic associations in response to changing conditions and changing populations is urgently needed. Strategy 7 will highlight two community events that build connections among community residents and at the same time attract participation from outside. The former is of greater importance here because, without the collective work of the community, there would be no event to draw others.

Since 1975, a Minneapolis-based puppet theater has mounted an annual spring celebration and created an increasingly elaborate process for involving hundreds of people in the diverse neighborhood in which the theater is located. This incredible mix of people participates both in the creative and the organizational processes.

Planners and a multitude of artists involved in the Delray Beach Cultural Loop found inventive ways to connect a wide range of people for the first time through community-based cultural organizations. This process crossed ethnic boundaries and helped people celebrate together in a rapidly growing area of south Florida.

An Act of Transformation

May Day Parade and Festival, In the Heart of the Beast Puppet and Mask Theatre, Minneapolis, Minnesota

www.hobt.org

STRATEGY ❼
Increase Civic
Participation
through Cultural
Celebrations

The Setting

The Minneapolis–Saint Paul metropolitan area has a population of more than three million. It's a prosperous center of finance, food production, medical, and high-technology industries and known widely for its active arts community. The Phillips and Powderhorn neighborhoods on Minneapolis' south side are home to about 40,000 residents. While the urban area, as a whole, is made up of a largely White European population, these neighborhoods contain large Native and African American communities, as well as immigrants from Africa, Latin America, and Southeast Asia. The Phillips neighborhood has long been the city's poorest and a primary port of entry for immigrants. Powderhorn, just to its south, is predominantly working class.

Snapshot •

May Day Parade and Festival

Minneapolis, Minnesota

Setting
Urban neighborhoods with diverse populations including longtime and new residents, population 40,000

Community Assets
• Large and high-quality public spaces
• Traditions of spring celebrations of multiple cultures
• Immigrants from many parts of the world building new lives

Strategies
• Use puppetry and public celebration to build community
• Involve the community in creating the parade and events
• Encourage diversity of participants and artistic styles

Outcomes
• Increased understanding and ownership of public places
• Increased capacity to organize across cultures
• Increased safety and sense of community

Lake Street, a primary commercial artery, separates Phillips and Powderhorn. It also transects the city, cutting a straight east-west path from the Mississippi River through working-class, poor, and immigrant communities, and an up-and-coming entertainment district known as Uptown. It eventually leads to upscale communities and suburbs on the city's western edge. About two miles south of downtown, Lake Street was once a streetcar "suburb" with a thriving retail strip featuring car dealerships and major retailers and employers. After decades of decay, its central portions have rebounded during the past ten years as a thriving Latino and East African center of commerce and culture.*

Organization Type/Description

The two buildings belonging to In the Heart of the Beast Puppet and Mask Theatre (HOBT) are situated on the poor-, immigrant-, and working-class stretch of Lake Street. HOBT began informally in 1973 and incorporated as a nonprofit in 1975. The spring of that year marked the group's first May Day ceremony. The theater troupe wanted to thank the community that supported its work and create a celebration to bring people together outdoors at winter's end. And the theater wanted to do so in a way that honored the collective and creative potential of people in the community. Today, the annual May Day Parade and Festival has become the company's signature event, building cross-cultural relationships and leadership and serving as common ground for exploration and action on issues of importance to the community. The event attracts more than 50,000 participants.

Mission or Statement of Purpose

HOBT embraces puppetry, ritual, and street theater inspired by cultures from around the world. In the process of building community, the theater brings people together to share the acts of building, performing, and celebrating. HOBT's season of original, company-generated plays is for both family and adult audiences. School- and community-based residencies teach puppetry and pageantry to students and teachers, and to people of all ages. The theater, which has grown to be internationally recognized, remains firmly grounded in the concerns of its home neighborhoods, and in both regional and global issues. It conducts national and international touring programs and produces ceremonial events and outreach programs that served nearly 100,000 in 2003.

Goals and Strategies

Throughout its artistic work and institutional practices, the company contributes as an active and vital member of its south Minneapolis neighborhood. Strategies include the following:

• Engage people in symbolic acts of transformation

---

* For a description of the work of In the Heart of the Beast Puppet and Mask Theatre, see Colleen J. Sheehy, ed., *Theatre of Wonder: 25 Years in the Heart of the Beast* (Minneapolis: University of Minnesota Press, 1999).

- Create original work that incorporates the issues, people, and cultures of the community
- Use "low-tech" artistry and high human energy
- Integrate visual art, movement, music, and the spoken word
- Value and engage the creative spirit of each person
- Incorporate diversity—economic, cultural, and age—among the theater staff and program participants
- Engage in dialog about the human, spiritual, and natural worlds
- Provide critical social analysis and commentary through puppet and mask artistry

General Description of Activity

The May Day Parade and Festival is an annual ritual for the Twin Cities. The event includes a parade and ceremony, followed by a festival in Powderhorn Park. Organizing the event has become a year-round task. Each February neighbors gather at the theater to share ideas and images to develop the year's parade theme. The theater staff shape a simple parade story and draw out a storyboard with specific parade sections, each designed to musically and visually tell the community's story. A month of workshops follows. Hundreds of neighbors build and paint the puppets, banners, and costumes, each making unique cultural and aesthetic contributions. Youth, adults, immigrants, and longtime residents of all ethnicities work side by side, sharing their skills and vision.

On the first Sunday in May, the parade transforms Bloomington Avenue—the route from the theater on Lake Street to Powderhorn Park—into a celebratory space. The theater and neighborhood "own" the street for part of the day. Hundreds join in, playing instruments, strutting in masks, and working together to animate giant puppets. A powerful bond is created that goes well beyond this one day.

Assets Employed

- Public spaces, including streets, sidewalks, and parks
- Creative talents of a diverse range of people from the neighborhoods
- Talented artists from the neighborhoods and beyond drawn to a large-scale celebratory event
- A long history of celebration and ritual based on an important spring date
- Desires for social engagement during late winter months and recognition of spring
- Spring rituals and artistic traditions from multiple cultures
- Immigrants and entrepreneurs seeking involvement with accessible cultural, social, and civic events
- Underused and vacant buildings

A girl creating a papier-mâché mask for In the Heart of the Beast Puppet and Mask Theatre's annual May Day parade.

It takes a whole village—
and then some—to put
together a May Day Parade and
Festival. If you want to plan,
brainstorm, organize, fundraise,
give money or supplies, sculpt,
sew, papier-mâché, staple, build,
paint, cook food, usher, clean
up, sing songs, play music, or
dance please join us!

—Heart of the Beast
web site[78]

Direct Outcomes

• New bonds and working relationships between neighbors

• Elevation of the role of artists as forgers of community vision and aspiration

• Development and emergence of new leaders

• Sense of ownership of public spaces as places to share ideas and visions

• Heightened cross-cultural understanding and sense of unity as community builders

• Familiarity and enhanced comfort level with neighbors and different neighborhoods

• Renewed and deepened sense of meaning in public gathering

• Rehabilitated, productive buildings with high-visibility street presence

Indirect and Potential Impacts

• Enhanced sense of neighborhood safety

• Development of skills and relationships useful in development of small businesses

• Formation of relationships transferable to civic action

• Economic revival through increased activity and sense of optimism

New Life for Decaying Buildings

In 1990, the Heart of the Beast Theatre purchased a defunct art deco movie theater to serve as its performance, studio, rehearsal, and administrative site. For over a decade prior to that, the building had been used to show pornographic films, a symbol of and contributor to the area's decline. The city took ownership of the building in the late-1980s to force out the film exhibitor. HOBT stepped forward to take it on. Gradually, the theater company repaired and renovated the space, always incorporating bright colors and the simple paint-ings of trees, suns, stars, and other designs for which the company is well known. Partnering with neighborhood groups and the city, HOBT also created designs for banners and light posts that brought further life to the street. But the theater company didn't stop there.

In 2004, HOBT took another bold step and became the lead partner in the purchase and renovation of an adjacent 40,000-square-foot building—once a Masonic Temple—that had also been vacant for years.

Renamed Plaza Verde, and painted a bold green color, the massive three-story building now houses several Latino retail businesses, a business development training organization, other nonprofits, and office and rehearsal space for the theater itself. Much of the top floor, a grand ballroom, is rented by HOBT and actively used for community social events.

An illlustration of the theatre can be found on page 21.

Keeping Everyone in the Loop

Delray Beach Cultural Loop and History Trail, the City of Delray Beach and Pineapple Grove Main Street, Delray Beach, Florida

www.delrayconnect.com
www.delraybeach.com

The Setting

Delray Beach, Florida, is located on the Atlantic coast in the southern end of Palm Beach County. It's about halfway between Fort Lauderdale on the south and West Palm Beach to the north.

With a population of more than 60,000, Delray Beach is an unusually diverse suburban community. As early as 1894, African American families bought property and farmed here, characteristically limited to the western side of town. White business and real estate investors acquired beach-front lands toward the east. With the completion of the railroad in 1896, the area's agricultural products became widely marketable. Farms and businesses prospered. The town's first recorded civic association was formed by the Black community at the end of the nineteenth century. It petitioned the county school board to establish a school for Black children.

After World War I, the population grew to more than 1,000, and beautiful beaches attracted tourists, artists, and writers. Haitian and Latin American immigrants also have long roots in the community. Their populations have grown dramatically since the 1960s. Arts and cultural celebrations among all Delray Beach's ethnic communities have flourished for a century.

As early as the 1920s and '30s, the all-Black "Silas Green" shows marched through town playing New Orleans jazz before presenting three days of vaudeville. In the 1940s and '50s, Delray Beach was the largest grower of gladiolas in the nation. An annual festival celebrating the flowers made Delray Beach widely known. Since 1966, the Delray Affair, which features artists and craftspeople, has attracted more than 200,000 visitors each spring. The Cultural Roots Arts Festival began in 1977 in the African American community, joined by Cinco de Mayo and the Caribbean Festival in the Latin and Haitian communities. There are numerous arts and cultural organizations with exhibitions, performances, and classes and an equal number of historic groups and sites. Many churches and other places of importance serve as sites for ritual, ceremony, and social activity.

Snapshot ●

Cultural Loop and History Trail
Delray Beach, Florida

Setting
- Agricultural and beach community over one hundred years old
- Established and expanding population of 60,000

Community Assets
- Established business improvement association
- Many cultural, historic, and civic organizations rooted in the diverse cultures of the community
- Expertise in planning public events

Strategies
- Create an event to celebrate diverse people, arts, history, and foods
- Facilitate crossing boundaries into less familiar areas
- Create partnerships between cultural and community-based groups
- Promote the city's cultural resources

Outcomes
- Increased interaction between community segments
- Increased cultural tourism
- New institutional relationships
- Wider awareness of local artists and cultural organizations

Organization Type/Description

The Delray Cultural Loop and History Trail was a one-time event on a weekend in November 2003. It consisted of a 1.3-mile rectangular route that led participants to sites representing all the city's major ethnic groups. In doing so, it showcased the community's rich and diverse cultural heritage.

Glenn Weiss, a Delray Beach public arts consultant, and Rick Lowe, a Houston-based artist, created the cultural loop. The City of Delray Beach and Pineapple Grove Main Street, Inc., a business improvement association, were sponsors of the effort. In addition, partnerships between cultural and community-based groups rooted in the African American, Haitian, Anglo, and Latino communities were important to the event's success.

Mission or Statement of Purpose

The mission of the City of Delray Beach is to create a renaissance that enhances the unique cultural, historical, and natural resources that make this an attractive community to a diverse population. It operates under a commission-management form of government.

Pineapple Grove Main Street was formed in 1994 by merchants and community leaders to revitalize a commercial district. A highly successful public art program known as the Pineapple Grove ArtWalk became a cornerstone of its work. Together with several annual arts events, the ArtWalk is a major draw to the district. Pineapple Grove is affiliated with the National Trust for Historic Preservation's Main Street Program, a Washington, DC-based network and support program for historic district revitalization.

Goals and Strategies

The Delray Cultural Loop used public space to link people across lines of race, ethnicity, age, gender, profession, and economic class. Goals included the following:

- Build relationships across ethnic communities by having participants visit partnering sites
- Share stories of diverse residents through existing organizations and artist projects
- Engage and empower youth and others in creating new artwork that reflects their condition and identity
- Provide free public access to historical sites and contemporary art
- Introduce participants to the diversity of contemporary art and artists
- Assist in the growth of a creative culture that is vital to the economic success of the city and the individual citizens
- Support cultural organizations and other organizations with cultural programming

- Emphasize the city's walkability and active streets
- Enhance civic involvement and reinforce a sense of ownership
- Promote interaction and cohesion among neighbors

General Description of Activities

Visiting artist Rick Lowe led the design of the loop, recruited participants, and helped partner groups design activities and exhibits. In addition to a self-guided walking tour, two trolley-buses circulated along the loop. The most remarkable aspect of the loop event was that it represented the first time that diverse groups worked together to better acquaint neighbors with each other, and to let people from far and wide know that Delray Beach is a destination rich in cultural resources.

Key partners—and stops on the tour—included the following

- Delray Beach Historical Society, which featured a local history archives and exhibits
- The Milagro Center, with a gallery, theater, dance studio, and classrooms
- Museum of Lifestyle and Fashion History, which displayed artifacts reflecting the lifestyles and people of diverse cultures of the world
- Old School Square, a renovated central cultural space with exhibits, theater, art classes, and concerts
- S. D. Spady Cultural Arts Museum, a historic house dedicated to the history of Delray's African Americans
- Toussaint L'Ouverture High School for Arts and Social Justice, based in Haitian culture and traditions with emphasis on empowering students and families
- Pineapple Grove ArtWalk, a self-guided tour of contemporary outdoor sculptures and murals in a commercial setting
- Women in the Visual Arts, exhibits and classes by an association of women artists
- Palm Beach Photographic Center, a non-profit photography center with a gallery, lectures, and workshops

The tour also included fourteen churches, six civic institutions, and twenty-three additional historic sites, all welcoming passersby. A variety of artists projects—on utility poles, trees, sidewalks, and kiosks—lined the way. Each told a story of the people and the place. A vacant lot was occupied by the Open Door Project, displaying over one

A map of Delray Beach's Cultural Loop, highlighting stops on the tour.

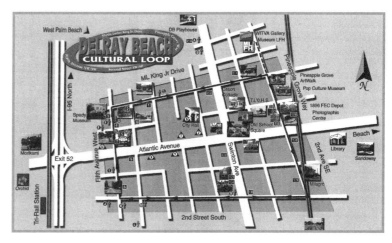

hundred used doors, painted and collaged in preceding weeks by people of all ages through workshops led by artist Sharon Koskoff. The spectacular collection of doors symbolized the people and events that helped open the doors of diversity and opportunity for individuals and the community.

A "green" market featuring fresh, locally grown foods, holiday craft show, and outdoor art fair were other attractions along the route, and Old School House Square near the center of the rectangle featured music and entertainment. Miami-based artist Gary Moore set up a temporary barbershop in a vacant house in the African American neighborhood, offering free haircuts and a glimpse into the world of Black hair for travelers on the loop.

Assets Employed

- A rich heritage of social, cultural, religious, and civic organizations and events within the diverse communities
- A tradition of valuing the arts and artists as forces in community and economic development
- A widely recognized program (ArtWalk) designed to encourage people to experience art in the public realm
- Active civic leaders intent on creating a welcoming, interactive community
- Visionary public arts administrator and lead artist
- Established Pineapple Grove Main Street program experienced at producing public events
- Activists from all sectors of the community eager to overcome ethnic and cultural divisions
- Public officials confident in the use of cultural activities to heal, connect, and build

Direct Outcomes

- Active "boundary crossing" from all segments of the community
- Several thousand participants in a one-time event
- Institutional relationships and partnerships spilling over to other areas of community interest and concern
- Wider appreciation of the talents and resources existing all around the loop

Indirect and Potential Impacts

- Increased tourism traffic
- Heightened awareness of the depth of cultural and historical organizations and sites
- More equitable opportunities for development and new businesses

City leaders said the organizers of the Cultural Loop shouldn't shy away from highlighting the city's past racial inequalities, since that could be a tool for talking about the incidents and working toward erasing pent-up racial tensions. But they stress that the information should be accurate, balanced and relevant to the tour meant to showcase the lives of blacks, whites and immigrants living near downtown.

— Leon Fooksman, *South Florida Sun Sentinel*[79]

Summary of Examples in Strategy 7: Increase Civic Participation through Cultural Celebrations

These projects are but two of many that build community through actively involving a diverse range of people in the process of planning and carrying out cultural celebrations. One is long-standing and has become an anticipated annual element of community life. The other was a one-time event that sparked collaborations across ethnic and economic divides. Both used public and private spaces, engaged diverse communities, and integrated artists and volunteers as leaders.

After thirty years, In the Heart of the Beast Theatre now involves a second generation of participants who grew up to know this unique and phenomenal event as part of what community life is about. The neighborhood is largely poor with a dynamic mix of ethnic groups and immigrants. Starting small and growing over time, the May Day Parade and Festival draws on the histories and cultures of the many people involved. It annually reinvents the community's story and vision for its future.

Delray Beach's Cultural Loop connected people in celebration of their own diversity. Although rapidly growing and predominantly prosperous, Delray Beach has ongoing healing and bridge-building work to do. The cultural loop was a unique event that helped locals to be tourists discovering their own hometown using familiar public spaces. At the same time, it gave visitors access to the diverse cultural riches and history of this south Florida beachside community.

In the next strategy, we'll see how involving youth in the arts can build social capital.

Every human being seeks to have his or her dignity recognized (i.e., evaluated at its proper worth) by other human beings. Indeed, this drive is so deep and fundamental that it is one of the chief motors of the entire human historical process.

— Francis Fukuyama[80]

Engage Youth

STRATEGY 8 IS ABOUT ENGAGING YOUTH to both build and ensure an economically and socially healthy future for your community. As public health researcher Felton Earls pointed out, children and youth provide a common ground on which adults and communities come together. In a sense, they are a catalyst to build cooperative relationships among adults and agencies of all types.

Including young people as meaningful contributors in the social and economic aspects of community building must not be overlooked and cannot be left to schools and parents alone. Many of the programs and communities highlighted in this book have youth components, but this section looks specifically at two outstanding ways in which youth are shaping their communities, building the economy of the future, and taking charge of the civic agenda.

People often say that youth are a top priority in U.S. society. However, facts show otherwise. Education is a declining portion of public expenditures. On average, parents now spend less time with their children than in previous generations. Young people spend only about one-quarter of their time in school. They have to make choices about what to do with nearly half their time outside school.

"The labor shortage of the end of the 1990s, along with highly innovative programs to subsidize transport from urban to suburban jobs, has enabled most young people who want to work to find at least minimum wage jobs. Few of these jobs, however, provide meaningful or developmental experiences in exchange for the meager pay," write researchers in youth development, Shirley Brice Heath and Laura Smyth.[81]

The workplace is but one of the many "spaces" in which youth shape their identity and worldviews. Researchers Lois Weis and Michelle Fine conclude that "much of what youths learn, teach, believe in, and long to know—and, most fundamentally, how they form and re-form identities—takes place within spaces both within and outside school." Schools do not deliver the extensive time for practice in forms of group interaction, problem posing, and problem solving needed by youth to become productive citizens, they contend. Youth need spaces "of meaning, recognition, and comfort," where they can restore "a sense of possibility for themselves and their peers."[82]

An asset-based approach is essential when thinking about youth. They have much to offer if their unique interests and skills are tapped.

Engaging youth has a dual benefit: it brings more adults into the picture. Research in civic engagement by the League of Women Voters indicates that the factor most likely to get people more involved in community affairs is helping to improve conditions for youth. "Issues related to children, including mentoring and coaching, and education are those most likely to mobilize the untapped reservoir of volunteers." [83]

The programs that follow do just that. These are exemplary in that they provide space for inquisitive and creative activity as well as productive and valued work where youth are engaged with adults as active collaborators.* The youth use more of their innate capacities and time to both learn and contribute—and their contributions are honored and rewarded!

Artists for Humanity in Boston provides avenues for youth to become socially conscious and engaged entrepreneurs who bridge economic and cultural differences. Youth build confidence and gain business experience while working with professional artists as mentors and instructors. Berkeley's Youth Radio outshines most professional media operations in the number of local and national awards it has received. The program meets youth where they are, on their terms, and empowers them with a voice heard far and wide.

STRATEGY 8
Engage Youth

Creative Entrepreneurs Earn Respect

Artists for Humanity, Boston, Massachusetts

www.afhboston.com

The Setting

One of the country's oldest cities, Boston embodies the old and the new—in regard to ideas, ethnic populations, architecture, and institutions. In the midst of a large and prosperous region of over 3.4 million people, Boston's 600,000 residents are highly diverse. In 2000, the White population ceased to be in the majority—just under half are now Caucasian, with rapidly growing communities of color, especially immigrants. The latter account for virtually all the city's recent growth. While participating within their own communities most of the time, these diverse groups regularly find themselves on common ground with the White population in public space and in the marketplace.

---

* There are many outstanding—and usually small—youth arts programs in the United States today. An excellent source for information on some of them is Coming Up Taller, an awards program established by the President's Committee on the Arts and the Humanities. See www.cominguptaller.org.

A 2002 study by the Boston Foundation examined the city's assets and major challenges for moving into the future as a prosperous and healthy community. With seventy-four area colleges enrolling 265,000 students, the region still saw an alarming decline in its percentage of youth. Over the past decade, Metro Boston's share of youth twenty to twenty-four years old dropped by 21 percent and by 13 percent for youth twenty-five to thirty-four years old. This is in contrast to a 7 percent decline of young adults in the U.S. population as a whole. "This decrease in energetic young people reflects a 'brain drain' that threatens the region's prosperity, unless the challenge is met by growing, retaining and attracting talented young adults—the drivers of innovation."[84]

Organization Type/Description

Artists for Humanity (AFH) began in 1990, when Susan Rodgerson, an independent artist, worked with students at Boston's Martin Luther King Middle School to paint a mural. After it was complete, six students asked her if they could paint something else. That summer they showed up at her studio every day as she found things for them to paint, eventually turning their attention to designing and producing T-shirts to earn money. In 1992, Rodgerson and the six students incorporated as a nonprofit. While they secured more commissions and product sales, they received grant money to lease warehouse space in Boston's Wharf District. As AFH grew, it developed studio production activities in graphic design, commercial photography, silkscreen printing, sculpture, theatrical set design, ceramics, and painting. The organization later added warehouse space for offices and a gallery.

In 2004, AFH opened a state-of-the-art, environmentally friendly "green" facility with 23,500 square feet of studio, gallery, performance, and office space in Boston's Fort Point Channel Arts District. The group named the new space the EpiCenter, and the youth are very proud of its environmentally conscious design. In describing itself, AFH cites its adherence to principles of social mission and businesslike discipline. "In 1991, we were the vanguard of programs encouraging youth empowerment through art and entrepreneurship. Today, we are applying the same forward thinking to empowering young people with the knowledge and understanding to make good decisions about their future and the future of their communities."[85]

Mission or Statement of Purpose

Artists for Humanity's mission is to bridge economic, racial, and social divisions by providing at-risk youth with the keys to self-sufficiency through paid employment in the arts. The organization is built upon the philosophy that art is a powerful force for social change, and that creative entrepreneurship is life-changing and productive work. AFH develops leaders in social change by providing a haven for Boston teens to explore and express their creative abilities, identify possibilities for continuing education, and, most importantly, dispel the myth that the world is forever closed to them. AFH

Snapshot

Artists for Humanity
Boston, Massachusetts

Setting
- Central city population of 600,000
- Ethnically diverse
- Out-migration of youth

Community Assets
- Artist mentors
- Ethnically diverse youth seeking creative activities
- Commercial and nonprofit client base
- Philanthropists focused on youth development

Strategies
- Create an artistic apprentice program for at-risk youth
- Provide an environment supportive of diverse forms and styles
- Facilitate creativity and critical thinking
- Develop marketable skills and youth-adult relationships

Outcomes
- Constructive creative economy employment for at-risk youth
- Positive cross-cultural working relationships among youth
- Increased diversity and creativity in labor force

works to dismantle economic and social barriers impeding inner-city communities, and to transform how youth view themselves and their potential.

Goals and Strategies

Artists For Humanity advances three goals designed to provide inner-city Boston teens with

- A safe, meaningful place where they are respected for their contributions
- An opportunity to have a voice through exhibitions, commercial services, and public presentations
- The responsibility of paid employment that promotes their own economic development and provides a springboard to postsecondary opportunities

The organization works with youth primarily between the ages of fourteen and eighteen from all parts of the city. Fundamentally, it is based upon a small business model, concentrating on what young artists can creatively produce, rather than following a social service model that attempts to address their shortcomings. Young artists are paid and participate in client meetings and contract negotiations. AFH joins creativity and street smarts with entrepreneurial spirit, engaging youth in all levels of business planning, marketing, production, and sales. Older youth mentor younger ones. The unique talents of each are cultivated and channeled into one of the areas or projects. AFH is careful not to draw boundaries between commercial arts and fine arts—art as personal expression and art as a product for sale. By embracing both, the organization encourages youth to tap their intrinsic creativity.

General Description of Activities

Artists for Humanity operates as a structured, paid apprentice program to pair teens with experienced artists in a broad range of fine and commercial arts for product development and services to the business community. In 2003, the program employed eighty young artists in its microenterprise programs and served more than three hundred through drop-in programs. The young artists receive an hourly wage and have the opportunity to earn a 50 percent commission on each individual work they sell through the gallery, shows, or negotiated contracts. Major clients have included Gillette Company, Filene's Department Store, the Boston Red Sox, local radio stations, Fleet Bank, and many other businesses and nonprofit institutions. T-shirts, murals, graphic design, and fine artworks are the primary earned-revenue sources. While AFH has earned more than $1.7 million since 1996, foundation grants and corporate sponsorships still account for the largest share of the organization's budget.

Participating youth represent the entire city and come primarily from low-income neighborhoods. The makeup is diverse: 52 percent male, 35 percent African American, 25 percent Latino, 13 percent Caucasian, 3 percent Haitian, 11 percent Asian, 2 percent Cape Verdean, 1 percent Pacific Islander,

Paying young people for their organizational work is something communities should be much happier about than paying them to flip burgers. Challenging, committed work by youth, work that demands creativity, needs to be recognized.

— Shirley Brice Heath, youth development researcher [86]

and 10 percent bi- or multiracial. In addition to the creative process, teens actively relate to others and exchange ideas. They serve as role models for each other and to other youth through their families and neighborhoods. During the school year, they work from 3:00 to 6:00 p.m., and during summer from noon to 5:30 p.m. As with any job, they are required to be punctual, treat the work seriously, and function as members of a team. Unlike most jobs available to youth, the teens are involved in meeting and negotiating with clients and funders, and they learn to balance creativity with the production and business activities necessary for economic survival.

Artists for Humanity has received widespread recognition. In 1999, the Carnegie Foundation for the Advancement of Teaching named AFH as one of four outstanding youth arts programs in the country. The organization was also awarded a coveted Coming Up Taller Award from the President's Committee on the Arts and the Humanities in 2001.

Artists for Humanity's EpiCenter—a state-of-the-art, environmentally friendly facility.

Assets Employed

- Entrepreneurial and creative drive of youth
- Enterprising artists committed to working with young people
- Appeal of creative work and response to recognition
- Commercial clients desirous of images and products attractive to youth and seeking to provide constructive avenues
- Microenterprise and small business skills
- Philanthropic sources seeking effective approaches to youth development

Direct Outcomes (for participants)

- Meaningful, part-time employment for low-income students
- Development of marketable arts production skills as well as creative problem-solving, teamwork, and business skills
- Reinforcement of having creative ideas taken seriously and rewarded
- A 100 percent graduation rate for high school seniors working at AFH in 2001, 2002, and 2004
- High rate of continued education through a dozen major East Coast arts schools, four-year colleges, and community colleges
- Highly developed cross-cultural communication and collaboration skills

Indirect and Potential Impacts (for community)

- Improved image of youth among general adult public
- Development of new styles and approaches that influence larger commercial and fine arts worlds
- Expanded creative labor force with greater levels of racial diversity
- Reduced levels of truancy and crimes by youth

Youth Fill the Airwaves

Youth Radio, Berkeley, California

www.youthradio.org

The Setting

The Bay Area—including San Francisco, Berkeley, Richmond, and Oakland—is one of the largest and most ethnically diverse urban regions of the United States. The youth population of the region has grown up in the context of a cultural mix unlike that experienced by older generations, yet there is still great division and tension around economics, culture, and geography. Youth Radio, centered in Berkeley, operates programs that parallel the experiences of its youthful radio broadcasters. They tap a rich tradition of social change activism and alternative media, including independent film, print journalism, and radio broadcasting. It is within this context that Youth Radio has grown, pulling from its community's many assets. Today, Youth Radio is national in scope with bureaus in Los Angeles, Atlanta, and Washington, DC. Youth Radio also has an international network of young reporters and plays a curatorial role with young people and groups around the country, including rural sites.

Organization Type/Description

A nonprofit organization, Youth Radio was founded in 1992 by Ellin O'Leary, an award-winning radio journalist and producer. It's a hands-on broadcast journalism training and production program, engaging low-income and at-risk youth in the Bay Area. It distributes a regular slate of news and public affairs programs through a dozen media outlets regionally and nationally. The work of Youth Radio goes well beyond technical training, helping youth strengthen basic life skills including verbal expression, writing, critical thinking, conflict resolution, and civic participation.

Mission or Statement of Purpose

Youth Radio's mission is to promote young people's intellectual, creative, and professional growth through training and access to media and to produce the highest-quality original media for local and national outlets. Through hands-on practice, working relationships with industry professionals, and production of award-winning programming, Youth Radio students learn the basics of broadcasting while being exposed to a broad spectrum of media-related careers.

Goals and Strategies

Youth Radio sets out to engage and empower young community members who have traditionally been left without a voice. This includes young

CORE student Oliver Rodriguez on the mic in Youth Radio's studio. CORE is Youth Radio's intensive ten-week training course in radio, web, television, and journalism fundamentals.

Snapshot

Youth Radio
Berkeley, California

Setting
- One of the largest U.S. urban regions
- Good public transportation
- Ethnically diverse population with high numbers of youth

Community Assets
- Experienced journalists and media producers
- Large population of media-savvy youth
- Regional and national media outlets
- Growing media-related job market

Strategies
- Provide training in broadcast journalism for low-income and at-risk youth
- Strengthen basic life skills
- Allow youth opportunities for self-expression
- Create stronger role of youth in community and civic affairs

Outcomes
- Increased youth involvement and influence in community activities
- Thousands of hours of youth-produced media programming
- Improved communication between youth and community

women, incarcerated youth, and low-income young people of color in inner-city schools. Structured training courses are the cornerstone of the program with participation and leadership in radio production leading to regular broadcasts. Partnerships with a dozen outlets provide the forum. They include weekly and monthly slots on both public and commercial regional stations such as KQED, KCBS, and KPFA, as well as periodic installments on national outlets including NPR (Morning Edition and All Things Considered), public radio's Marketplace, Public Radio International, CBS HealthWatch, and the Pacifica Radio Network.

Youth Radio provides constructive after-school activities, mentoring, job training, career development, and life skills training. Youth are involved in creating positive social change by bringing media attention to issues affecting youth and taking on leadership positions at Youth Radio and in their communities.

General Description of Activities
Youth Radio offers free classes in the fundamentals of radio, web, and television production, in journalism, and in areas such as DJ'ing, audio streaming, and business skills. Classes are conducted in a professional setting twice each week in ten- and twelve-week intensive sessions, and they are led by some of the Bay Area's most accomplished journalists, audio engineers, and music programmers. Students learn how to conduct workshops and thereby become peer teachers. Youth Radio also provides college and career guidance.

Through a project called Community Action Street Team (CAST), youth use a mobile DJ setup to take part in community events and school assemblies. They bring music, knowledge, and peace to the streets through live events.

Both in-school and after-school activities are provided through other agencies, sometimes in conjunction with recreation, tutoring, conflict resolution, mentoring, violence prevention, and job placement programs. Civic participation and community-asset-mapping projects have been undertaken, which resulted in one city setting up a youth commission to recognize the input of youth. In another city, the mayor committed to making improvements to a community center. Such victories provide lifelong motivation for young people who realize their capacity to make change.

Since the early 1990s, Youth Radio has garnered a remarkable list of regional and national awards. These include such prestigious awards as the DuPont/Columbia Award, two Edward R. Murrow Awards, and the George Foster Peabody Award. However, Youth Radio has increasingly been acknowledged for its wider impacts, receiving awards from the California Public Health

Association, California Teachers Association, National Council on Crime and Delinquency, Girl Scouts of America, National Anti-Defamation League, and Planned Parenthood Federation of America.

Assets Employed

- Highly skilled broadcast journalists and producers committed to youth
- Media tools attractive to youth seeking self-expression and connection to media culture
- Regional and national media outlets seeking programming relevant to the enormous youth community
- Schools, social service agencies, and other community organizations open to partnering with a hands-on media arts program
- Growing job market for creative media and technology-savvy workers

Direct Outcomes

- Increased energy and time of thousands of Bay Area youth devoted to school and community activities
- Thousands of hours of youth-produced radio, web, and television programming that connects with millions of youth nationwide
- More adults hearing directly the voices of youth on important social concerns
- Youth reporting significantly greater levels of communication with parents and friends about community and personal issues

Indirect and Potential Impacts

- Media and public attention more attuned to the needs and interests of youth and youth culture
- Public policy more influenced by youth and more favorable to youth

> Conventional media tells us who youth are, but youth-produced radio lets young producers speak for themselves. . . . They experiment, express themselves and push the boundaries of what radio can sound like. As youth producers make their voices heard, they are changing the face of media.
>
> — Johanna (Jones) Franzel, MediaRights[87]

Summary of Examples in Strategy 8: Engage Youth

There are many exceptional youth activities in communities across the United States. Even the most troubled school systems have noteworthy teachers and programs. The programs highlighted here gained widespread recognition because the work created by the youth is artistic and contributes in meaningful ways to the social, civic, physical, and economic life of their communities. The youth come from diverse backgrounds, work collaboratively with highly skilled and caring adults, and together create products that contribute to change. Everyone is respected and acknowledged for the gifts they bring.

While their outputs are different, Artists for Humanity and Youth Radio provide a variety of avenues for youth to find how they can best contribute. Young artists at Artists for Humanity meet with corporate clients, theater directors, or protest groups. They use their imagination and skill to make T-shirts and other creative products for their clients. Youth Radio broadcast production involves young people in the community with people across the spectrum of professions. Construction workers and mayors have their own stories to tell, and it is those stories the youth seek. Both programs recognize the dignity, the talents, and the uniqueness of each participant.

The next strategy examines ways to engage people in the creation (or re-creation) of important places in their communities.

Promote Stewardship of Place

STRATEGY 9 IS ABOUT INVOLVING PEOPLE in the design, creation, and upkeep of "places" or meaningful public spaces in their communities. When people become involved in this way, they develop a vested interest in using and maintaining the space. When people have a true sense of "owner-ship" or connection to the spaces they inhabit and frequent, the community becomes a better place to live, work, and visit. The residents' feelings of respect and responsibility for the place bonds them to that place and to each other. No architect or town planner can design or build a place that does that.

The idea of effective "place making" has been the subject of renewed discus-sion in planning and design during the past two decades. Though hard to define, the elevation of space to the level of "place" is essential to effective community building. The task requires grassroots engagement, creative think-ing, and the participation, but not domination, of professionals. Ownership or stewardship of place is a fundamental element of a strong social fabric.

"For a process of urban refurbishing and remaking to take hold among an urban populace, and to become adopted as a fundamental part of a new image for the city, those in government and civil society naturally must find the right level at which decision making matters most," writes former Dean of the Harvard Graduate School of Design, Peter G. Rowe. "In urban design, this invariably means identifying the scale at which there is sufficient congruence between city form, social purpose, and cultural values to make a palpable difference in the daily life of citizens." [89]

Finding that "right level" for decision making around the design and cre-ation of spaces, public or private, requires significant commitment and a willingness of leaders and professionals to listen and to trust the people who use, or will use, that place.

"The sooner the community becomes involved in the planning process the better—ideally before any planning has been done," write Kathleen Madden and Fred Kent of New York's Project for Public Spaces. "And people should be encouraged to stay involved throughout the improvement effort so that they become owners or stewards of the place as it evolves." [90]

Citizen involvement in public decision making is too often reactive and negative in character. People are inclined to involve themselves when the status quo is threatened. But citizen involvement is best when community members and grassroots organizations take the lead and engage professionals

Culture is the "glue," the shared values and meanings that bind us together, that shape our lives and, indeed, shape our attitudes about development and stewardship. Yet it is this intangible dimension of culture that is frequently ignored in public policy discussion, where culture is too often seen as a "soft" topic or an impediment to progress.

— Caroline Marshall [88]

and policy makers only after community members know what they want. Landscape architect Lane L. Marshall advocates that the planning and decision-making processes be "fueled by the energy and creative juices of the citizens of the community." [91]

In this section we'll see how the residents of two communities creatively came together to shape the places in which they live.

Hope Community in Minneapolis stimulates the creative juices of its citizens in shaping and uplifting their community's self-image. The organization has not only made people believe great things are possible but also it has already accomplished many great things. Through an asset-based community-organizing strategy and "listening process," Hope Community brought people of multiple ethnicities together in small-group dialogs. Hope has organized three major listening projects—each including more than three hundred adults and youth—focused on jobs and education, the meaning of community, and the design of a park. In fact, the organization designed an entire neighborhood with concern for children as the unifying factor based upon what it learned from listening. Engaging people through their cultural traditions and involving artists as catalysts have become key parts of Hope's strategy.

In the suburban community of Tamarac, Florida, a very different process unfolded. Residents of this "new" and sprawling community responded to opportunities to create public space that would enhance and connect existing amenities. In partnership with the county cultural commission and an artist-led design team, citizens came together to plan a parkway and, along the way, developed new standards for community participation.

STRATEGY ❾
Promote
Stewardship
of Place

Building the Urban Village

Hope Community, Inc., Children's Village and Peavey Park Designs, Minneapolis, Minnesota

www.hope-community.org

The Setting

The Phillips neighborhood, which has nearly 20,000 residents, is the poorest and most racially diverse of Minneapolis' eighty-six neighborhoods. It serves as home to a long-standing and politically organized Native American community, as well as burgeoning Latino and East African immigrant communities. It has accommodated virtually every immigrant population that has come to the city, having once had a large number of Swedes and Norwegians. While many immigrants move on to other parts of the region as their fortunes improve, some put down roots and remain their entire lives. Phillips is just south of downtown and is defined on three sides by major freeways. In decline since the 1960s, the neighborhood long held a reputation as the city's center of homicides, drugs, and prostitution.

Organization Type/Description

Hope Community, Inc., is a community development corporation steeped in a tradition of community organizing, creating "not just housing but community." This Minneapolis-based group operates affordable housing, education, leadership development, and cultural programs. It facilitates community involvement in envisioning and reshaping the neighborhood. As of 2005, Hope owned and managed 89 units of housing and over 6,500 square feet of community space, with plans in motion for 250 more units and 20,000 square feet of new commercial space. Among the group's hallmarks are its Listening Project and cultural programs, vehicles it employs to facilitate involvement in visioning and actively reshaping the neighborhood.

Hope's vision for Children's Village and Peavey Park came from its years of listening and from the active involvement of residents with artists and planners in a variety of culturally centered creative projects.

Mission or Statement of Purpose

Hope Community was founded in 1977 to provide emergency shelter and hospitality for women and their children. It later expanded its mission and vision as it began to acquire, renovate, and manage housing for families. The group's work builds upon a tradition of community organizing and valuing people as the building blocks of community. Hope's leaders frequently partner with other organizations that put people first, including education and arts groups.

Hope embraces active listening and cultural practices in all it does. "We work in a multicultural environment where culture is always present in the strengths and relationships people bring, sometimes in the tensions among people from different cultures, in language, in people's perspectives and stories," according to Deanna Foster and Mary Keefe, Executive and Associate Directors.[92]

Goals and Strategies

Hope Community is committed to providing quality low-income housing while developing a healthy mixed-income neighborhood. Hope approaches its work using asset-based community development and community-organizing strategies and sees the diverse cultures of its residents and neighbors as key assets. It focuses on long-term capacity development versus crisis

Snapshot

Hope Community, Inc.
Minneapolis, Minnesota

Setting
- Low-income, racially diverse urban neighborhood, population 20,000
- High rate of homicides, illegal drug activity, and prostitution
- Negative stereotypes applied by outsiders (and some residents) to the neighborhood

Community Assets
- Experienced community organizers
- Accessible location
- Available real estate
- Multiple cultural communities, including Native American, African American, low-income European American, and diverse immigrant communities

Strategies
- Create a respectful environment for all cultural traditions centered around children
- Balance housing development with a strong community environment
- Facilitate community involvement in planning and employ good place-making design principles

Outcomes
- More than 1,000 participants in dialogs
- Multiple blocks of housing, play areas, indoor and outdoor public spaces
- High levels of stewardship in a low-income area
- Improved public safety

response, and it values process and product equally. The design of both Children's Village and Peavey Park were guided by the following strategies:

- Integrate the processes of real estate development with community organizing, relating to people as citizens not clients
- Use listening and observation as key organizing, design, and management strategies
- Draw people into social and educational activities in safe, attractive, and welcoming gathering places
- Nurture and acknowledge indigenous leadership
- Engage in concerns expressed by the surrounding neighborhoods
- Foster an environment where culture is respected and where people can relate to each other across cultures through what they have in common
- Assert leadership in municipal, philanthropic, educational, and other institutions within the wider community based upon the expressed vision of the neighborhood
- Build partnerships with people and with other organizations that believe in people

General Description of Activities

Hope began its development activities in the 1990s with the acquisition and renovation of adjacent two-, three-, and four-family houses on several blocks. It gradually integrated each block with public spaces behind and between homes, creating passageways visible from kitchen windows designed to let adults watch for and protect children.

In 1997, Hope began its Listening Project to help learn about residents' ideas on education and jobs. More than thirty dialog groups helped deepen Hope's relationships with the community and its understanding of these issues. A larger project with more than three hundred participants, including many youth, later focused on the meanings, struggles, and hopes people attach to neighborhoods and communities. People talked about the multiple communities in their lives, the power in building relationships across cultures, and the importance of public spaces and opportunities to work together toward common goals.

These discussions led into a project to redesign Peavey Park, an underutilized, crime-ridden park that the Minneapolis Park Board had scheduled for an overhaul. The listening and visioning process enabled Hope to engage broad-based participation and to recognize that building community was the central purpose of the park. Hope arrived at the design through a series of creative workshops that were later translated into a formal design and adopted by the Park Board to guide the renovation.

Intermedia Arts participants play homemade instruments at a dedication event. Through mosaic art, murals, and music, participants explore the cultural traditions of their community.

As the neighborhood began to change, concerns grew about gentrification and dislocation. In response, Hope began an arts-based project with nearby Intermedia Arts, a community-based center for art and activism. Artists worked on-site at Hope with youth and others to explore the community's many cultural traditions and to create permanent murals and mosaics as well as music and spoken word arts. The project created cross-cultural dialog about gentrification and other issues and helped guide design efforts. It also helped build a sense of ownership and respect for others while creating stronger working relationships among residents. Hope later decided to add an artist-organizer to its staff to lead ongoing arts programs.

As Hope brought together what it learned with its core activity of creating a safe environment for children, it embarked on a bold project to envision a larger community it called Children's Village. The organization commissioned professional planners to draw up designs for this sixteen-block area and presented them to city leaders and the media. In 2003, Children's Village Center opened. It is a four-story, thirty-unit, low-income housing complex that includes offices for a staff and a community center. It sits prominently as the first of four developments at the intersection of two major city thoroughfares. When complete, these well-designed centers of community activity will signal a massive turnaround for a neighborhood long infested with drugs, poverty, and hopelessness.

Assets Employed

- Experienced community organizers who straddle the worlds of the powerless and the powerful

- Neighbors of diverse cultures who seek peace and security

- Ability to tap the power of cultural understanding to strengthen human connections

- A tradition and a process centered on listening to what the community values, thinks, and hopes

- Prominent location near downtown and at intersection of key traffic arteries (Children's Village Center)

- Development opportunities on abandoned and deteriorated real estate

- Desire of Minneapolis Park Board, city government, and philanthropies to try new approaches (Peavey Park)

Direct Outcomes

- More than 1,000 participants, adults and youth, in the community visioning dialogs with concrete results of their civic participation

- Housing representative of the very diverse neighborhood

- A community-driven park design adopted by the Minneapolis Park Board

We think about what would have happened if we had demonstrated and tried to force people with power to do the right thing. People with power would have had no idea what to do. We had to shape the vision and then make our vision happen. We stirred people up. And it's working.

— Deanna Foster and Mary Keefe, Hope Executive and Associate Directors [93]

- Blockwide design standards for over fifty housing units that create play areas, public gathering places, and safe passage for children
- A thirty-unit, low-income housing property with unusually high-quality design, materials, and construction
- Unusually high rate of tenant retention
- An informal neighborhood gathering spot with an unusual mix of community spaces, offices, and housing
- Ongoing youth and family activities, leadership and organizing training, art and community projects, community-based education, and community celebrations and cultural events

Indirect and Potential Impacts

- Altered perceptions about the wider Phillips neighborhood, bringing increased business and investment
- Healthy mixed-income neighborhood that retains cultural diversity and is an alternative to unchecked gentrification
- Reduced crime and improvement in neighborhood safety
- Reduced city cost for park and public area maintenance
- Increasing property values and desirability of neighborhood
- Broadened understanding of diverse cultures and of the ability of people to work together across cultures

STRATEGY ⑨
Promote
Stewardship
of Place

The Green Connection

Southgate Linear Park Project, City of Tamarac, Florida, and Broward County Cultural Affairs Division

www.tamarac.org
www.broward.org/arts

The Setting

Tamarac, Florida, is a recently developed community sitting on twelve square miles of land between the Atlantic Coast and the eastern edge of the Everglades. A water management canal draining from the Everglades to the Atlantic begins in Tamarac and runs east to the town's edge and beyond. In 2004, Tamarac's population was 56,444. Its economy is mixed. Although it is home to several large employers, it serves partly as a bedroom community for employment centers such as greater Fort Lauderdale and West Palm Beach. Tamarac has many retirees, and it boasts one of the lowest crime rates in Broward County.

Organization Type/Description

As a growing and relatively young community with an emerging network of public services, institutions, spaces and civic practices, the Park had potential to become both a real place and ground on which to develop practices for building future civic amenities.

The City of Tamarac was incorporated in 1963. It has a council-manager form of municipal government serving a rapidly expanding population, most of whom have come to the community during the past twenty years.

The Broward County Cultural Affairs Division is a public agency chartered by the County Board of Supervisors. It was created to coordinate the county's increasing number of commitments to cultural activities. With thirty-two full-time and part-time employees, it works with a population of 1.8 million residents, more than 450 nonprofit cultural organizations, innumerable government offices and private businesses, and more than 10,000 artists and community organizations in the county's thirty-one municipalities.

Mission or Statement of Purpose

The City of Tamarac states that it "constantly strives to meet the needs and improve the health, welfare, and safety of its residents." Its web site says that honesty and integrity are the city's core values, through which it is "prepared to continue delivering the highest level of city services to residents and businesses in the twenty-first century."[94]

The Design Arts Grant Program of the Broward County Cultural Affairs Division, established in 2002, is an innovative program to foster and assist partnerships between municipalities and nonprofit organizations to cooperate on aesthetic and functional improvements to the built environment. The program endeavors to foster excellence in public- and private-sector community design and historic preservation and to establish private development initiatives for public art.

Goals and Strategies

In planning the Southgate Linear Park, residents set out to define a community identity and to project Tamarac's personality through this park. They also wanted to add environmentally friendly biking and walking trails. An underlying objective was to explore ways to include culture and artists in community planning and to launch an independent arts council and an ongoing public arts program.

Snapshot

Southgate Linear Park Project
Tamarac, Florida

Setting
- Growing South Florida community with a population of 56,444
- Location bordering eastern edge of the Everglades

Community Assets
- Focused civic leadership
- East-West canal draining to the Atlantic Coast
- Publicly held land corridor
- Visionary county cultural commission

Strategies
- Nurture community identity
- Develop public space that reflects community interests
- Connect neighborhoods, community organizations, and public service facilities
- Strengthen citizen experience in civic design and decision-making processes

Outcomes
- Increased community ownership of public places
- Higher standards of community design
- Community identity that influences ongoing development
- Ongoing public art and design programs

There were four stated objectives of the project:

1. Complete the conceptual plan for Southgate Linear Park

2. Identify proposed public arts projects for the new park

3. Develop a public arts program

4. Identify an identity or cultural theme for Tamarac

General Description of Activities

In 2002, the City of Tamarac asked for and received a grant from the Broward County Design Arts Program that allowed Tamarac to engage a design firm and local artist in a public planning process. Four public workshops were held to articulate the city's cultural identity, address public concerns for the park, review draft plans, and prepare for a presentation to the Tamarac City Commission.

The community and designers put forth a plan for a multipurpose scenic trail and park to connect with neighboring communities, provide a respite from urbanized areas, and preserve areas of native Florida landscapes. Informal partnerships with several adjacent homeowner associations were formed through the process. Nearly $7 million in costs were identified and a variety of public concerns resolved through this planning and design project. These included issues around traffic management, environmental protection, youth opportunities, access for people of all ages and abilities, evolving cultural diversity, and access to other public amenities.

In addition to the plan, a location for a gateway plaza was established and a public artist engaged for the gateway project. Library and community center expansions were incorporated into the park design. The residents felt that the personality of Tamarac was reflected and that they met their goals of a park blending the city with the natural environment while enhancing recreation opportunities. Importantly, the community developed new skills to apply to the design of other parks and public spaces. In addition, leadership emerged, and city officials and citizens alike gained experience in the decision-making processes necessary to implement a successful public arts program.

Assets Employed

• A community of engaged citizens who desired to increase their sense of ownership and empowerment

• Opportunities to build new facilities and amenities in a growing economy

• Well-qualified design and arts professionals

• Progressive county cultural affairs commission

Many communities do not realize that qualified designers and artists can help a community visualize appropriate environmental options, capitalize upon unrecognized resources, solve long-standing problems, and provide a framework for managing change.

— National Association of Counties[95]

CHAPTER 3 Building Social Connections through Arts and Culture   111

- A strategic location that serves as a trailhead and connection point for a water management canal to the western conservation area
- Public land held for water management and future recreation
- Cooperative public and private sectors, including private homeowner associations

Direct Outcomes

- Amenity-rich, multipurpose recreation areas for people of all ages and abilities
- Heightened sense of community ownership of new public amenities
- New outdoor public space and public art reflective of the community's personality
- Opportunities for the community to share its culture and history with thousands of annual visitors
- Connections to adjacent neighborhoods, city library, and community center, including bicycle and walking alternatives
- New opportunities for face-to-face connection among residents
- Key part of a link to adjacent towns and beaches
- New standards in community design, incorporating extensive public input
- Enhanced awareness of design and participatory practices
- Newly launched public arts program

Indirect and Potential Impacts

- Improved design for other public spaces, including streets and transit hubs
- Civic leadership attuned to the expression of the community's aesthetic tastes
- Heightened sense of community identity affecting other development strategies

Summary of Examples in Strategy 9: Promote Stewardship of Place

The two communities profiled here are about as different as their climates. The Phillips neighborhood in Minneapolis has a very diverse population that struggles with economic, physical, and social deterioration. It is rebuilding infrastructure put down over a century earlier. In contrast, Tamarac was incorporated in 1963. It is expanding, thriving economically, and homogenous. Its infrastructure is still being built.

Hope Community and the City of Tamarac used creative participatory processes that resulted in better design and increased social capital, and elevated residents' personal stewardship of the places in which they live, socialize, work, and play. They used familiar spaces and created new ones.

Hope Community, a people-centered community development corporation, applied its organizing principles and practices to neighborhood planning. It combined three processes: listening patiently to the community, cross-cultural activities, and the use of artists to uncover the values and visions of the people in the neighborhood. It saw design as both a participatory art and an important subject for public policy.

The Broward County Cultural Arts Commission assisted suburban Tamarac to bring artists, community leaders, and neighbors together to create a vision for a multipurpose park. The process also resulted in an emerging municipal public arts program to involve residents on an ongoing basis to build a unique community.

The next and final strategy highlights different ways artists have helped members of their communities navigate difficult civic and social issues.

Broaden Participation in the Civic Agenda

SELF-EXPRESSION IS A CRITICAL INGREDIENT of democracy. Strategy 10 makes use of community-centered arts and cultural practices to solve problems in a way that simultaneously broadens people's involvement in civic issues. In this section we'll see how artists helped community members get at core values, deal with difficult issues with an open mind, and leave with new tools to face future issues and solve problems.

Some people have argued that social capital has eroded steadily over the past two generations, noting drops in participation in social and civic groups. This crisis may really be one in which the old tools for involving people in civic issues are no longer sufficient to meet new challenges. The tools may have lost effectiveness as the population diversifies.

At the same time, many social, civic, and cultural functions have been "professionalized" in ways that exclude participation of ordinary citizens. From city to city across the United States, professional arts organizations have grown up where voluntary groups once stood. This trend has severed the practice and experience of the arts from day-to-day life. Participation in cultural activities (as opposed to spectatorship) connects people to each other and to their community institutions, providing pathways to other forms of participation.[97] Thus, arts and culture can create opportunities for political expression, community dialog, shared cultural experiences, and civic work.

Within the arts, there is a vital yet lesser-known field of practice that strives to develop cultural understanding and civic engagement. Community-based arts practitioners bring members of a community together to solve problems, build relationships, and get involved in ways that rebuild social capital.[97]

This section features two different ways that artists and citizens have worked together to facilitate change. Road projects have often been divisive and ultimately destructive to community fabric and to the infrastructure of communities. In rural Danville, Vermont, artists and highway planners engaged citizens to solve a road construction dilemma. The Danville Transportation Enhancement Project found a unique way to identify and resolve touchy issues of values and aesthetics.

In Anchorage, Alaska, artists and activists helped people wrestle with the issue of same-sex relationships. Understanding Neighbors brought together people of diverse values and opinions to process this difficult and divisive

The correlation between survival/self-expression values and democracy is remarkably strong. Do they go together because self-expression values (which include interpersonal trust, tolerance, and participation in decision-making) are conducive to democracy? Or do democratic institutions cause these values to emerge? It is always difficult to determine causality, but the evidence suggests that it is more a matter of culture shaping democracy than the other way around.

—Ronald Inglehart[96]

issue. A filmmaker, two performance artists, and other artists facilitated the dialog. Unlike road construction there was no concrete result, but neighbors walked away understanding each other better.

Where Artists Meet the Road

Danville Transportation Enhancement Project, Vermont Agency of Transportation, Vermont Arts Council, and Town of Danville

www.danvilleproject.com

The Setting

Danville is a community of 2,200 people in the northeastern part of Vermont. It sits on U.S. Highway Route 2, part of the National Highway System and one of the major east-west roads across northern New England. With the White Mountains as a backdrop, Danville boasts some of New England's most unspoiled and spectacular scenery.

The town is anchored by a classic village green with a Civil War monument, bandstand, distinctive school, general store, courthouse, and churches. The Danville Village Improvement Society was formed in 1896 to beautify the town. The following year it placed an elegant stone watering trough on the green, an amenity still in use today. The society also installed street lamps and planted rows of shade trees on the green and along the streets surrounding it. The past one hundred years have brought little change to the town and its appearance.

Organization Type/Description

The Danville Transportation Enhancement Project brought together the Vermont Agency of Transportation, the Vermont Arts Council, and the Town of Danville.

The Vermont Agency of Transportation (VTrans) is a leader in the national movement among transportation agencies toward context-sensitive design solutions and public involvement. VTrans aims to bring communities together early in the planning process to help design environmentally responsible transportation infrastructure that promotes safety and efficiency while preserving the community's vision of itself.

The Vermont Arts Council, founded in 1964, is an independent nonprofit that receives and distributes state, federal, and other funds to support the arts in Vermont communities.

The Town of Danville incorporated in 1784. Legend has it that it was named for a French admiral by the name of d'Anville.

Mission or Statement of Purpose

The purpose of the Danville Transportation Enhancement Project was to plan for the redevelopment of a portion of U.S. Highway 2 through the town's village center. The Danville project needed to find a way to upgrade road conditions and meet federal highway requirements, while respecting the aesthetic, economic, and cultural fabric of the community.

Highway expansion in a rural area, where the most valuable currency is often aesthetic, can be difficult and controversial, pitting residents, businesses, local officials, and state officials against each other. Many quaint towns and villages have lost all sense of place and have been economically and socially devastated by such expansion—widened highways sending cars speeding through; rerouting through residential areas; diverting essential business and tourist traffic to outer areas where big-box retailers sprout up. This last-mentioned impact can wind up gutting downtowns, draining a town's established, local economic base, and exporting local dollars to distant headquarters and indifferent shareholders.

Goals and Strategies

A local review committee was formed as part of the legislated highway planning process. This group set a goal to "bring a sense of visual unity between the highway and the already-present characteristics of the town by considering the artistic and aesthetic aspects of the area, while also addressing public safety and accessibility."[99]

The Danville project implemented the principles of context-sensitive design and the time-honored Vermont traditions of public meetings, civil discourse, and representative democracy. Artists, working closely with engineers and residents, infused the process with creative problem solving and openness to new ideas.

General Description of Activities

The process began in early 2000 when the Vermont Arts Council conducted the search for an artist to oversee the design of artistic enhancements and to involve the community in the redevelopment of the highway through Danville. With the help of the local review committee, two artists were selected—landscape architect David Raphael as lead artist and sculptor Andrea Wasserman as creative consultant. These artists joined the local review committee, which

Snapshot

Danville Transportation Enhancement Project
Danville, Vermont

Setting
- Older rural village, population 2,200
- Location on principal, arterial east-west state highway designated as part of the National Highway System
- Few changes in more than one hundred years

Community Assets
- Scenic beauty
- Strong tradition of civic engagement
- Historic town green and architecture
- Strong support for school and local institutions

Strategies
- Reconstruct highway while respecting community fabric
- Develop transportation facility to fit the physical setting and preserve aesthetic, historic, and environmental resources, while maintaining safety and mobility
- Involve an artist with the community design process
- Build community consensus and ownership through the establishment of a local review committee
- Incorporate public art
- Create a plan that supports the existing economic base

Outcomes
- Preserved and reinforced community identity
- Safer, more efficient transportation infrastructure
- Continued economic stability
- Sense of accomplishment
- New activities and amenities involving youth

included nine local residents, representatives from VTrans and the Vermont Arts Council, and a state-paid transportation consultant. Additional artists were later selected for the proposed enhancements and for the arts-based activities and projects that spun off from the planning process.

Raphael and Wasserman led community meetings, interviewed residents, and circulated questionnaires. They helped residents envision the future of the village and its central green, and they took the community through a review of preliminary VTrans designs.

The civic engagement process was the most important aspect of the project. It was purposefully inclusive, sensitive, engaging, and ongoing. Having artists, rather than highway engineers, lead the process seemed less threatening to community participants, and they were more effective at devising satisfying alternatives.

A final design and enhancements were presented to the Danville community in late 2002. Construction and completion are scheduled through the latter part of the decade. Enhancements include gateways with signage, lighting, landscaping, granite posts, and sidewalk markers to alert motorists that they are entering a village center. Streetscape designs reinforce the village character and improve aesthetics and pedestrian comfort.

Almost as important as the road design, a number of related activities emerged from the community process, especially those involving youth—projects that got started right away. They include a student photography project that led to postcards and a Danville calendar. Other students carved stone figures to be embedded along three miles of concrete sidewalk. Youth planted seedlings in the project's right-of-way, and they designed tile markers, a ceramic playground mural, and clay cutouts of hands to hang in the village green.

Assets Employed

- Scenic beauty and rural way of life
- Tradition of volunteerism and civic engagement
- Creative artists skilled in community process
- An important major transportation route
- A prized center and symbol of community life in the village green and the structures surrounding it
- State arts and transportation agencies willing to collaborate and work with a small town
- Residents who welcomed the rejuvenation of community and creative spirit
- A state arts agency willing to invest in a creative planning process

> Ultimately the success of the project will be reflected by how completely the experience incorporates all that the community has to offer, while encouraging exploration and discovery throughout the process. A participatory process that supports a community in learning from its past to inform its present and guide its future will, in turn, be supported by the community.
>
> — Danville Transportation Enhancement Project web site[100]

Direct Outcomes

- Invigorated sense of collective efficacy
- Strengthened community problem-solving capacities
- A positive, invigorating experience where there was great potential for division
- Preservation and enhancement of community aesthetic value, sense of place, and sense of belonging
- Affirmation of creative possibilities and contributions of citizens
- Intergenerational respect and working relationships
- Appreciation of the multiple roles art plays in daily life

Indirect and Potential Impacts

- Economic stability for a village center whose survival was threatened
- "Spin-off" arts and cultural civic projects
- A model artist-led community planning process cited by VTrans as "satisfying both economically and aesthetically"
- Discovery by transportation planners that involving artists in infrastructure design can result in increased public support for construction projects
- Documentation of a successful methodology for maintaining momentum and public interest in highway planning

Melting Barriers in the Far North

Understanding Neighbors, Out North Contemporary Art House, Alaska Common Ground, and Interfaith Council of Anchorage, Anchorage, Alaska

www.outnorth.org
www.artsusa.org/animatingdemocracy/reading_room/case_studies/ interdisciplinary.asp

STRATEGY 10
Broaden Participation in the Civic Agenda

The Setting

Anchorage, the largest city in Alaska, is an international center of trade and transportation. The city is a major ocean shipping port with a relatively small downtown, and residents spread suburban-style across a vast and spectacular landscape. The population of 260,000 is comprised of a significant number of Alaska Natives, together with newer populations of U.S. military and ex-military, rugged individualists, recently arrived professionals in financial,

Understanding Neighbors
Anchorage, Alaska

Setting
- Remote northern city, population 260,000
- Regional ocean and air cargo shipping port
- Small traditional downtown with much of the city widely dispersed

Community Assets
- Active gay and lesbian community
- Tradition of individualism
- Art center highly engaged in civic issues
- Leaders from multiple communities eager to build bridges

Strategies
- Use art to begin conversations about a divisive topic
- Create understanding through a structured dialog process
- Help develop tools for understanding and solving other issues

Outcomes
- Participants more comfortable discussing same-sex relationships
- Organizations formed new partnerships
- Increased community capacity to respond to social change

oil, government, tourism, and other industries, and a wide assortment of people who tolerate long, dark winters and long summer days. Due, in part, to its relatively short history, Anchorage has a fledgling social and civic infrastructure. Its rugged, individualist culture brings equally diverse political, religious, and social beliefs.

Organization Type/Description

Understanding Neighbors was a joint project of three Anchorage groups: Out North Contemporary Art House, Alaska Common Ground, and Interfaith Council of Anchorage. It was created to carry out a dialog project around issues related to same-sex couples.

Out North Contemporary Art House is a nonprofit arts center. It was founded in 1985 by a small group of artists seeking to produce plays not generally seen in Alaska. It grew to commission, produce, and present a mix of community-based and visiting artist exhibits, screenings, and performances for diverse Alaskan audiences. The center is led by Gene Dugan and Jay Brause, a long-term gay couple. They are also activists in various civic causes and have publicly advanced issues around homosexuality and gay marriage in Anchorage for more than a decade. As community builders, they approached potential partners and secured funding from Animating Democracy, a Ford Foundation project, and other groups seeking to stimulate civic dialog around contemporary issues through the arts.

Alaska Common Ground collects and disseminates information on public issues and problems in Alaska. It uses the information to facilitate discussion and seek consensus on issues, to develop solutions, and to encourage adoption and implementation of these solutions. Alaska Common Ground seeks to provide a forum for Alaskans from all walks of life and all parts of the state to address public policy issues and find areas of mutual agreement. The group was founded as a nonprofit in 1991.

Interfaith Council of Anchorage is a consortium of spiritual communities committed to finding effective ways to plan and work together for the sake of peace and justice in the community. Its mission is to serve others and to be present in all areas of the human situation. It believes that all faiths teach that wisdom must be coupled with actions if the world is to be transformed.

Mission or Statement of Purpose

The Understanding Neighbors project was created to convene people who would not usually come together to discuss issues related to same-sex couples, to help people in Anchorage understand each other, and to train community facilitators in a dialog methodology that could benefit the community in the future.

Goals and Strategies

The goal of the Understanding Neighbors project was to explore the question, What is the place of same-sex couples in our society? Its strategy was to use artists to stimulate dialog that would result in greater understanding. A pre- and posttest were included in the plans to gauge the outcome of the project. Project leaders also chose to use professional dialog facilitators so as to allow partnering organizations to remain neutral on the issue and to encourage participation from a wide range of Alaskans.

General Description of Activities

The project engaged three artists who had been trained in dialogic methods by the Public Conversations Project. Performance artists Peter Carpenter and Sara Felder and filmmaker Stephan Mazurek conducted community interviews with seventy Alaskans of diverse viewpoints, from which they created short performance works and videos to spark small-group discussions.

Considerable planning and negotiation went into the front end of this project. Ninety participants who identified themselves as conservative, moderate, or liberal on the issue of same-sex relationships were recruited. They were pretested on their views and then carefully divided into twelve facilitated-dialog groups, with a spectrum of views in each group. Each group met four times. The short videos were shown at the start of each session and followed by discussion. Twenty-five volunteers recruited from sponsoring agencies and trained in dialogic methods facilitated the discussions.

After these dialog sessions ended, the artists developed a final performance work, to which all participants and general audiences were invited. Dialog participants were posttested to examine changes in attitudes. In addition, posttesting looked at the effectiveness of the process—whether participants had changed their comfort levels in discussing homosexuality, and whether they felt they had gained new skills for approaching other tough topics.

Results of this post-analysis revealed that 86 percent of participants agreed that the artworks presented were instrumental in sparking meaningful dialog on a controversial issue; 94 percent of participants reported a positive experience; only 4 percent reported the experience as negative. All but 6 percent of participants agreed that they left with new tools for engaging in dialog about controversial topics.

Assets Employed

• An organized and assertive gay and lesbian community

• Social issue and religious organizations willing to tackle sensitive issues

By witnessing the stories of eleven courageous neighbors, I was returned to a place of hope, faith, and trust in the goodness and humanness of us all.

— Frankie Barker,
volunteer dialog
facilitator[101]

- An art center with national fundraising connections and relationship-building savvy
- Leadership with connections and personal relationships in multiple communities
- Commitment of participants to cross traditional barriers

Direct Outcomes

- Greater comfort levels among participants when discussing same-sex relationships
- New tools introduced to help participants engage in dialog about controversial topics
- Considerable local media coverage

Indirect and Potential Impacts

- Sponsoring organizations motivated to partner on other issues
- Greater openness and comfort addressing the same-sex topic among partner groups
- Stronger infrastructure and skills for navigating social and economic changes in the community

An Understanding Neighbors test dialog group held at Out North Contemporary Art House in Achorage, Alaska.

Summary of Examples in Strategy 10: Broaden Participation in the Civic Agenda

Artists develop their ability to work with multiple layers of meaning, some of which may not be readily apparent to the observer. In Strategy 10, we saw how artists applied these skills—seeing and symbolically reconstructing the world differently—to facilitate and improve debates over social issues and public policy.

Putting a team of artists at the helm of highway design may seem risky. However, when the most difficult part of highway construction is sorting out and negotiating individual and community values, feelings, and aesthetics, it makes sense—and it works. The Danville Transportation Enhancement Project made everyone an expert in highway construction. In so doing, the Danville project met the needs of local residents and the state highway department. Community members of all ages gained a new understanding of the function and possibilities of highways, as well as a greater understanding of what they can do when they work creatively together.

Citizens of Anchorage tackled the controversial issue of homosexual relationships through an extended artist-led dialog process. Artists were able to make breakthroughs by respecting and including divergent viewpoints. They provided a new context for ideas and were able to pull apart layers of feelings. Understanding Neighbors expanded the ways participants could understand and talk through controversial topics.

Best Practices in Using Arts and Culture to Build Social Connections

Chapter 3 examined five strategies for the social, civic, and physical revitalization of communities. The were

Strategy 6: Promote Interaction in Public Space

Strategy 7: Increase Civic Participation through Cultural Celebrations

Strategy 8: Engage Youth

Strategy 9: Promote Stewardship of Place

Strategy 10: Broaden Participation in the Civic Agenda

Two case studies illustrated each strategy. They were chosen to demonstrate a wide range of community types and sizes, as well as a variety of organizations and partnerships. However, they all exemplified all or some of the following best practices.

- Build on the history and unique qualities of place, drawing on the community's creative assets and cultural traditions
- Begin small, employing visible aesthetic and symbolic actions that reframe the value of diversity, youth, and creativity to build momentum
- Acknowledge everyone as "expert" with regard to their culture and their community; exercise respect and include divergent viewpoints
- Incorporate learning as an ongoing process to enable people to respectfully cross boundaries into unfamiliar cultures; embrace difference and controversy as opportunities

- Engage diverse stakeholders, especially youth, in visioning, planning, and sharing ongoing responsibilities; use participatory processes
- Conduct events and activities in familiar public spaces understanding that people have different culturally based relationships to these spaces
- Build organizational and cross-sector partnerships, working with existing groups including those involving neighborhood residents and stakeholders
- Value and elevate design and the planning process both as art forms and as the subject of public policy
- Coordinate activities to complement other economic and civic projects that build upon human and economic assets

This ends Part 2 of the book. We have explored ten strategies and twenty examples. The first five strategies revolved around improving the "hardware" of community—its economic infrastructure. The second five strategies looked at the "software" of community—social connections among individuals and groups. In all cases, arts and culture were integrated strategically and provided extraordinary benefits.

Part 1 of this book looked at the ideas that underlie these strategies.

But the ultimate goal of this handbook is to help you become a more creative community builder, and to discover ways to implement these strategies in your neighborhood, village, town, or city. And that is the focus of Part 3.

Endnotes for Part Two

[29] Mariano Grondona, "A Cultural Typology of Economic Development," *Culture Matters*, 46.

[30] Charles Landry, *The Creative City: A Toolkit for Urban Innovators* (London: Earthscan Publications, 2000), xiii.

[31] Brian Headd, "The Small Business Economy: A Report to the President" (Washington, DC: Small Business Administration, 2004), 5.

[32] Maria-Rosario Jackson et al. "Investing in Creativity: A Study of the Support Structure for U.S. Artists" (Washington, DC: Urban Institute, 2003). www.usartistsreport.org

[33] Americans for the Arts, "Arts and Economic Prosperity: The Economic Impact of Nonprofit Arts Organizations and Their Audiences," 2002. www.artsusa.org/information_resources/economic_impact/

[34] Jane Jacobs, *The Death and Life of Great American Cities* (New York: Vintage Books, 1961), 188.

[35] Shop Mainstreets Pittsburgh: Garfield/Friendship Commercial District, web site, 2005. www.ura.org/shopmainstreets/districts/garfieldfriendship.html

[36] Laurel Jones and Bay Consulting Group, "Assessment/Evaluation of Arts Programs, City of San José," Report commissioned by San José Office of Cultural Affairs (August 2002), 5.

[37] Chris Walker, Maria-Rosario Jackson, and Carole Rosenstein, *Culture and Commerce: Traditional Arts in Economic Development* (Santa Fe, NM: The Fund for Folk Culture and the Urban Institute, 2003), 10.

[38] Partners for Livable Communities, "Cultural Heritage Tourism: How Communities Can Reinvent Their Future" (Washington, DC: Unpublished paper, 2004), 32.

[39] Dee Davis, "Full Faith and Credit," in *Community, Culture and Globalization*, 185.

[40] Interview with Bill Bulick, Creative Planning, Inc., Portland, OR, September 2005.

[41] Partners for Livable Communities, "Cultural Heritage Tourism," 28.

[42] Juana Guzmán, quoted in "Cultural Quest: Juana Guzmán Wants You to See Another Side of Chicago," by Yolanda Perdomo. Hispanic Magazine.com, January/February 2004.

[43] Hal Cropp, as quoted in Carlo M. Cuesta, Dana M. Gillespie, and Padraic Lillis, *Bright Stars: Charting the Impact of the Arts in Rural Minnesota* (Minneapolis: The McKnight Foundation, 2005), 71.

[44] John Villani, "A Call to Art," *Urban Land* (July 1999):58.

[45] Davis, "Full Faith and Credit," in *Community, Culture and Globalization*, 175.

[46] Stuart Rosenfeld, "Crafting a New Rural Development Strategy," in *Economic Development America* (Washington, DC: U.S. Department of Commerce Economic Development Administration, Summer 2004), 13.

[47] Ann Markusen, "Creative Space," *Minneapolis Star Tribune*, Sunday, May 8, 2005, sec. D, p. 4.

[48] Villani, "A Call to Art," *Urban Land*, 78.

[49] State of the City Address, February 23, 2004.

[50] Marian Van Landingham, *On Target: Stories of the Torpedo Factory Art Center's First 25 Years* (Alexandria, VA: Self-Published, 1999), 2.

[51] "What We Do and Why We Do It," MASS MoCA web site, February 28, 2005. www.massmoca.org/about.html. February 28, 2005.

[52] Bill Hudnut, Presentation of findings of an Ernst and Young study entitled "The Economic Impact of Arts Centers: A Real Estate Perspective," at the Mayor's Forum on Culture and Community Development (Orlando, FL, February 2000).

[53] Candelaria Silva, interview by author, April 2003.

[54] From Linda F. Kinsey, *Voices of North Adams: A Booklet Commemorating the 100th Anniversary of the Incorporation of the City of North Adams, Massachusetts, April 8, 1895* (North Adams, MA: Beck's Printing Company, 1996), 25.

[55] Stephen Sheppard in a report to the Ford Foundation, January 31, 2006, page 1.

[56] Tara Bahrampour, "A 'Plague of Artists' Is a Battle Cry for Brooklyn Hasidim," *New York Times*, February 17, 2004, sec. C, p. 16.

[57] Robin Pogrebin, "Report Says Artists' Arrival Can Push Out Neighbors," *New York Times*, November 11, 2002, sec. B, p. 1.

[58] Ibid.

[59] Lynda McDaniel, "Using Our Strengths: The Grassroots Leadership of Becky Anderson," *Appalachian Magazine* (January–December 2002) as shown in web site www.arc.gov/index.do?nodeId=1562

[60] Quoted by Julie Ball Hambrick, "Paducah's New Direction: The Fast Lane to Neighborhood Revitalization . . . Artist Relocation," *Dialogue Magazine* (January–February 2003):16. www.paducaharts.com/articles/dialogue103.pdf

[61] Robert D. Putnam and Lewis M. Feldstein, *Better Together: Restoring the American Community* (New York: Simon & Schuster, 2003), 294.

[62] See "Project on Human Development in Chicago Neighborhoods," www.hms.harvard.edu/chase/projects/chicago/index.html

[63] Neil Bradford, "Creative Cities: Structured Policy Dialogue Backgrounder" (Ottawa, Ontario: Canadian Policy Research Networks, 2004), 2.

[64] Fred Kent and Kathleen Madden, *How to Turn a Place Around: A Handbook for Creating Successful Public Spaces* (New York: Project for Public Spaces, 2000).

[65] William H. Whyte, in Albert LaFarge, ed., *The Essential William H. Whyte* (New York: Fordham University Press, 2000), 256.

[66] Kent and Madden, *How to Turn a Place Around*, 75.

[67] Lake Snell Perry and Associates and the Tarrance Group. "Working Together: Community Involvement in America." The League of Women Voters, 2004. www.trustingov.org/research/other/civic/lwv.htm

[68] Jack Becker, "Goodbye Plop Art," *Utne Arts Extra* (November 15, 2002), 28–29.

[69] Barnaby Evans, as quoted by Bill Rodriguez in "Blazing Glory: The Elemental Splendor of WaterFire," *Providence Phoenix*, June 20, 1997. www.providencephoenix.com/archive/art/97/06/19/WATERFIRE.html

[70] Ibid.

[71] David I. Kertzer, "WaterFire as Community Ritual," *Illuminating the Mirror: Reflections on WaterFire: On the Occasion of the 100th Lighting of WaterFire* (Providence, RI: WaterFire Providence, undated), 26.

[72] Baker County Cultural Plan, page 3. Baker County, 2004. www.bakercounty.org/Commissioners/CulturalTrust.html

73 Mark J. Stern, "Performing Miracles," Center for an Urban Future, October 17, 2002. www.nycfuture.org/content/reports/report_view.cfm?repkey=86

74 Mark J. Stern, "Communities and Culture: Lessons for Practitioners from Our Research," Presentation at the Ford Foundation (New York, NY, December 2003).

75 Francie Ostrower, *The Diversity of Cultural Participation: Findings from a National Survey* (Washington, DC: The Urban Institute and Wallace Foundation, 2005), 5. Also see 2002 *Survey of Public Participation in the Arts: Research Division Report #45* (Washington, DC: National Endowment for the Arts, March 2004), 1.

76 Alaka Wali, *The Informal Arts in Chicago: Finding Cohesion, Capacity and Other Cultural Benefits in Unexpected Places* (Chicago: The Center for Arts Policy, Columbia College, 2002).

77 Pia Moriarty, *Immigrant Participatory Arts: An Insight into Community-building in Silicon Valley* (San José, CA: Cultural Initiatives–Silicon Valley, 2004). www.ci-sv.org/cna_imm_pa.shtml

78 From In the Heart of the Beast Theatre web site. www.hobt.org/mayday/part/index.html

79 Leon Fooksman, "Charting the Path of Delray History," *South Florida Sun Sentinel,* October 18, 2003 as cited in www.racematters.org/chartingdelrayhistory.htm

80 Fukuyama, Trust, 6–7.

81 Shirley Brice Heath and Laura Smyth, *Art Show: Youth and Community Development* (Washington, DC: Partners for Livable Communities, 1999), 35.

82 Lois Weis and Michelle Fine, eds., *Construction Sites: Excavating Race, Class, and Gender among Urban Youth* (New York: Teachers College Press, 2000), xi, 3.

83 Lake Snell Perry and Associates and the Tarrance Group, "Working Together: Community Involvement in America" (Washington, DC: League of Women Voters, 2004).

84 "Creativity and Innovation: A Bridge to the Future" (Boston: The Boston Foundation, 2002). www.tbf.org/indicators/summary/index.asp?id=1393

85 Artists for Humanity web site: www.afhboston.com/Epicenter/Green. EnvironmentalDesign.html

86 Brice Heath and Smyth, *Art Show*, 36.

87 Johanna (Jones) Franzel, Generation PRX: Amplifying Youth Voices," *MediaRights: Media That Matters,* September 19, 2005. www.mediarights.org/news/2005/09/19/generation_prx_amplifying_youth_voices

88 Caroline Marshall, *Envisioning Convergence: Cultural Conservation, Environmental Stewardship and Sustainable Livelihoods* (Santa Fe, NM: The Fund for Folk Culture, 2004), 3.

89 Peter G. Rowe, *Civic Realism* (Cambridge, MA: MIT Press, 1997), 52.

90 Kent and Madden, *How to Turn a Place Around*, 35.

91 Lane L. Marshall, *Action by Design* (Washington, DC: American Society of Landscape Architects, 1983), 97.

92 Deanna Foster and Mary Keefe, *End of One Way* (Minneapolis: McKnight Foundation, 2004), 30.

93 Ibid., 41.

94 City of Tamarac web site www.tamarac.org

[95] From a nomination statement provided by Broward County Cultural Affairs Division, 2003 National Achievement Award.

[96] Ronald Inglehart, "Culture and Democracy," in *Culture Matters,* 81.

[97] Walker et al., *Culture and Commerce,* 8.

[98] See Community Arts Network, www.communityarts.net

[99] From Danville project web site: www.danvilleproject.com/files/enhancement.htm

[100] From Danville project web site: www.danvilleproject.com/files/guide.htm

[101] Frankie Barker, quoted by Lynn E. Stern, "Animating Democracy Case Study: Understanding Neighbors: Art-Inspired Dialogue Bridges Diverse Viewpoints About Same-Sex Relationships" (Washington, DC: Americans for the Arts, 2005), 5. www.artsusa.org/animatingdemocracy/reading_room/case_studies/interdisciplinary.asp

When Artist Laura McLaughlin purchased a run-down building on Penn
Avenue, the Penn Avenue Arts Initiative
(PAAI) supported her through its renovation. They provided interior loans and
a façade grant via their Artist Loan and
Grant Fund. Laura collaborated with
PAAI's youth arts program and Unblurred
events to create the mosaic glass-tile façade on the exterior of the building. PAAI
promotes Clay Penn on its web site, tours,
and monthly Unblurred events.

To learn more about PAAI and creating
jobs through economic development
strategies, see pages 24–27.

LEFT: 5111 Penn Avenue before it was
renovated into artist Laura McLauglin's
Clay Penn. Laura created two loft
apartments on the top floor of the
building. Photo courtesy of Friendship
Development Associates, Inc.

BOTTOM LEFT: A glass-tile mosaic
façade was created during PAAI youth
arts programs and Unblurred events.

BOTTOM RIGHT: Artist Laura
McLaughlin stands in front of Clay
Penn. Photo courtesy of Friendship
Development Associates, Inc.

Lanesboro, population 788, is nestled in the Root River Valley of southeastern Minnesota. The transformation of the abandoned rail line to a bicycling and walking trail in the 1980s set off the community's revival. When the trail system began attracting more tourists, the council convinced Eric Bunge, a native of the community, to return and start a theater company. The Commonweal Theatre Company began in 1989 with an eleven-week summer season. Word-of-mouth and hard work built a widespread audience, and, by 2004, it operated an eleven-month season with a full-time staff and eight hundred subscribers—more than the entire population of the town.

The Commonweal Theatre and the Root River Trail have created a wave of tourism to Lanesboro. This, in turn, has created opportunities for restaurants, bed-and-breakfasts, and shops to flourish in this small town. More than $1.2 million has been spent in the community by tourists attending Commonweal Theatre since 1989.

To learn more about Lanesboro and stimulating trade through cultural tourism, see pages 38–41.

TOP: Scenic Lanesboro, Minnesota, lies at the foot of dramatic river bluffs and among tree-covered rolling hills uncharacteristic of the Midwest. Photo by Tom Borrup.

MIDDLE: The Lanesboro Art Council bought the St. Mane, an old theater space on the virtually abandoned main street in the 1980s. The St. Mane Theater has housed the Commonweal Theatre Company since 1989. Photo by Tom Borrup.

BOTTOM: Commonweal's 2003 world premiere production of *Beautiful Again* by Melanie Marnich. Photo courtesy of the Commonweal Theatre Company.

Arts, Culture, and Trade (ACT) Roxbury's mission is to use arts and culture to enrich and strengthen the physical, economic, and social revitalization of the Dudley Square Business District and Lower Roxbury community in Boston, Massachusetts.

ACT carefully restored Hibernian Hall, a historic four-story former Irish social club. This building now serves the community as a center for cultural activity and can be rented for business conferences, theater productions, concerts, and receptions.

The renovation was also meant to spark the revitalization of an important block in Dudley Square. Newly restored and active storefronts will invite the community to eat at restaurants, visit the businesses and offices, attend workshops and events, and draw people to the Dudley Square Business District.

To learn more about ACT Roxbury and using arts and culture to diversify a local economy, see pages 54–57.

ABOVE: Built in 1913, Hibernian Hall featured one of the largest dance floors in Boston and was a favorite place for dances, receptions, and fundraisers. The building fell into decay as the community around it lost businesses and crime and poverty increased. Outside photo by Tom Borrup, inside photo by Lolita Parker, Jr.

BELOW: Carefully preserved, the building is now home to the Roxbury Center for the Arts at Hibernian Hall, and once again serves the Lower Roxbury community as a gathering place. Outside photo by Jonathan Bonner, inside photo by Lolita Parker, Jr.

North Adams, Massachusetts, was once the largest city in the Berkshire Hills and one of the most prosperous, but by 1990 it ranked as the poorest.

The Massachusetts Museum of Contemporary Art (MASS MoCA) was created, in 1999, by a partnership that included the City of North Adams, the Commonwealth of Massachusetts, and nearby Williams College. While the museum fosters exciting new works of art, it also acts as a vibrant catalyst for community revitalization and economic diversity.

To learn more about MASS MoCA and using arts organizations to generate and attract other enterprises, see pages 57–61.

ABOVE: The museum has a large outdoor space that hosts summer performing arts events—including this showing of the animated movie, *Iron Giant*. Photo by Kevin Kennefick.

RIGHT: Trees grow upside down outside MASS MoCA. Property values for homes near the museum increased more than $10,000 in 2004. Photo by Kevin Kennefick.

Built at the convergence of two rivers, Providence covered its polluted downtown waterways in the 1950s with roads, rail yards, and expanded parking lots. In the early 1990s, the city uncovered, or "daylighted," the rivers and lined them with public promenades and pedestrian-friendly parks.

Artist Barnaby Evans conceived WaterFire as a one-time event in 1994. Private citizens recognized the power of Evans' spectacle, in which fire evoked a ritual feel and the flames symbolized the renaissance of the city. Their support, seconded by the city's mayor, led to the institutionalization of WaterFire as a community ritual in 1997. Today, twenty-five events, or "lightings," are held each year.

For more information about WaterFire and using public spaces to engage community members, see pages 77–80.

TOP: Each event attracts as many as 100,000 people to downtown Providence's public spaces. Photo by Eric Gould, copyright 1998, WaterFire Providence.

MIDDLE: Volunteers stoke the fires built in basins along Providence's canals. Photo by Thomas Payne, copyright 2005, WaterFire Providence.

BOTTOM: Performance artist Spogga performs at a WaterFire event. Photo by Thomas Payne, copyright 2005, WaterFire Providence.

In the Heart of the Beast Puppet and Mask Theatre (HOBT), located in a working-class neighborhood in Minneapolis, wanted to thank the community that supported its work, and create a celebration to bring people together outdoors at winter's end. The theater also wanted to honor the creative potential of people in the community. Today, the annual May Day Parade and Festival has become HOBT's signature event, building cross-cultural relationships and serving as common ground for exploration and action on issues of importance to the community.

To learn more about HOBT and using celebrations to strengthen neighborhoods, see pages 85–88.

ABOVE: Flower bearers participate in a May Day parade. Photo by Warren Hansen. Masks by Sandy Spieler. Performed by women from At the Foot of the Mountain Theater.

RIGHT: A papier-mâché yak saunters down the parade route. Photos courtesy of HOBT. Puppet by Andrew Kim.

A 2002 study found that over the past decade, Metro Boston's share of young adults had dropped by 21 percent. Artists for Humanity (AFH) began in 1990 as a way to empower young people with the knowledge and understanding to make good decisions about their future and the future of their communities. AFH's paid apprentice program pairs teens with experienced artists in a broad range of fine and commercial arts for product development and services to the business community.

For more information about AFH and engaging youth in civic affairs and enterprises, see pages 95–98.

ABOVE: Youth participants working in the EpiCenter's painting studio. The EpiCenter is AFH's state-of-the-art, environmentally friendly facility.

LEFT: To celebrate a Paul Gauguin exhibit at Boston's Museum of Fine Arts, FleetBoston commissioned AFH to create a large-scale painting of modern-day Boston based on Gauguin's masterpiece, "D'où venonsnous? Que sommes-nous? Oùallons-nous?" Photos courtesy of Artists for Humanity.

Danville is a community of 2,200 people in the northeastern part of Vermont. It sits on U.S. Highway Route 2, one of the major east-west roads across northern New England.

The Danville Transportation Enhancement Project was created to plan for the redevelopment of a portion of U.S. Highway 2 through the town's center. The Danville project needed to find a way to upgrade road conditions and meet federal highway requirements, while respecting the aesthetic, economic, and cultural fabric of the community.

The process began in early 2000 when the Vermont Arts Council conducted a search for artists to oversee the design of artistic enhancements and to involve the community in the redevelopment of the highway through Danville. Two artists were selected—landscape architect David Raphael as lead artist and sculptor Andrea Wasserman as creative consultant. These artists joined the local review committee, which included nine local residents, representatives from VTrans and the Vermont Arts Council, and a state-paid transportation consultant.

To learn more about the Danville Transportation Project and broadening community participation in a civic agenda, see pages 114–117.

TOP: Boasting some of New England's most unspoiled and spectacular scenery and anchored by a classic village green, the town of Danville has seen little change over the past one hundred years. Photo by Tom Borrup.

MIDDLE: Existing photograph of U.S. Highway 2 running through Danville, VT. Photo courtesy of the Vermont Agency of Transportation and Stantec (formerly Dufresne-Henry.)

BELOW: An artist rendering of proposed changes to U.S. Highway 2 in Danville. Illustration courtesy of the Vermont

PART THREE

Steps for Creative Community Builders

IN CREATING A COMMUNITY MURAL, the lead artist draws upon the unique qualities of place and people, their history and stories. She also builds upon the knowledge and talents of participants with all levels of skills who join together to work on the project. She guides them toward a collective theme and expressive style. Participants engage in research, gather stories, and contribute ideas, images, and labor. As a result of this process, the mural has deeper meaning, power, and beauty. Members of the community feel a profound sense of ownership and pride in what they or their neighbors have done. Participants share a common bond with each other for having created something of significance together. Within the community, talents are unleashed and new connections are made. Visitors to the community can see that it's a place people care about.

Skilled community muralists lead people to create a unified scene or image that represents their identity, hopes, and dreams. Their genius is in bringing forth and integrating the ideas of many, putting those creative minds and hands to work in a process that will be celebrated for years to come. The added value is that the community is invested in that work of art and, as stewards, will supply its long-term maintenance and protection.

As a creative community builder, you are like the muralist. Your tools and mode of expression differ, but the process is similar: you harness the assets, history, and creativity of the people to make the community a richer place.

This handbook does not prescribe solutions for your community. Only you and your partners in community building—perhaps with the strategic help of some outside eyes and ears—can determine what will bring about the results you're looking for. Reflect on the stories of successful projects in Part 2, and follow the steps in Part 3. The community building steps in Part 3 can help you arrive at strategies suited to your place.

Culturally based strategies rooted in the unique assets of your community are essential components of equitable and lasting revitalization. Just remember, no single strategy is a magic bullet. Your plan will work best if it complements or synergizes with other revitalization or development efforts.

While the steps described here are generic, the way you proceed should be tailored to the conditions of your community and to the skills and resources at your disposal. This process starts with many assumptions about people, place, and scale. You'll need to adapt it to fit your situation. As a creative community builder, you'll find ways to blaze your own trail as circumstances dictate, as did those creative community builders profiled in Part 2.

The steps in Part 3 lead you through an assessment of your own, your organization's, and your community's strengths. They help you assess your community's cultural assets and unique character. The steps guide you through essential and thoughtful collaboration, and they employ culturally centered and creative methods to help you reach meaningful strategies for your revitalization plan.*

There are five major steps in the process, organized one to a chapter. They are as follows:

Step 1: Assess Your Situation and Goals (Chapter 4)

Step 2: Identify and Recruit Effective Partners (Chapter 5)

Step 3: Map Values, Strengths, Assets, and History (Chapter 6)

Step 4: Focus on Your Key Asset, Vision, Identity, and Core Strategies (Chapter 7)

Step 5: Craft a Plan That Brings the Identity to Life (Chapter 8)

Chapter 9 contains tips to use during implementation—ways to position your project for attracting funding, ways to lobby and advocate for your community, and ways to get the message out about your goals and successes.

The five steps can occur over approximately ten to twelve meetings, including two or three more lengthy sessions, over the course of ten to twelve months. The number of and agenda for these meetings and an approximate timeline are shown on page 162. This is not a prescription but a guide. Your situation has its own requirements, preferences, and scale of work to tackle—you may require more or fewer meetings. It helps, though, to estimate the time requirements to let people know up front what you need from them. If in mid-process it's clear that meetings need to be added or an extension of a few months is required to reach a good outcome, ask the group's permission to make the additional time commitment. However, don't let schedule changes become a recurring event, or the project and your credibility are in trouble.

Electronic versions of the worksheets in this book can be downloaded from the publisher's web site. Use the following URL and code to access these worksheets.

http://www.FieldstoneAlliance.org/worksheets

Access code: W474ccB06

These worksheets are intended for use in the same way as photocopies, but they are in a form that allows you to type in your responses and reformat the worksheets to fit your community building work.

* It should be noted that this author's perspective is shaped by nearly thirty years of working in and with community-based nonprofit organizations. While local governments and businesses are essential partners and leaders of this process, this book is limited by the vantage point of the author. The process that follows may require "interpretation" and some modification if put to use by a local government or business leader.

In Part 3, we'll follow a fictional small town—a rural midwestern place named "Midville"—and how it addresses the five steps. Our Midville has some fame as the hometown of a popular superhero, but has its own unique assets and culture. While the qualities of that place evolved over time, they were not well understood by the community as *assets* until it engaged in this planning process. As you read through the steps, you'll see Midville's concept paper, list of values, survey of assets, conclusions, and stated goals.

Worksheets will help you create an asset inventory, assess key organizational and leadership strengths, create a plan (including timeline and budget), evaluate prospective partners, and define outcomes that are measurable and helpful to making a case for continued support.

It must be noted that the five steps represent an idealized process. I know of no community that has followed this or any other logically designed process in perfect order. Community building, like life, does not unfold linearly. The process is just a map to get you on your way and point out the overall direction. Don't be afraid to wander around and enjoy the territory!

I hope these steps and Midville's story will spark new ways of seeing possibilities in your community and the multiple assets you have at your disposal. Like the community mural process, they are designed to empower voices, ideas, and creative talents. They aim to tap and celebrate the wells of cultural meaning in each participant and each place.

Let's begin!

CHAPTER 4

Step 1: Assess Your Situation and Goals

EVERY COMMUNITY HAS UNIQUE and powerful assets, the most important of which reside in its people—their creativity and cultural traditions. Most places also have things that people care about or value, and every community has social and ethical values that allow it to function. These are the primary raw materials for creative community building.

The key to building a stronger community is the ability to see and understand the things that make it special, along with the ability to motivate people to act. These abilities are the central tools you need to do creative community building—the most valuable skills you need to seek out and nurture.

Artists and community developers may seem like polar opposites, but they have much in common. Both learn to see possibilities in raw materials, and both understand how to work with those materials to create something of value and meaning. Both rely routinely on creativity to solve problems and overcome obstacles. The creative community builder adds values, or a healthy dose of social purpose, to this process.

A holistic community vision incorporates environment, social vitality, economics, culture, health, and other fundamental elements affecting human community. This vision has to be both inward looking (analyzing both the obvious and the hidden assets) and outward looking (considering the community's special place in a larger region or world). Few developers or policy makers think so holistically about creating sustainable communities. Creative community builders work to have all these elements and the people advocating for them as part of the process.

Whether it be a city neighborhood, a small town, or a suburb, your community's assets are lodged in its history, geography, traditions, people, natural environment, economic endeavors, and physical structures. While assessing all those features is important, your particular community's assets may be more strongly vested in one of these areas. Regardless of which asset is your community's greatest strength, its most important and versatile assets are less tangible—the people, their cultures, their creativity, and their sense of identity.

> Creative persons operating in the civic realm perceive value, create value, and add values. It is a precious resource to be nurtured.
>
> — Charles Landry [102]

Whether you are starting as an individual, group of individuals, or existing organization, as a creative community builder, you will need the support and enthusiasm of other people, organizations, and opinion makers. The vision you help bring forth must be one that is shared. It begins with your ability to articulate your community's assets and your capacity to bring those people and their ideas together into the marvelous mural you're about to paint.

The importance of local assets

Familiarity with the principles of asset-based community development and the work of John P. Kretzmann and John L. McKnight is helpful to begin your work. As authors, consultants, and teachers, Kretzmann and McKnight have articulated and demonstrated an effective community building philosophy and have detailed methods that will help you seek out and bring to the table a multitude of overlooked resources. Places they suggest looking include the following:

• Local institutions: schools, libraries, colleges, hospitals, parks, and businesses

• Citizens' associations: block clubs, cultural groups, and churches

• Individuals: artists, people with disabilities, welfare recipients, elderly, youth, and people of varying incomes [103]

Their methods represent an *ongoing* practice and way of seeing the world, not a one-time planning exercise. This practice will help you reexamine your community's physical and economic attributes and find ways to turn things long-considered liabilities into assets.

Developing capacity to see assets is not about looking at the world through rose-colored glasses, putting positive spin on bad situations, or ignoring problems. Asset-based approaches may appear to be in stark contrast to old approaches of first identifying and addressing deficits, problems, and limitations. These old approaches only perpetuate the sense that communities are powerless and have to depend upon outside intervention, resources, and problem solvers.

Asset-based strategies mobilize strengths to leverage change and to overcome deficiencies. Simply in terms of rallying people's energies to a cause, it's more effective to lead with vision and possibility rather than with stories of defeat. This is one way artists' special capacities contribute to community building.

This book and the process that follows focus on identifying and working with assets. Spending time describing how to see problems seems unnecessary. Most people have learned to do so automatically and, in fact, have difficulty *not* seeing problems! Seeing assets requires special effort.

In this book, we'll look for assets even beyond the places outlined by Kretzmann and McKnight. You, the creative community builder, must dig to a deeper, less tangible level. You have to locate the distinctive qualities that shape the *identity* of your community—that thing which defines and connects the people of the place. It is this identity that can motivate people to act and invest resources. Ultimately this identity is what will enhance the meaning of living in and contributing to your special place. As you move through the steps, coming to this identity is the single greatest creative challenge!

Getting started

Chapter 4 looks at things you must do to lay the groundwork. These include a variety of readiness factors, such as how to assess your own capacities and position in the community, how to take stock of what and whom you've got to work with, and, finally, how to test the currency of your idea—or your first instincts. This is important preliminary work to do before going public.

You're at the stage where you, and possibly a group of people around you, are thinking of making change in your community. Perhaps you feel ready to implement a project that grew from your instincts, or perhaps you want to try something you've seen work elsewhere. Maybe you've already got something going that you want to formalize or better define.

First you need to organize your ideas, shape them with the help of close confidants, and find the energy and partners to get a planning process off the ground. To do this, you need to complete six tasks:

1. Define the community
2. Identify your strengths and leadership capacity
3. Identify community assets
4. Clarify values and goals
5. Write a concept paper
6. Review readiness

TASK 1.1   Define the community

Your initiative should be a big idea addressing a small enough place to make big change.

You'll be more effective if you take on a small area—a geographically limited community—and let your efforts radiate outward as you get your footing. Earlier you read about Hope Community in Minneapolis (Strategy 9: Promote Stewardship of Place) as it began with one house, expanded to several, then to a block, and later to a sixteen-block area. Artists and arts advocates in Alexandria, Virginia, began by setting up shop temporarily in a waterfront industrial building (Strategy 3: Attract Investment by Creating Live/Work Zones for Artists). The building eventually became the centerpiece of a dramatic revitalization of a historic and cultural district. An artist in Paducah, Kentucky, saw old homes in his neighborhood crying for attention (Strategy 5: Improve Property and Enhance Value). His efforts to attract other artists to move in set off a town-wide revitalization.

It's best if the community has a preexisting identity or a defining characteristic or the clear potential to come together around a lesser-known or newly constructed identity. The small town of Lanesboro, Minnesota, contained enough distinctive recreational and artistic assets around which an identity could be built to attract thousands of visitors (Strategy 2: Stimulate Trade through Cultural Tourism). Boston's Lower Roxbury had become known as one of the city's roughest areas. By asserting its cultural identity as its strength, it built a positive identity as a lively center for African American arts that fueled grassroots economic revival (Strategy 4: Diversify the Local Economy).

To define your community, ask yourself these questions:

- What is the geographic area you or your organization serves, impacts, or relates to in your work?
- Where is the place in which you have the strongest connections and relationships and know the most about?
- Is this a manageable area within which to launch a community building initiative?
- Is there a neighborhood where your work and where relationships are already strong that you'd like to focus upon?
- Does the area fit within a predefined identity or political boundaries, or is it a natural geographic area?
- Is there a core community or neighborhood immediately surrounding your central facility or headquarters upon which you want to focus?

Trust the asset identification process and believe in your community. The identity—the engine of regeneration—will come from the assets of the people and the place. The creative process is in being able to see them and understand the meanings and possibilities they have. But first you have to land on that geographic definition. Later, as you assess your assets, you can think anew about qualities you associate with, and want to include in, your community. If they exist on the periphery, you can revise the geographic definition to include them.

ACTION ▶   *Outline on a map the geographic parameters of the community you want to directly affect.*

TASK 1.2   Identify your strengths and leadership capacity

As you think ahead about the skills and partners needed in a planning process, you want to be clear about what *you* bring to the table. Conduct an inventory of strengths and leadership capacity for yourself and your organization. Worksheet 1: Strengths Inventory, page 144, helps you list your greatest strengths in areas such as visioning, planning, management, marketing, fund development, advocacy, and organizing. Personal strengths you assess should include group leadership skills and knowledge of various sectors and professions within your community. Also important is your familiarity with political, philanthropic, nonprofit, and business leadership, as well as readiness to learn and venture into new territory! Be honest about your strengths and the areas in which you need to find partners who complement what you bring. (These strengths will be listed again in Task 3.3 as you create a strengths inventory for all the partners who will be involved in the community building process.)

In addition to the strengths inventory, ask these questions about yourself and your organization:[104]

• Do you understand how decisions are made in the community?

• Do you understand the history of the community?

• Do you understand the demographic makeup of the community and how different groups relate to one another?

• Are you committed to the community's holistic and long-term well-being?

• Do you have a substantial attachment to or positive reputation among key community members and leaders?

• Will you be perceived as acting primarily to serve the interests of the community at large or of an internal or external group?

• Do you have the ability to work with and motivate a wide range of people?

• Can you plan group activities that will be productive?

Complete an inventory of your organizational (or personal) strengths. Use Worksheet 1: Strengths Inventory, page 144.

 ACTION

WORKSHEET 1   Strengths Inventory

Give an honest assessment of yourself (if starting alone) or your organization with regard to each of the categories below. Rate the category as +1 for strong, O for neutral, and -1 if weak. You may total the strengths, if you wish, but this is not a formal process wherein a score of 16 earns an A+ and –16 is an F. It's just an honest assessment of strengths.

Name of organization: _____

Organization's leaders: _____

Strength	Comments	Rating
1. Capacity to invest time		
2. Experience with collaboration		
3. Positive profile in the community		
4. Staff/board stability		
5. Demonstrated depth of constituency		
6. Demonstrated breadth of constituency		
7. Demonstrated broad concern for community		
8. Bring key perspective to the work (name it)		
9. Bring key skills to the work (name the skills)		
10. Share information openly		
11. Represent group or position strategic to cause		
12. Holds a special leadership position		
13. Holds a symbolic position		
14. Positive reputation among key civic and business leaders		
15. Ability to participate in or lead groups through planning		
16. "Gut" assessment of "fit" (Do I want to do this? Is it right at this time?)		

TASK 1.3   Identify community assets

Remember, recognizing assets is an art! For those not in practice, it can be approached systematically. However, there's nothing better than insight and creative thinking. Worksheet 2: Community Asset Inventory, pages 146-148, provides a way to begin. Use it as a tool to think through the types of assets your community contains. Be sure to consider the categories listed by Kretzmann and McKnight (see page 141). Walk though this process yourself; informally ask others in your organization or your immediate circles to name what they consider the community's assets. You may not want to tell them what you're doing yet; just take a poll of what they consider the most unique, interesting, or important things about your community.

Don't get invested in your conclusions at this point. Keep your focus on assets, not problems. If you, or people in your community, haven't adopted asset-based approaches, this first pass helps you practice thinking and talking about assets with others. Pay particular attention to the "Other" categories. The most unique characteristics of your community cannot be anticipated in a worksheet!

Providence covered its downtown waterways in the 1950s. In the early 1990s, the city uncovered, or "daylighted," the rivers and lined them with public promenades and pedestrian-friendly parks.

Later, as you bring partners on board, you will engage them—and possibly other community members—in the same asset-identification process (see Task 3.4). They will see assets you don't or see them differently than you do.

Complete a community asset inventory from your perspective. Use Worksheet 2: Community Asset Inventory, pages 146–148.

 ACTION

WORKSHEET 2   Community Asset Inventory

For each item below, describe your community in terms of its strengths, characteristics, and/or unique features.

1. **Geographic parameters and demographics**

2. **History and industries**
    2a. Native American/pre-colonial

    2b. Significant events and people

    2c. Products manufactured and grown

    2d. Cultural and technological innovations

    2e. Economic base and employment

    2f. Other

3. **Geography**
    3a. Natural or geological features

    3b. Climate

    3c. Recreational amenities

    3d. Other

4. **People** (Give special thought to historic or recent uncelebrated heroes, especially women and people of color whose contributions mirror the spirit of community building)
    4a. Openness

    4b. Age range and balance

    4c. Ethnic mix

WORKSHEET 2   continued

4d. Economic status

4e. Education levels

4f. Outstanding individuals

4g. Other

5. Public sector

5a. Effective leadership

5b. Communications and accountability

5c. Service quality and capacity

5d. Versatility and innovation

5e. Other

6. Reputation

6a. Identity to outside world

6b. Receptivity to visitors

6c. Location and accessibility

6d. Navigability

6e. Safety

6f. Aesthetic experience

6g. Other

WORKSHEET 2　continued

7. Nearby features and attributes

7a.　Natural amenities

7b.　Widely known attraction(s) or features

7c.　Urban center or district (includes or is how far?)

7d.　Major or unique service(s)

7e.　Well-known institution(s)

7f.　Special places

7g.　Other

8. Infrastructure

8a.　Transportation

8b.　Education and culture

8c.　Housing stock—quality, mix of owner and rental

8d.　Architecture or built environment

8e.　Power, water, and sewer adequacy and capacity

8f.　Underutilized structures and real estate

8g.　Healthcare

8h.　Other

TASK 1.4   Clarify values and goals

Are you clear on your organization's or group's values and goals as they relate to larger community challenges—as well as your personal values and goals? Do they give you latitude to take a leading role in community building work, a role that may be more comprehensive than your customary position? Do you have—or can you easily gain—the support of your board, members, funders, and staff to think bigger and step onto a larger stage? Creative community building is not necessarily about expanding your organization; it's about leading a larger, more holistic, and collaborative effort to build a vibrant, sustainable community. It will probably return benefit to your organization, but only as all partners benefit. To invite others to a visioning and planning process, you'll need to articulate your broader values and goals. Do they provide a big enough canvas where your vision and the vision of others can be combined into one or be painted harmoniously side by side? Like the community mural artist, can you as the creative community builder integrate these visions into a whole picture?

To help clarify the congruence between the project you envision and your organization's goals, write your personal goals for the community side by side with the goals of your organization. If you see consistency or synergy, then you're in good shape. Completing this task will help you in conversations with and presentations to your board, funders, staff, and others. It will help you articulate how the project is relevant to your organization.

> *Make side-by-side lists of goals you and your organization have for the community.*  ACTION

TASK 1.5   Write a concept paper

At this point, a concept paper should not be mistaken for a blueprint; its job is to set out an idea, a broad vision, and a process. As such, it should be brief and simply highlight key attributes of the community.

The process of writing a preliminary concept paper helps you clarify your vision of the *possibilities* for your community. The concept paper itself then becomes a great tool to get other people interested in bringing their ideas to the table.

The best way to understand what should be in a concept paper is to study an example (see the sidebar Concept Paper for Midville on page 150). Here we'll begin to examine our hypothetical community—Midville—whose progress we will follow through the coming chapters.

> *Write a concept paper describing your community and its possibilities.* ACTION

Concept Paper for Midville

To set the context for this example, imagine that you've been the director of the Midville Chamber of Commerce for two years. You have a vision for expanding the chamber's impact, and you want to make Midville a more prosperous and rewarding place. You spent five years running a small retail business on Main Street and, before that, five years selling advertising for the *Midville Gazette*. You've devoted considerable volunteer time working with youth and still find time for your personal artistic pursuits. A few of your.collages have been on exhibit at the local nonprofit gallery.

From informal conversations with community leaders, you've been inspired by stories of Midville's history. There's a sense that the community has much unrealized potential and a concern from some leaders that changes in the economy and population are going to present difficult challenges if not addressed soon. Rumors have circulated that the fertilizer plant, the town's largest employer,

may relocate out of state or eliminate many jobs. You've taken stock of your capacities and the resources at your disposal, and you've taken your own informal inventory of community assets. You're thinking about how to design and launch a community transformation over the next twenty years. Numerous possibilities swim in your head. With those in mind, you draft a concept paper for Midville's future.

Midville is a midwestern agricultural community, population 8,500, built on the Clark River and on a transcontinental railroad. It has a traditional town center and serves as a commercial and service center for a county with a population of 18,000. Its population makeup is 22 percent under eighteen and 12 percent over sixty-five; 70 percent Caucasian, 4 percent Native American, 7 percent African American, 9 percent Latino, 8 percent Asian/Pacific Islander, and 3 percent Other.

Midville is a special place. It began as a bountiful fishing and trading site for Native ancestors. Over the last 150 years, it has grown through the work of industrious, creative people. Its present-day residents come from many corners of the globe and other parts of the United States. They proudly work and play together to make life better for their children and families.

The economy is rooted in transportation and agriculture. Midville is sited on a key tributary to one of the world's great river systems, and it is on an important rail line and highway. Besides its role in transport, Midville's economy includes a major fertilizer manufacturer, many farms, small manufacturers, and services for locals and visitors traveling to and from regional farming and food-processing centers.

Throughout Midville's history there have been many fascinating and unique individuals, natural phenomena, and inventions.

The Midville Chamber of Commerce is proposing a planning task force to better identify the community's unique qualities and to focus on opportunities for the future. Through a ten- to twelve-month planning process, the task force will arrive at strategies that highlight Midville's special character and mobilize its citizens. It will require strengthened cooperation among businesses, organizations, and institutions. By engaging a broad range of community members, this effort will build upon the community's positive attributes, and create a more diverse and dynamic economy to benefit all residents over the next ten to twenty years. These strategies will further diversify the economy, stimulate trade, build bridges among a changing population, and keep youth involved in the community.

TASK 1.6   Review readiness

Reflect on what you have learned from Parts 1 and 2 of this book and from the tasks you've undertaken so far. Review the checklist below.

Readiness Indicators:

- ❑ You have clear, value-driven, and flexible community building goals.
- ❑ You can describe the geographic area of your "community" and its current identity.
- ❑ You are aware of, and have connection to, your community's populations.
- ❑ You can articulate your key leadership strengths and capacities.
- ❑ You know the general history of your community.
- ❑ You know many key leaders in your community and how things get done.
- ❑ You understand asset-based organizing and development and can articulate what you consider key assets of your community.
- ❑ You understand and can articulate what cultural assets and culturally based development strategies are and why they're important.
- ❑ You have the support of your board, staff, and/or constituency to take a leadership role in a project of this type or size.

Complete the Readiness Indicators checklist.   ACTION

Summary

In Step 1, you moved through a series of tasks that brought clarity about what you want to achieve and what you're starting with. You also know that you have the support of the particular organization you represent.

But this work cannot be done by one agency alone—in fact, one can't "build community" without involving the community. In Step 2, you will identify partners, develop expectations of them, and begin recruiting.

CHAPTER 5

Step 2: Identify and Recruit Effective Partners

No one organization, no matter how wealthy or multifaceted, can do community building alone. Success is bred in the diversity of players, interests, sectors, differences, and imaginations. The creation of good strategies and plans requires you to reach out to business, government, nonprofit, cultural, voluntary, and religious organizations. You'll need their expertise, creativity, and resources.

Most communities are fraught not only with problems but also with divisive issues and complex interpersonal histories. Thus, Step 2 is particularly important to setting the stage for a productive process. You need to identify people who play well with others. You need to do the homework that results in a dynamic mix of dedicated community builders coming together.

One very important principle as you move through every step in the community building process is to maintain a high level of transparency and provide multiple levels of involvement. You'll have a highly engaged working group, but it must not become a closed group. You need to be sure that you're communicating with as many people as possible, that your community is aware of the planning process, and that they have opportunities to provide input. Depending upon the size of your community and the scale of your process, involving community members could take many forms. Some are detailed in the steps that follow; others you will invent as you go.

Step 2 focuses upon identifying and recruiting the partners that will generate and act upon a truly compelling vision. Three essential tasks are involved in Step 2:

1. Identify potential partners
2. Develop expectations for potential partners
3. Recruit partners

> Collaborating is a relationship in which each organization wants to help its partners become the best that they can be at what they do.
>
> — Arthur Himmelman[105]

TASK 2.1   Identify potential partners

You've identified the community you hope to impact. You clarified your own values and strengths, inventoried the assets your community possesses, and wrote a preliminary concept paper.

You're moving into the creative community building process with little more than an unrefined vision and personal confidence. Now you're going to seek others to join in. It's time to listen and learn, tapping the expertise of others across sectors and professions. You'll venture into areas where you may have little experience. Ultimately, you'll identify the key players you need. You may add or lose others at implementation and other points along the way. Initially, you want to talk one-on-one.

Think about the skills, resources, and leadership it will take to design and build a project to improve the economic and social capital of your community. Who will supplement, relate to, or complement the work of other leaders and groups in the community? Think broadly. Be sure you're considering people, institutions, and citizens' associations who have a key relationship to what you see as the community's major assets. Be sure to include someone in local government, elected and appointed. Not all ideas or potential partners will make sense or pan out, but keep a list of prospects—even if you need blank spaces for a "type" of person not currently known to you. As you move forward, some people will reveal surprising insight or skills. One way or another, you'll find the right person to fit those slots. Worksheet 3: Partner Checklist, pages 156–157, can help you sort out the best fits.

As you brainstorm organizations and people, keep in mind the qualities partners might bring. Each individual should embody one or more of the following:

- *Collaborators.* Put their own self-interest honestly on the table, respect the self-interests of others, and commit to long-term shared goals that meet broad community interests as well as self-interests.*

- *Intermediaries.* Mediate (or translate) between the jargon and mindsets of creatives, businesses, government agencies, and grassroots communities—especially between the often nontraditional jargon and actions of artists and other creatives and more traditional or mainstream parties.**

- *Visionaries.* See the big picture, imagine the future, and often have a holistic view. Also known as outside-the-box thinkers.

---

* For tools to practice collaboration, see Michael Winer and Karen Ray, *Collaboration Handbook: Creating, Sustaining, and Enjoying the Journey* (Saint Paul, MN: Fieldstone Alliance, 1994).

** Walker et al., *Commerce and Culture,* found that when artists and economic developers joined forces, the best results came when a key player had well-developed "intermediation" skills. By this they mean a person or entity that can "translate" between the languages and practices of each sector. Each of the examples in Part 2 of this book included leaders or key partners who possessed these skills.

- *Synthesizers.* Find and connect common values and visions.
- *Culture Mavens.* Represent and connect to the arts and cultural activities in the community—visual artists, cultural historians, dancers, and composers and leaders of organizations that employ them.
- *Doers.* Get the job done and have skills, contacts, and access to resources.

In Delray Beach, Florida, cultural loop organizers brought together people who represented distinct cultural assets within the community (Strategy 7: Increase Civic Participation through Arts and Culture). While these people had much in common and much invested in Delray Beach, they rarely had a reason to work together. In Danville, Vermont, artists, merchants, school children, and highway engineers joined together to redesign a highway (Strategy 10: Broaden Participation in the Civic Agenda). Through such diverse groups, out-of-the-box thinking can spring.

Your community's assets will provide clues as to what kinds of partners can bring resources to the creative community building process. For instance, if natural resources play a prominent role as a community asset, be sure to identify one or more people or groups that understand and advocate for natural resources. If the community is rich in historic but crumbling architecture or underutilized industrial space, think about who might have ideas or experience with renovation—historians, realtors, homeless advocates, and even police may have valuable contributions. However, be very careful not to overload the group with too many similar people. If you bring together the usual people, you'll get the usual results.

Generate a long list of prospective partners, and then begin to evaluate it. As you evaluate each individual, ask these questions:[106]

- Do prospective partners understand—and are they aware of—how broad community issues affect them or their constituents?
- Do potential partners consider themselves part of the same community?
- Are potential partners open to change?
- Do community norms place rigid restrictions on the methods of a community building process?
- Are there groups in the community that are not well connected? Are there ways to strengthen the relationships among these groups so all can participate more fully?
- Do the prospective partners have a history of working together?

First, brainstorm a list of potential partners. Then complete Worksheet 3: Partner Checklist, pages 156–157.   ACTION

WORKSHEET 3   Partner Checklist

As you fill in prospective partners, check which of the following assets they may bring. Use the categories (for example, "Social/Civic/Social Justice Partners") to help you think through the types of partners you might recruit—but don't be limited by these categories or the number of spaces. Color outside the lines!

Prospective partners	Capacity to invest time	Positive current rela- tionship to community	History of collaboration	Positive public profile	Staff and board stability	Demonstrated depth of constituency
Social/Civic/Social justice partners						
Economic development/Housing partners						
Environmental partners						
Education/Youth partners						
Cultural/Arts partners						
Other:						

Demonstrated breadth of constituency	Demonstrated broad concern for community	Brings key skill or dimension	Represents key group	Holds special leadership position	Holds symbolic position	Positive reputation among key civic and business leaders	Ability to participate in or lead groups through planning	Gut instinct

Navigating Turf Issues among Arts and Cultural Groups

Turf issues are a part of all community work. You and other members of your alliance are going to strategize ways to leverage cultural assets for economic and social development. Institutional players from the cultural sector may feel threatened, or choose not to take you seriously, if they are not invited to participate. This is true even if the broader definition of "culture" you use doesn't seem like the same one they're organized around. At the same time, you want to be certain that the creative community building effort isn't hijacked by cultural organizations or any single interest. Like any organization seeking to remain viable, arts groups will resort to old ways of thinking to advance their institutional interests.

You are putting together a broad community rejuvenation project. Established arts groups can bring important resources to the table. *But this is not an effort to advance the arts groups—whether institutions or informal groups—by rallying the community around "the arts."* At hand are overarching community concerns. You're not setting out to advance the arts, nor the chamber of commerce, nor any other one group or sector.

Of course, the intent is that all groups will benefit in the long run—and therein lies the root of each participating organization's self-interest.

Joseph Thompson, founder and director of MASS MoCA (Strategy 4: Diversify the Local Economy), did not rally just his academic community to support the creation of a museum. He made the case that this new institution would be an economic engine for the entire community. The Pilsen/Little Village Information Center (Strategy 2: Stimulate Trade through Cultural Tourism) was formed to support *all* the community-based enterprises in those Chicago neighborhoods. Had any of the partnering organizations, especially the Mexican Fine Arts Center Museum, expressed anything but sincere interest in the fortunes and well-being of the entire community, the information center would not have succeeded. The process and the product in these cases brought the community together and all participants benefited.

A second, more complex, and possibly less obvious, turf issue has to do with debates and divisions among arts and culture practitioners. These divisions include elitist versus populist, formal versus informal, "high arts" versus "low arts," and art versus craft. When defining art and culture, many practitioners assume an either-or way of thinking. Binary thinking divides people. As the creative community builder, you need to make it clear that all ways of looking at culture and art are welcome. The quilter and the sculptor, the symphony conductor and the community video activist are *all* important contributors. The practices and value systems of one group cannot be positioned as better than or more worthy than another.

People who cling to the supremacy of one cultural practice or ethnic form can make many assumptions and take much for granted. This is especially true if they are not accustomed to being challenged, which tends to be more often the case among the more privileged. If you are outside the artistic professional area, you may find this elitism irrational. The creative community building process may not be the right forum for tackling the issue, but as a leader you'll need to recognize the phenomenon and strategize how to engage diverse groups and individuals constructively, and elevate the process to a level so that elitism won't be an obstacle.

You'll identify overarching community values through this process, especially issues of equity and fairness. You want people from the creative sector—and from all parts of the community—who can focus upon those larger values. Make your best efforts to be inclusive and to clarify the larger values that bring people together.

TASK 2.2   Develop expectations for potential partners

You have just created and evaluated a list of potential partners. When you recruit them, you have to be able to tell them what you are recruiting them for (that's your concept paper), why you are recruiting them (that's the information you generated in Worksheet 3), and what, at least to begin with, they will need to commit—the focus of this task.

Community builders Linda Hoskins and Emil Angelica in *The Fieldstone Nonprofit Guide to Forming Alliances: Working Together to Achieve Mutual Goals*[107] describe relatively simple steps for gathering partners and coordinating efforts around a goal. Their ideas have been adapted here for the task of developing expectations for potential partners. (For detailed guidance on forming alliances, please see their text.)

The best way to be clear on your alliance is to ask partners for a commitment of time and resources that is appropriate for the project and for their capacity to contribute. At the beginning, a fitting commitment will be to attend a set number of 90- to 120-minute meetings. Beyond that, lots of other help will be needed—copying, mailing, writing media releases, sharing costs, providing in-house technical expertise, contacting a legislator, rallying constituents from a neighborhood, rounding up artists, hosting a reception.

Be realistic with your expectations. Each person brings different assets and resources. Some partners earn a salary and are expected to participate in community planning. Other partners—such as small business owners, self-employed people, and artists—only earn a living when they're working. The amount of time they can commit may be limited.

Be respectful with the time people *do* commit. Accomplishing, or even exceeding, your task-at-hand—something as simple as finishing a meeting early—is a bonus for everyone and indicates that you can deliver.

Planning out the number of meetings and the amount of time each will require is an important step. However, nothing will go exactly as planned. There will be unexpected detours and delays when complex agreements need to be hammered out or when participants can't follow through or have unexpected illnesses and other emergencies. Good leadership will keep the group moving forward, overcoming obstacles and resolving differences. Figure 2: Sample Timeline, page 162, will provide guidance about how much time and how many meetings the key planning steps should ideally require.

Excellent meeting leadership and planning facilitation are key to keep everyone on board and motivated. If all goes well, your group members may ask for additional meetings or assignments because they're enjoying the experience and it's stimulating their imagination!

Excellent meeting leadership and planning facilitation are key to keep everyone on board and motivated.

Your unique situation and mix of partners will have their own requirements, preferences, and scale of work. Keeping those things in balance is the trick. The task is to estimate the time you'll need from partners, alerting them that change can happen as the project evolves, but that changes would not occur without their consent.

On the financial and resources front, be equally clear. What will the planning process cost? Think about things such as meeting space, refreshments, copying, mailing, a consultant or facilitator, speaker honorarium, research costs, photo or map printing, or publishing a report or plan. Do you have participants who need childcare assistance? Are there key self-employed people or artists who could participate if given a stipend? Do you need an intern or part-time assistant to help keep communication flowing? Based upon what you think the scale of the project will be, make a budget and identify potential funding sources. Figure 3: Sample Budget, page 163, can help you with this task.

It's best if multiple partners contribute. If one larger institution, city agency, or philanthropy pays the major share of the bill, the process can lose its broad footing. It's like the mural artist doing all the painting herself, rather than sharing the work with many eager volunteers: she may get the mural done, but, in the process, everyone else loses all sense of community ownership. However, if you do have a local philanthropy or highly placed business executive or government official willing to put not only money but also their influence behind the process, negotiate their active participation. Their presence can usually motivate others to bring resources to the table to broaden ownership.

As mentioned, once you've created your timeline and budget you'll have a clearer idea of what to ask of potential partners. Along with your invitation to participate, tell them specific expectations, whether it's to pay photocopying expenses for six months, to sponsor a luncheon, or to assign an administrative assistant to the project one-half day a week.

Answering some additional questions about resources may help as you move forward: [108]

- Have we examined community building efforts like ours, so we can learn from them?

- Does our community building effort have both long- and short-term goals as a way to develop community members' skills?

- Does our community building effort have enough information about the issues to take action?

- What options exist to reach out to groups not already involved (at the appropriate time)?

- Does communication about community building activities occur in a timely way?

- Is there a balance in our community building efforts between achieving ultimate goals and paying attention to the process?

- Could we advance our community building process faster with the help of an outside expert?

- Will the technical experts we hire support our community building process?

Your process may vary depending upon your starting point and the level of resources you and your partners can muster. With greater resources, you can engage a consultant or a firm to take you through key parts of this process; but there is an advantage, too, in a more grassroots approach with consultants in a minor role. Devise a timeline and budget; write in steps and dollars you think are appropriate. After reading the rest of this book, come back and review them. You'll probably need to revise your timeline and budget as you go, but don't pull any huge surprises on your partners.

> *Create a timeline and budget; establish expectations of partners.*
> *Use Figure 2: Sample Timeline and Figure 3: Sample Budget*
> *(pages 162–163) as models.*

 ACTION

Figure 2. Sample Timeline

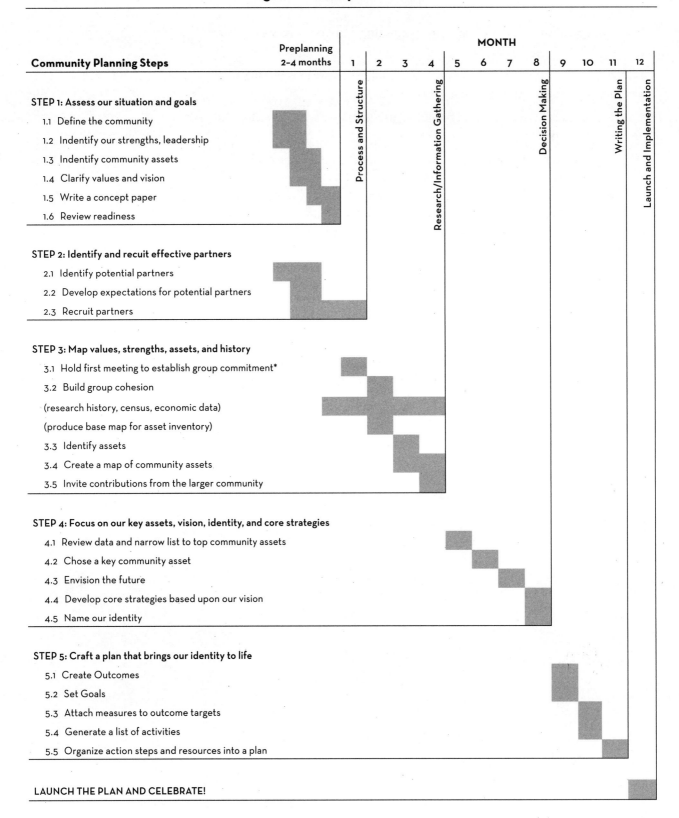

Figure 3. Sample Budget*

Expenses	Cost	Private Funder	City Econ. Devel. Dept.	Partner 1 Art Ctr.	Partner 2 CDC	Partner 3 Bank	Partner 4 Grassroots	Total
Contract Services								
Guest Speaker	$200					$200		$200
Planning Consultant	$12,000	$6,000	$4,000		$2,000			$12,000
Travel Expense	$3,000	$1,500	$1,500					$3,000
Asset Map Artist	$600			$500			$100	$600
Researcher - History	$1,100	$1,000					$100	$1,100
Researcher - Demographic	$250				$250			$250
Photographer	$1,000			$500		$500		$1,000
Designer - brochure/press kit	$750					$750		$750
Meeting Expenses								
Lunches (10 meetings x 15 x $14)	$2,100	$630	$420	$210	$420	$420		$2,100
Photocopying	$400			$400				$400
Space (12 meetings @ $100)	$1,200			$400	$400	$400		$1,200
Planning pads, markers, misc.	$200				$200			$200
Recognition Gifts	$500			$500				$500
Staffing Costs								
Meeting Planning	$2,400					$2,400		$2,400
General Communications/Notes	$3,600				$3,600			$3,600
Communications Planner	$2,500			$2,400			$100	$2,500
Materials, Office Costs								
Postage	$300				$200		$100	$300
Photo printing	$600			$300	$300			$600
Brochure/press kit production	$3,000				$1,500	$1,500		$3,000
Total Costs	$35,700							$35,700
Cash		$9,130	$5,920	$1,210	$3,920	$3,370	$100	$23,650
In-Kind		$ -	$ -	$4,000	$4,950	$2,800	$300	$12,050
Total Cost Share		$9,130	$5,920	$5,210	$8,870	$6,170	$400	$35,700

* This budget is designed for a community the size and nature of Midville. Larger communities or complex urban neighborhoods typically require a larger commitment, especially in the area of consulting expertise and communications and/or coordination costs.

TASK 2.3   Recruit partners

You've made your list of alliance partners and evaluated their respective strengths. You have a sense of the skills and resources you need. You can articulate your expectations of potential partners. Some potential partners have floated to the top, and you've kept a few in the "maybe" column. As you meet with potential partners and your conversations progress, you'll get a better picture of who you think will be great contributors. Remember, you're beginning by listening and learning.

With your concept paper in your back pocket, begin to meet one-on-one with prospective partners. To help you develop your approach and to build momentum, start with two or three you know the best and believe to be the strongest candidates. Branch out quickly and try your ideas on someone who will ask you tough questions. Be careful not to stay only within your comfort zone as you move through your list. You'll talk with people who speak different professional languages and have different ways of seeing the community's assets and problems. It will be a learning experience. Your alliance will need members who function in areas with which you're less familiar and with whom you have been less likely to have a professional relationship. Go to breakfast, lunch, or coffee with these leaders and activists. If you have no previous contact with someone on your list, have a mutual friend invite the person and come along to introduce you.

Talk about the idea and allow your vision to evolve as a result of lively, open conversations. Share your concept paper with potential partners only if you feel comfortable doing so. Some people think because something is on paper it's already decided upon. You want their ideas, not their approval. Your original concept may grow in scope, it may shrink, or it may shift direction. Don't let anyone else push you into premature action, and don't get too set on a specific approach that may arise from one conversation. You're inviting partners into a group planning task force.

Be cautious if you run into a naysayer or person with negative energy. While you want people who are inventive and challenge assumptions, use your judgment to discern people who may hinder the process. For example, if someone is overly cynical about getting people to work together or expresses major doubts about culture as the center of any initiative, he or she could hold the group back. Be sure to engage people in conversation about the assets inherent in culture and cultural diversity. If they refuse to let go of deficit-based thinking or dismiss the significance of culture or cultural differences, they will not be helpful. If someone prefers to criticize other community leaders rather than look for common ground, thank this person for his or her ideas, and move on.

If you have doubts about someone before the meeting, begin on a general premise of wanting to learn about his or her organization and areas of interest. Don't invite people to join the task force before you've assessed their appropriateness or readiness.

These are some questions to ask yourself in evaluating the mix of alliance partners:[109]

- Do the people participating in the community building initiative represent the population? Are some community groups not involved? How will this affect problem solving and decision making?

- What organizations or groups in the community, such as religious congregations, parent-teacher groups, or business associations, have strong ties to the community?

- Are the activities planned for this effort reasonable, given community members' ability to accomplish tasks?

- Do participants see a need for training in a particular area? What would be most beneficial?

- Do mechanisms exist to help new participants feel accepted and part of the process?

- Are leadership and resources in this community building effort stretched because of competition between groups?

- Do community members agree upon important aspects of their identity? Whom they represent? What geographical area they represent? What their purpose is?

Complete one-on-one conversations and finalize your list of partners to invite.

 ACTION

Summary

The identification and recruitment of partners is a difficult job—you need the right mix of leaders, enthusiastic supporters, well-networked people, and truly creative types, as well as a mix of resources. Take your time, trust your instincts, try to seek out more than the "usual suspects," and, as partners join the effort, ask them to help you expand and improve your original list. If you need additional help with Step 2, *The Fieldstone Guide to Forming Nonprofit Alliances*[110] is an excellent and easy-to-use resource.

In the next step, the group will start work—beginning by identifying and mapping the community's values, strengths, assets, and history.

Leadership

There are many styles of leadership and types of leaders. Rarely does any one person possess all the attributes we'd like to see in a leader—and that is a good thing in community building. In the planning phase of a community building project, key qualities include the ability to listen, synthesize ideas, manage good meetings, and keep focused upon the prize. There are quiet leaders and there are loud leaders. Early parts of the process may be better served by the former, and latter parts or implementation may benefit most from the cheerleader. Building ownership among a broad range of stakeholders is the key in the beginning. A community building project requires many people with different kinds of leadership skills to carry it to fruition, so the less it belongs to one person, the better. Understanding your own strengths and the areas where you need complementary partners is critical. If you're a visionary but not the leader called for to carry out this process, use your power of persuasion to find a co-leader early on and work as a team.

In thinking about leadership, ask yourself these questions: [11]

- Does this community building effort rely too heavily on the person who provided the spark for initiating the group?

- What needs does our effort have for leadership from many sources and for leaders with different styles?

- Does the community have members who are already taking on visible leadership positions? Are these people available and interested in doing additional community building?

- Does the community have a reservoir of leadership, as yet overlooked (for example, Head Start parents or block watchers)?

- Does this community have a history of community building? Has community building been a successful experience?

- If it was unsuccessful, what needs to be done to increase trust and confidence in the present community building process?

CHAPTER 6

Step 3: Map Values, Strengths, Assets, and History

T HERE'S NO BETTER WAY TO START a project that involves many players than to acknowledge the value of each player and to engage in discovery and creativity together. Building an asset inventory, a community asset map, and a history of your community gets everyone involved and can be fun at the same time.

It's important that the process you're launching not be tedious or contentious. You'll begin your planning as a group by taking stock of the assets each partner brings to the table, and then by taking stock of the assets in your community in which your partners feel pride. Somewhere among these assets you'll eventually find the program, plan, or project you want to work together to build. You already took stock of your own strengths and developed your personal list of community assets. Now the group you've assembled needs to repeat these exercises and bring even more people into the process. This will develop a broad base of ownership in the plan the group develops. It will spread the practice of asset-based thinking, and it will build momentum.

Keep the list of strengths and assets you generated (Step 1.3) in your back pocket. Start from scratch and let everyone pitch in their ideas—peek at your list only to be sure assets you thought of weren't missed. With good facilitation, the group will mine the assets in your community more deeply, and see the community's strengths in different ways. Learning new things and actively contributing make meetings more enjoyable.

Leave no stone unturned in your search for assets. As we saw in the case studies, Delray Beach (Strategy 7: Increase Civic Participation through Cultural Celebrations) looked back at an illustrious history of multiple ethnic groups living and celebrating their cultures side by side and then created a cultural event that connected the community as never before. Providence (Strategy 6: Promote Interaction in Public Space) reopened its once-dirty and hidden rivers and staged a spectacular waterfront event to make its downtown thrive. Rather than wiping clean the abandoned 150-year-old mill in its town center, North Adams (Strategy 4: Diversify the Local Economy) re-purposed the vast structures as symbols of imagination and hope. The contemporary arts

P erhaps authenticity is a better concept to apply in this context than distinctiveness. That is, it may be more productive to concentrate on ensuring that the cultural manifestations in a community have a direct relationship with the culture of that community than to obsess on what makes a particular community different from, or better than, any other.

— Jon Hawkes[112]

and business enterprises that now inhabit the former industrial space borrow from the best of the past while they look to the future.

Identifying the historic and contemporary assets of your community is truly a creative exercise. The goal is to uncover or create an identity built upon the best of the past with a vision for what's to come.

Your one-on-one meetings are complete, and—assuming you've found enough interest among your colleagues to work together—you're ready to call your first meeting. Better yet, issue an invitation for everyone to share cultural experiences. Make sure everyone knows what to expect. Get the process moving by instilling a sense of discovery and learning, helping participants see their community and each other anew—recognizing assets, cultural richness, and creative potential.

The step involves five tasks:

1. Hold the first meeting to establish group commitment
2. Build group cohesion
3. Identify assets
4. Create a map of community assets
5. Invite contributions from the larger community

TASK 3.1   Hold the first meeting to establish group commitment

Meetings should be fun. Participants enjoy learning something new, seeing familiar faces, and meeting new people. Everyone should come away knowing they accomplished something and contributed to it.

Find a welcoming space that's convenient, where everyone can look across the table at each other, hear without shouting, and eat together. This may be a private room at a popular restaurant, one that has a diverse patronage in the community, and not one closely associated with any single group. It could be a public or private institution that is equally welcoming and may, in fact, sponsor the breakfast or lunch. If your resources are scarce, make it a "brown-bag" lunch.

Inform people of the meeting's length—probably two hours. It's better to overestimate a little. There's nothing better than getting done early. Invite a guest speaker, and let everyone know about the speaker in advance. The more known the name, the better. If you're not able to pay fees and travel expenses for a "name" speaker, look closer to home. This may be someone from a neighboring community who successfully pulled off a community-based improvement project, or someone from your community who recently visited an exciting community project and has pictures and stories to share.

Ask the speaker not to "sell" your community on what he or she did or saw. Rather, have the speaker focus on why that project was right for that particular place and on how that community mobilized its unique assets. Too many civic leaders are eager to copy something that worked for others rather than learn from it. Others fail to see relevance in another project built upon assets completely different from theirs. Both miss the point. The speaker is not the focus of this meeting, but a conversation starter, someone to introduce a new way of thinking about seeing and mobilizing assets.

At the beginning of the meeting, be sure everyone introduces themselves fully—ask each person to answer a question as you go around the circle, such as, What was especially interesting about a place you've recently visited for vacation or business? or What is the one thing you value most about your hometown or neighborhood? You want to stimulate thinking and conversation about quality of place, community assets, and how people find common ground.

Allow enough time for introductions, for the speaker, for presentation of your planning proposition, and for questions and discussion. Remember, your premise is to invite your audience to participate in a task force that will explore and develop a community improvement strategy built upon the community's assets. Be sure group members understand that the proposed initiative is meant to have a comprehensive impact upon the well-being of all residents, businesses, and organizations, and is not meant to promote an art program, tourist business, or any other single enterprise. At the same time, you want to be sure the initiative is rooted in the cultures (emphasize the plural) and unique qualities of the community. As such, part of the process will be experiencing and learning about what the community has to offer.

Before the meeting adjourns, seek an expression of interest and agreement to "sign on." You asked everyone individually, but committing in front of each other is an important step. Be careful with asking for a commitment publicly if you know there are people who are unclear or hesitant. If you ask for a show of hands and get few, if any, and lots of questions, it's like throwing a wet blanket on your attempt to start a fire. If group members seem tentative or unsure, tell them you'll be inviting them to a series of meetings to further discuss ideas for community building. Ask for preferences for days of the week and times of day. If someone needs to think about their participation or has questions, follow up with a call to talk over their questions or reservations and extend an invitation to continue.

> **AGENDA—Meeting 1**
>
> *Task 3.1—Hold the first meeting to establish group commitment*
>
> **Preparation**
> Choose a comfortable, accessible location. Be sure each member knows the purpose of the meeting and what's on the agenda.
>
> **Agenda**
> 1. Introductions
> 2. Sharing quality-of-place experiences
> 3. Speaker presentation
> 4. Presentation of community building initiative
> 5. Questions and discussion
> 6. Commitment to planning schedule and process
>
> **Homework**
> If your budget calls for a potluck, have each member bring a food item representing his or her culture for the next meeting.

Conduct a first group meeting to introduce ideas and formalize participation.

 ACTION

TASK 3.2   Build group cohesion

The second group meeting will have two parts. First, members of the group will work to understand something about each other's cultural roots. Then the group will begin to identify shared values. This meeting should be fun. It helps group members build relationships and learn to work together. Cultural sharing propels this meeting.

Share cultural roots (Task 3.2.a.)

The family and personal backgrounds of most Americans include ethnic diversity among parents and grandparents (German and Irish, or Mexican and Puerto Rican, or African American and Native American, for example). Most people belong to a number of different organizational cultures through social or professional groups. Some cultures are entered into by choice, while others are birthrights. Most people enjoy talking about who they are, once they feel safe with each other and they understand the relevance. Your job is to create that safe space and make the relevance clear.

The second meeting includes sharing and appreciating the cultures, qualities, and perspectives each person brings to the group. Often, you can start this meeting as a potluck, with each person bringing a food that represents their personal or cultural history. If the budget allows you to have food provided, vary the menu to include foods from the different cultures in your community. If you're meeting in restaurants, vary the choice of cuisine (although having one consistent location helps eliminate confusion about meeting place).

Start with a warm-up exercise. Ask individuals to move into pairs and take ten minutes to "interview" each other, seeking stories about their cultural roots or favorite holiday practices. Have partners report back to the entire group things they learned about the other. More ambitiously, participants can choose to express what they learned about their interviewee in a drawing, dance, or poem. You will not only learn about each other, your ways of thinking and what guides different ways of working, but also you'll develop a group vocabulary and some collectively understood metaphors. This sharing helps create group cohesion. It's the beginning of a new group or organizational culture!

It is important to begin the community building process on a person-to-person level within your alliance not only to have a better functioning group but also to model the way you want the group to work and relate in the wider community. You're keeping people and culture at the center of your process. If some are uncomfortable with a "touchy-feely" process, let them know that part of community building is to respectfully cross personal boundaries and to define when they shouldn't be crossed. Try to keep a light-hearted tone without losing sight of the serious purpose. Tell them that at the next meeting, you'll "get down to business."

AGENDA—Meeting 2

Task 3.2—Build group cohesion

Preparation
Plan a potluck or an interesting menu. Bring brainstorming supplies (large sheets of paper, markers, color dots).

Agenda
1. Pair off for cultural history interviews
2. Share findings with the group
3. Brainstorm statements of valued community attributes
4. Consolidate list
5. Vote and arrive at six to eight items
6. Distribute blank copies of Worksheet 1: Strengths Inventory, page 144

Homework
Each member should fill out the strengths inventories assessing personal and organizational strengths as appropriate and bring resources, items, and ideas for historical research.

Identify what people value about a community (Task 3.2.b.)

As this project moves forward, it will face distractions and disagreements that could derail it. The group's collective belief in the people, the place, and the ideas, and in what it sees as community values will keep everyone on track.

At this same meeting, after you've opened the door to talking about diverse backgrounds, create a list of values that everyone agrees are important for community. You (or your facilitator) can elicit the list from the group using brainstorming methods. This needs to be an *in*clusive exercise that builds consensus, not an *ex*clusive exercise that defines a narrow set of standards. This is important for the facilitator and group to understand.

The difference between *values* and *assets* can get fuzzy in this discussion. For example, someone may say they "value the community's great school." The school is an asset. Instead, help reframe that comment to find out if the community shares a value of supporting good education.

Begin the brainstorming by explaining (and giving examples of) the kinds of items that are appropriate. (See the sidebar Midville Values.) Encourage everyone to speak and don't let one or a small number of people dominate. Set ground rules that stop cross-talking or judgments during brainstorming. You might go around the room asking each person for their contribution before opening up for additions. Elicit a list of twenty to thirty items or statements of what people value in a community. Write the items on large sheets of paper and post them around the room. Take only a few minutes to talk about what people observe about the list. Quickly edit or consolidate duplicate items, but don't allow the group to get hung up on refining the list at this point.

Next, have group members use adhesive dots or color markers to indicate four or five items they think are most important. Underline the top six to eight vote getters. Those items can then be discussed—but don't spend time finding the perfect words for each one. Someone can edit the final choices later. Unless you plan to publish them at some point, they're for use as *internal* guidelines and don't need to be stated perfectly. If you do refine them for external use, be sure they're brought back to the group at a later time for approval. The values become the filter through which assets and plans pass to determine your final strategic plan.

Give each group member a blank copy of Worksheet 1: Strengths Inventory. Ask them to fill out the inventory to indicate their personal strengths and bring it to the next meeting. These inventories will stimulate thinking about the group's assets for community building.

> **Midville Values**
>
> The Midville community planning task force ended up with the following short list of shared values.
>
> **We value**
>
> - **Face-to-face relationships with people across generations and ethnic groups**
> - **Midville's friendly and welcoming atmosphere**
> - **Respect for the natural environment**
> - **Inventive and creative people**
> - **High level of volunteerism in community and civic projects**
> - **Opportunities for social gathering**
> - **Intellectually stimulating environment**

Establish a set of group values.   ◖ ACTION

TASK 3.3   Identify assets

Task 3.3 can take place in the third group meeting, and there are two parts to it. First, the group needs to identify the assets of its members. This task helps the group know its own strengths (for example, it's helpful to know if someone has extensive background in finance, public relations, photography, or working with craft artists). At the same time, it prepares the group for the task of identifying community assets. The second part of this meeting requires preparation that you might start weeks or even months earlier. It involves assembling a concise review of the community's history and population and economic trends.

Identify group assets (Task 3.3.a.)

The goal here is to have the group dialog about its own assets and to discover hidden talents and interests. If the group enjoyed the creative exercise at the second meeting, and you think it helped build camaraderie, try the exercise outlined in the next paragraph. If the group seems to want a more linear process, simply have each person list his or her skills and assets—from political connections to technical skills to strategic planning experience—and compile and post those for all to see. How you handle this exercise depends upon the size of your community and how familiar people are with each other. No matter how well people might think they know each other, there are always hobbies, talents, and skills that will be uncovered.

The following asset-identification exercise should be both fun and serious. Break the group into threes, and give each trio a large sheet of paper and a set of color markers. Have them ask each other questions about personal hobbies or special skills that are generally *outside* what they're best known for professionally. In addition, have each person state the top three professional skills they bring to the community. These can include both personal and organizational capacities they bring. Ask one member to create a collage or drawing representative of the skills and abilities of the three-person team. After twenty to thirty minutes, reassemble the larger group. Have someone report on the team's collective abilities while showing off the drawing and talking about the connections and similarities among the trio's qualities and capacities. You'll also find out who can draw!

Follow up this exercise by collecting the more traditional inventory you distributed at the previous meeting. Have someone combine the inventories into one document (removing duplications but citing multiples—for example, "small business management skills [3]"). Report on this list in summary format at a subsequent meeting without attaching names to the roster of skills, so the group gets a sense of its strengths. But keep the raw data so you know whom to call on for appropriate help!

AGENDA—Meeting 3

Task 3.3—Identify assets

Preparation
Arrange a short presentation by a history project leader. Conduct census and economic research and prepare an overview including trends. Bring community asset inventory forms.

Agenda*
1. Breakout groups assess individual and organizational strengths
2. Report to larger group and/or collect forms
3. Presentation by a historian with an invitation for group members to contribute
4. Presentation of census data and economic trends
5. Explain community asset inventory process

Homework
Each member should go through Worksheet 2: Community Asset Inventory, pages 146- 148, and jot down ideas to share at the next meeting.

* *This meeting requires concise presentations. Some items can be carried to the next meeting if needed.*

The first part of Task 3.3 has four outcomes: people get to know each other better, they learn to focus on strengths, and they begin to think about creative endeavors as useful community skills, and it helps you build a "file" of skills that you will call upon later.

Complete an inventory of partner assets through a group process.  ◀ ACTION

Identify community history, census, and economic data (Task 3.3.b.)

For this part of the meeting, you'll need to invite a person with deep knowledge of or curiosity about the community's history (if not already included as a partner). Find someone who is inclusive in his or her thinking and research, and who will assemble a history that is well considered. They should account for multiple points of view, incorporate contributions from others, and address questions from the group. If you can't find a historian or local storyteller who meets these criteria, form a research team including group members, a local college or high school class, and/or others who together represent a broad-based view of the community's past (for example, Native Americans, descendants of early immigrants, children of founding families).

However you proceed, be sure to bring out different perspectives and out-of-the-ordinary figures and events. This is where new ideas will emerge. For example, the people designing Baker City's Leo Adler Memorial Parkway (Strategy 6: Promote Interaction in Public Space) looked into their past and included gardens and parks named for miners, timber workers, Native Americans, Chinese railroad workers, and others who had been part of the region's history. Had their vision been limited to White pioneers on the Oregon Trail, for instance, the project would not have been successful community building.

Be sure your history goes WAY back! It should begin with the geological formation of the ground upon which the community stands. What momentous events formed a lake or river? Have there been discoveries of prehistoric creatures or the first humans in the area? What has been the ebb and flow of people and cultures over millennia? Who are the key figures in recorded history, and what are the significant events? What mythologies or unconfirmed but popular stories exist? What are the artistic, literary, or technological creations or inventions? Most likely, some segments of this wide-ranging story have been collected. The more hands contributing to this process the better.

At your third meeting, after your skills inventory, have your historian give a sketch of community history. He or she should note various places where more needs to be learned and ask group members for items they have to contribute. Launch further research with an invitation for involvement and contributions.

Discovering Your Community's Economic Story

The U.S. Census Bureau web site (www.census.gov) contains a wealth of information to help you tell your community's economic story. Go to http://censtats.census.gov/cbpnaic/cbpnaic.shtml or use Google to search for "county business patterns." Enter a ZIP code for a profile of all the types of businesses in your community and their employment patterns. Repeat as needed if your area includes more than one ZIP code. You can also compare the numbers and types of businesses in your area with those in other parts of the county. For instance, this information might tell you that you have a concentration of auto repair shops, furniture retailers, or small manufacturers.

Census Bureau data is usually at least two years old, but you can paint a historic picture by tracking changes with past years. You can also project trends with current anecdotes from your own knowledge, such as the new housing development or industrial space conversion now under construction or the new Asian food businesses that opened during the past year.

Examining general trends in employment can also help paint that picture. Again, using the web and looking at America's Career InfoNet (www.acinet.org/acinet), you can see broader patterns in job types that are expected to grow or shrink. This information is especially useful if any kind of job training or professional development services might be on your radar.

Mike Temali, community development leader and author, lays out a detailed process to assess your neighborhood or community's economic conditions in his 2002 *Community Economic Development Handbook*.[113] He recommends drawing a map of your primary commercial corridor or district, labeling all the known businesses. The map should also include vacant properties. Often, this visualization can help you see clusters or combinations you otherwise hadn't noticed.

You're looking for ways that creative entrepreneurs and the cultural bonds that people share can generate new industries or activities to stimulate the local economy. You're also looking for ways that cultural organizations can play a pivotal role in nurturing enterprises or in leveraging development or investment that lands new businesses or transforms existing community assets. These assets might range from vacant buildings to the community's image, both of which have been transformed by creative thinkers in many places.

Part of the overall mapping you will undertake (Task 3.4) is to know more about the people and business enterprises in your community. You, someone from the group, or another guest speaker should present a profile of your community from recent census data. Find someone in city, county, or state planning to help prepare this profile. Perhaps there's a newspaper reporter looking for an interesting story who will research census data and work up a profile. (See the sidebar Discovering Your Community's Economic Story.)

You want to track and comprehend changes that have taken place, especially during the past few decades. Those changes usually provide a good indication of what to expect in the future. Changes in population related to both ethnicities and ages are central to your community's story because they represent culture change.

Historically, your community's economy may have been based upon one industry, such as resource extraction, food or raw material processing, manufacturing, county or state government, or education. If so, the community's story may be the story that is all too common among small and midsize cities: when the major manufacturer or single industry packed up and moved or faded away as markets shifted to other products, the community deteriorated.

Twenty-first-century success stories are communities that have diversified or become centers of creative industries—businesses whose raw material is human ingenuity. Understanding the origins and trajectory of the community's economic base is essential to projecting and envisioning its future. Success lies in creatively building upon the assets and identity of the place—even when these assets include abandoned buildings or an idle workforce!

Finally, as this meeting wraps up, distribute blank copies of Worksheet 2: Community Asset Inventory, pages 146–148, and take a few minutes to introduce it. (You will recall filling out your personal version of this worksheet during Step 1.3.) Have partners begin to fill out their inventories, and encourage them to take these home and continue to identify assets.

> ***Share preliminary history, census, and economic data; get members involved in further research.***    **ACTION**

TASK 3.4   Create a map of community assets

Task 3.4 will require one group meeting; however, the task could be extended to involve community members through community meetings or workshops. Focus this fourth meeting upon starting the community asset map.

A community asset map documents and displays the community's strengths. It can show both physical strengths, such as infrastructure, buildings, museums, hospitals, walkways, parks, and geographic features, as well as intangibles, such as cultures, history, and events.

It's fun to have a big base map of the community on a wall throughout the planning process. You can hire an artist to draw or paint the base map, or use creative talents in the group. Reasonably to scale, the map should represent the geographic parameters of the community with the basic street pattern and natural and institutional features—lakes, rivers, schools, hospitals, and so forth—but otherwise little detail. If the map is made of canvas or other heavy fabric, it can be rolled or folded, and moved to other locations for visual reference and additional contributions. Make the map colorful, maybe cartoon-like, and not so precious that anyone is intimidated from writing or sticking items on it.

Group of people working on a community asset map for a Minneapolis community.

AGENDA—Meeting 4*

This meeting is designed to be fun and stimulate creative thinking.

Task 3.4—Create a map of community assets

Preparation
Have an artist prepare a large map of the community. Arrange appropriate space for displaying the map. Bring materials for adding assets to the map.

Agenda
1. (Presentation of census and economic data carried over from the previous meeting, if needed)
2. Group discussion of important assets to place on the map
3. Individuals place items on the map
4. General discussion about nature and importance of assets
5. Discussion about further community participation in mapping

Homework
Each member should think further about the community's assets and their potential role in community revitalization.

* Consider setting aside time following this meeting for community workshops with the asset map.

During this focused group session, combine fun and serious conversation to identify key community assets. Have group members use their completed community asset inventories to stimulate ideas. Provide construction paper, fabric, markers, scissors, and glue. Have the group represent assets with images and text on fabric or construction paper, and then adhere them to their appropriate spot on the map. Make sure to use an adhesive that allows items to be removed, relocated, or replaced as the map grows. Give group members some time to work on their own.

Such a large, visual, and collectively generated representation of your community allows people to see relationships and types of community assets they might not otherwise discover. It also can make clear that similar attributes appear in multiple locations or that, together, make up a new characteristic or quality not previously appreciated. You're allowing people to see their own community from a different point of view. They take part in expressing and visualizing things that make it special. Create blank space on one side of the map to write in less tangible assets people think of—and encourage them to do so. These might be items having to do with identity and other important qualities related to the character of the people, the history, and the place.

If your community or neighborhood has access to geographic information system (GIS) mapping through your city or county, you can create a parallel GIS map that will result in a more precise positioning and juxtaposition of assets. Generate this map later. It's the creative activity and the imprecision of a big wall map—the process of abstraction—that unleashes imaginations. That is more important now than exact representations. Stick to paper, glue, and scissors. If you're interested in exploring a variety of mapping techniques, PolicyLink has excellent resources in print and available on the web.[114]

Based on the map, begin to develop a collective inventory of community assets. Distribute additional copies of Worksheet 2 for this inventory. (See the sidebar, pages 177–179, for Midville's community asset inventory.) Ask group members to point out what the map reveals about the community's assets. Revisit the map at subsequent meetings.

ACTION ▶ *Create a physical map and add assets. Begin to develop a collective inventory using Worksheet 2.*

Community Asset Inventory for Midville

WORKSHEET 2   Community Asset Inventory

For each item below, describe your community in terms of its strengths, characteristics, and/or unique features.

1. **Geographic parameters and demographics**
   Midville—twenty square miles at the northwest corner of Headwaters County; intersected by the Clark River; population 8,500— 22 percent under eighteen and 12 percent over sixty-five; 70 percent Caucasian, 4 percent Native American, 7 percent African American, 9 percent Latino, 8 percent Asian/Pacific Islander, 3 percent Other

2. **History and industries**
   2a. Native American/pre-colonial: **Key regional fishing and trading site**

   2b. Significant events and people: **Freak meteor shower 1936; movie superhero birthplace (deceased)**

   2c. Products manufactured and grown: **Fertilizers, corn, soybeans**

   2d. Cultural and technological innovations: **Fertilizer odor control system, popular card games**

   2e. Economic base and employment: **Agriculture, fertilizer plant, local trade, light manufacturing, services to through traffic**

   2f. Other: **Allegedly site of stagecoach stop where "Wild West" luminaries met untimely demise**

3. **Geography**
   3a. Natural or geological features: **Lovely, natural, glacier-formed lake; origin of largest Missouri River tributary; boulder fields and meteor craters**

   3b. Climate: **Hot summers, cold winters, moderate humidity**

   3c. Recreational amenities: **Popular, deep lake for swimming, boating; wooded creek-side hiking trails**

   3d. Other:

4. **People** (Give special thought to historic or recent uncelebrated heroes, especially women and people of color whose contributions mirror the spirit of community building.)
   4a. Openness: **Widely known as welcoming to visitors, immigrants**

   4b. Age range and balance: **Shrinking youth population**

   4c. Ethnic mix: **Rapid changes in past 20 years with some long-established communities of color; interesting mix emerging representing global spectrum**

Community asset inventory for Midville (continued)

4d. Economic status: **78 percent considered middle class; 18 percent in poverty; 4 percent considered well-off**

4e. Education levels: **Most have high school degrees and some community college; higher-than-average dropouts among more rural sections**

4f. Outstanding individuals: **Movie superstar; inventor of fertilizer process**

4g. Other: **Highly active in social events, especially in winter**

5. Public sector

5a. Effective leadership: **Honest, hardworking town council and mayor**

5b. Communications and accountability: **Good local paper, recent use of web, too much word-of-mouth information, which fails to reach all citizens; high voter participation**

5c. Service quality and capacity: **Friendly public servants; some favoritism to downtown business**

5d. Versatility and innovation: **Some leaders willing to take risks**

5e. Other:

6. Reputation

6a. Identity to outside world:

6b. Receptivity to visitors: **Exceptionally friendly, fun-loving**

6c. Location and accessibility: **Central location, downtown visible from major east-west highway and key Amtrak/rail route**

6d. Navigability: **Easy to navigate, get around; compact central street grid, in walking distance from historic train depot**

6e. Safety: **Virtually no crime**

6f. Aesthetic experience: **Pleasant and distinct, quick transition from commercial district to farm/rural/recreational areas**

6g. Other:

Community asset inventory for Midville (continued)

7. Nearby features and attributes

7a. Natural amenities: **Vast farming lands to the west**

7b. Widely known attraction(s) or features: **Meteor fields; boyhood home of movie/superhero**

7c. Urban center or district: **Major metropolitan center 100 miles east**

7d. Major or unique service(s): **None**

7e. Well-known institution(s): **Award-winning high school newspaper; Franklin's Museum of Farm Implements**

7f. Special places: **Sunset Ridge overlooking lake**

7g. Other:

8. Infrastructure

8a. Transportation: **Major freight rail siding; cross-country highway; Amtrak station; daily bus service to metropolitan center**

8b. Education and culture: **Excellent high school; community college branch; thriving forty-year-old community theater; two art galleries; active cinema club and two-screen commercial movie house; nonprofit artist collective; eight card clubs; mayoral-sponsored community book reading**

8c. Housing stock: **Quality is good, mix of owner and rental**

8d. Architecture or built environment: **Largely intact 1920s commercial district with art deco movie house; Arts-and-Crafts-era hunting lodge on lake; two dozen elaborate, Victorian-style homes on south side near railroad tracks**

8e. Power, water, and sewer adequacy and capacity: **Excess capacity, upgraded with fertilizer plant expansion in 1983**

8f. Underutilized structures and real estate: **Abandoned 1890 mill building, some underutilized warehouses, designated industrial site near Amtrak station**

8g. Healthcare: **Small regional hospital near downtown, community clinic attached**

8h. Other:

TASK 3.5   Invite contributions from the larger community

Once you've started your map, you can invite the larger community into the process, especially if you want visibility at this stage. Inviting the community is a great way to build momentum, increase support, and gather more creativity to your work.

One option—provided you have the right venue and sustained energy—is to display the map in a more public place and invite community members to add to it. Conduct workshops for specific groups who aren't often included in community planning. Perhaps one of your planning partners is an arts group that can fund an artist to lead workshops—or simply incorporate this

Intermedia Arts created a community asset map of its Minneapolis neighborhood and displayed it outside.

mapping activity into an artist-in-residence program already under way. It's a nonscientific way to survey a community's sense of self and what it values. You may discover—even simply by how often they are repeated—some of the things the community embodies and holds most dear.

An art center, school lobby, public building, shopping mall, or empty storefront are possible homes for this activity. Conduct workshops with senior citizens, school groups, youth groups, professional associations, unions, church groups, recreation clubs, or other groups that meet regularly for civic or creative activities. Be careful to draw participants who represent the diversity of your community. Let them know that mapping the community is an important step in a larger revitalization project and that their ideas and input will make a difference. If a certain demographic group is growing particularly fast, such as youth, elderly, Latinos, or immigrants, seek out their input and pay particular attention to it. They speak best to the future. Even if you don't gain too much information from these activities, you'll build community ownership and awareness of the process. Later, as your work unfolds, be sure to acknowledge all the hands that were part of it.

ACTION ▶   *Conduct open and/or targeted participatory meetings or workshops to build upon the asset map.*

Summary

Your group has covered a tremendous amount of ground in this step. It has met for the first time. Members have begun to learn about each other and work together. And real, concrete work is taking place! You've identified each other's assets and collective values, and, more importantly, you've built a community asset inventory and map. People from every walk of life have had a hand in this effort. In many communities, this much alone would be a monumental accomplishment.

But you're just getting started. In the next step, you will capitalize on this work to distill an identity for the community—something that captures it at its best and energizes people. This identity is the key to your plan and an exciting future.

CHAPTER 7

Step 4: Focus on Your Key Asset, Vision, Identity, and Core Strategies

YOU'VE ALREADY DONE the most labor-intensive part of the planning process. Your initiative is now in the spotlight. You've raised expectations and developed a broad base of participation. You've generated excitement, or at least curiosity, and people are thinking about ways to put community assets to work. Now you're entering the most tricky stage, where critical decisions have to be made and your group's creative powers will be challenged. The good working relationships you've built will be tested. You have to keep everyone focused as you move toward developing your plan. In Step 4, you'll decide the main elements of that plan: key asset, vision, identity, and core strategies.

Creating a vision and finding the identity for your community can be the most stimulating part of the process—but it is also the most hazard-prone. These tasks call for imagination and creativity. They present the highest stakes and the biggest payoff.

Community identity is a concept that embodies the community's strengths. It both describes the inhabitants and makes them proud. While there may be a marketing tone to this identity, take care. When you find the identity that represents the uniqueness and integrity of the community, *DO NOT try to find an image or a marketing phrase that you THINK will be attractive outside your community*. First and foremost, this identity needs to be for and about your community, and it needs to be simple and straightforward. It may build upon an existing identity or it may take a new spin. What's essential is that it has authenticity and meaning to the people in your alliance and in your community.

It takes time for ideas to incubate and settle. Once in a while, after significant time and effort, a group cannot arrive at consensus about a community identity. If this is the case in your alliance, consider whether you chose the right key asset or if you have the right people involved or if you just need more time. *Failure or abandonment of the effort at this stage can set your community back years*. If there is stubborn disagreement or an inability to come together, you'll have a hard time starting over.

In today's global environment, pressures for economic renewal drive innovation. Such renewal involves identifying a "niche" in the global new economy, based on distinctive local assets including location, geography, culture, skills and knowledge. Developing the niche requires a multi-faceted approach: retaining and attracting mobile citizens, investment, and jobs; improving the "quality of place" . . . and building local identity and pride through "branding" or place marketing.

—Nancy Duxbury[115]

If there's one place where you can use an outside facilitator or consultant—someone familiar with both group process and asset-based community building—Step 4 is it! If the process fails at this stage, you can blame the consultant rather than the people in the alliance. Blaming the consultant increases the possibility of re-starting the process after some rethinking and repair work.

Some planners would argue it's important to decide on outcomes before deciding on an identity. In other words, they believe you need to determine what your community wants to do first, such as create jobs, diversify the economy, or promote social interaction, and then build a "marketing" plan that includes an identity to support the outcomes.

This author argues that such an approach is less likely to be rooted in your community's values, assets, and creativity. The approach here asserts that sustainable development cannot be based upon today's needs or short-term conditions. Rather, this approach focuses on the character and cultures of the community and its indigenous assets. It entrusts the creative process into the hands of the community. It begins with a focus on what you've got, rather than on what you don't have.

Boom-and-bust cycles may be unavoidable. However, the community that knows how to assess, reassess, and take advantage of its assets is better able to weather economic and social changes. The process described here is therefore not backward. It's designed to instill a way of thinking about and a way of building upon strengths, rather than throwing all you've got at your deficiencies.

In Part 2 of this book, you saw many examples of communities that grew their own success stories. Neither Paducah (Strategy 5: Improve Property and Enhance Value) nor Roxbury (Strategy 4: Diversify the Local Economy) imported skills or major financial contributors. Paducah assembled a package of incentives from locally available resources and recruited one artist at a time until a critical mass signaled major change in the city's image and economy. Roxbury nurtured one indigenous cultural project after another until a buzz got started about the creative goings-on there, thus attracting more creative entrepreneurs. *In Paducah, in Roxbury, and elsewhere, "investors" were attracted to what was already there.*

Through Step 4, you will clarify the broader strategies you're best equipped to pursue, such as stimulating trade, promoting social interaction, and involving youth. Your plan will not be based upon need but upon what you're best positioned to do successfully. When you gain momentum, other options and other capacities will open up. In some sense, you're starting by reaching for the low-hanging fruit. After being nourished by these, you'll be able to reach higher.

At this point, you're swimming in data, historical facts, and people's ideas about what makes the community a special place. It's time to assemble your group in another working session and move toward naming the community's most unique and special feature. This process is not about neglecting or eliminating the many other assets present, but finding one that defines the place and is capable of reinforcing—and being reinforced by—the others.

Tasks in Step 4 are

1. Review data and narrow list of top community assets

2. Choose a key community asset

3. Envision the future

4. Develop core strategies based upon your vision

5. Name your identity

TASK 4.1   Review data and narrow list of top community assets

Your first task is to arrive at a short list of community assets. Plan a meeting at which this will occur. In preparation for the meeting, assign several people to collect all the information you've gathered in previous steps. Have them prepare reports to review the community's assets, history, census and economic trends, and other important findings.

Before the meeting, compile the long list of community assets based upon the map, group members' individual asset-inventory forms, and the collective asset-inventory form. Eliminate duplication, and select items that seem unique, especially important, and/or received repeated recognition. Write these assets on large sheets of paper and post them around the room. This could be a big job, so plan ahead.

At the meeting, have several members report on the history, population and economic trends, and other findings. Briefly discuss the updated information. However, if the information is new to most people and your group is eager to discuss it, this task may require an additional meeting. On the other hand, don't spend so much time on discussion that group members become bored or feel they're not getting anywhere. Judge an appropriate pace that allows for processing information while maintaining interest.

Call attention to the list of assets on the wall. Ask the group to review the list and provide any additions or clarifications.

By this time, everyone in the room has a clear and shared picture of the community's background and assets. Have group members use adhesive dots (or markers) to vote for their top three or four community assets. Use the top four to six vote getters for your short list. (For an example of a short list, see the sidebar Midville's Most Unique Assets—The Short List on page 186.) If the spread of votes is too wide and there's no clear short list emerging,

---

AGENDA—Meeting 5

Task 4.1—Review data and narrow list of top community assets

Preparation
List fifteen to twenty of the community's assets on large sheets of paper. Ask a small group or several groups to be ready to present history, census, and economic summaries. Bring supplies for voting (adhesive dots, color markers).

Agenda
1. Listen to report on history project findings; review findings from census and economic data

2. Discuss data

3. Present community asset list

4. Discuss, add to list as necessary

5. Narrow list to three to six assets

Homework
(Optional—see Task 4.2)
Assign small groups to develop scenarios around each asset on the short list.

you'll have to do a run-off vote by re-writing the top eight to twelve, and re-voting. This could also indicate some disagreement in the group which may require more time to work through.

At the next meeting, the group will select one asset from the short list to be the key asset. To help in this selection, group members will formulate scenarios, or descriptions of the future, that depict what might happen if a particular asset were the foundation of the community building project. To save time, you might divide the group into teams and have them develop scenarios before the meeting, or ask a group of team leaders to each take on an asset and develop a scenario around it.

ACTION ▶   *Review information collected and arrive at a short list of community assets.*

Midville's Most Unique Assets—The Short List

The town of Midville, a midwestern agricultural community of 8,500 residents, serves as a county seat and commercial center for an area of 18,000. The town has a long history as a place where people work and play together, and it has been the site of some unusual natural phenomena. Concerned with its economic future, town leaders decided to seek a strategy to re-invigorate both community life and financial fortunes. Through an asset-based planning process, the leaders generated the following short list of what they believed to be Midville's most unique assets.

• Site of major meteor strike

• Hometown of superhero

• Home base of state's largest manufacturer of chemical fertilizers

• Birthplace of several widely known card games

• Headwaters for tributary that provides 60 percent of water flow of the Clark River

• Transportation access point to the Wheat Belt

TASK 4.2   Choose a key community asset

Allow three to four weeks between the meeting for Task 4.1 and the meeting for Task 4.2. This scheduling lets people think about the short list as they prepare to arrive at a single, key asset around which an identity and revitalization strategies will be built. Members might consult others in the community or have conversations among themselves during this time. As a group, you'll be finding the nugget that speaks to your community's greatest strengths—the special quality that elicits community pride and that residents will rally behind.

Selecting one key asset does not diminish others. In fact, the strategies built around this key asset will make use of and help build upon all of the community's strengths.

Don't rush this pivotal task, which is probably the most important. Finding a key asset around which to build your strategies *is* sensitive business. It's also a very creative process! And don't spend too much time wordsmithing as you describe this asset. The *precise* words and images you use to represent this idea may take more time and work to find and agree upon. In this task, you are choosing the foundation upon which you'll build an identity and a set of core strategies.

To get started, post the list of values developed in Task 3.2. Take a few minutes to discuss them and remind people what they said they value in a community.

Next post the short list of community assets. If you haven't already done so (see the Homework for Task 4.1, page 185), divide the group into teams and have them develop a brief scenario for each asset. The scenario should describe how the asset might be mobilized into a revitalization plan. For instance, Midville's asset of being the site of a major meteor strike might be leveraged into a center for astronomy and mineralogical studies. The center could attract university partnerships, new highly skilled workers, education programs for local youth, and tourists. Maybe a network TV series could be based upon the strange phenomena or rumored alien presence afflicting a quiet midwestern community.

If your alliance is small (fewer than eight members), it could be best for the entire group to talk out a scenario for each asset. However, if discussion usually depends upon one or two creative "spark plugs," or tends toward contentious or competitive behaviors, small groups may be best.

Have each group share its scenarios verbally. In hearing the scenarios spoken aloud, the entire group will notice that some stand out above others. Once your group has examined the options, the members need to choose one asset. If one doesn't jump to the top of the list, take a preference poll by

AGENDA—Meeting 6*

Task 4.2—Choose a key community asset

Preparation
Check in with team leaders on scenario development. Prepare members for a deliberative meeting. Engage a facilitator if the budget allows. Have lists of the group's values (Task 3.2) and major assets (Task 4.1) ready to display in the meeting room.

Agenda
1. Develop scenarios in small groups (if teams didn't do so before the meeting)
2. Present and discuss scenarios around each asset
3. Decide on one key asset to pursue

Homework
Draft a scenario around the selected key asset to present to the group at the next meeting. This scenario would be a description of how a community revitalization plan based on this key asset might play out. It is simply a rough vision for what activities and what results you'd hope to see in ten to twenty years. Don't get too specific or "name names." At this stage it needs to be visionary but believable. (See Midville example.) Discussion of these scenarios will help your group decide on which is most exciting and feasible.

* *This task could require an additional meeting and deserves full consideration and evaluation in the community.*

using the dot method or a show of hands. If you can't come to a consensus at this meeting, you'll need to give the process more time and that's okay. You might be able to narrow the number of scenarios to two or three favorites that the group can flesh out further before the next meeting. Members can discuss pros and cons informally and take time to evaluate the ideas with community leaders who may not be part of your working group.

Some questions to ask in assessing how your prospective key asset plays out include the following:

- Is it rooted in important aspects of the community's cultures and values?
- Will it be inclusive of the community's diversity?
- Does it build upon multiple local assets (business, institutions, associations, individuals, reputation, natural amenities, etc.)?
- Does it address the future as well as the past?
- Can it be initiated with existing local resources (doesn't require infusion of external expertise or capital to get it started)?
- Does it have appeal to draw the participation of other volunteers and leaders?

Once your key asset has been decided upon and prior to the next meeting, update and flesh out the scenario that illustrates it. This will be the starting point for the vision you'll develop. Write it yourself or ask a trusted colleague (see the sidebar Midville Community Task Force Results, page 191).

> ACTION ▶ *Choose a key asset upon which to build your identity and work.*

TASK 4.3   Envision the future

A vision for the future expresses how the identity you're in the process of creating will look in real life—usually in ten to twenty years. Visioning exercises are most productive when led by an experienced and impartial facilitator. It is less important in this case that the facilitator is from outside the community, but more important that his or her impartiality or commitment to fairness is well established.

Set a meeting specifically to envision the community's future—one that is built upon both the key asset and the other assets now in the group's inventory. Post and reflect upon both the list of values and the longer list of fifteen to twenty assets. You're not disregarding your many assets; you're looking at them in the context of how they support—or will be supported by—the key asset. Spend time talking about what the key asset means to different people in the group. Break into small groups of at least three and no more than five per group. Have each group brainstorm ideas related to the key asset, describing in broad strokes what members want their community to look like and what conditions they want to exist at the end of a twenty-year effort.

This brainstorming should be a highly creative activity. The facilitator may want to use tools to warm the groups up and stimulate creative and visionary thinking. You can use maps, models, or drawings. Particularly when arts and culture are central, some facilitators use song, dance, drawing, or poetry to engage people with different expressive strengths and to tap ideas that might not arise through a process requiring strict rational or linear thinking. Such tools often bring about wonderful results.[116]

This is brainstorming! As with previous brainstorming tasks, don't let anyone stifle ideas, no matter how unusual (or dull, for that matter). Remember that silly or ineffective ideas can be weeded out later. Sometimes a silly idea contains the seeds for a more profound idea. Give the groups about thirty minutes for brainstorming. Have them write out or illustrate the central elements of their vision on large sheets of paper that are posted on the wall when they present their results.

Have each small group report back to the larger group. Each should take no more than five minutes. When all the groups have finished, circle and discuss the common elements found in each report. Sometimes one group may like the ideas of another group more than its own. If there is a diversity of ideas, use the adhesive-dot-voting method to focus in on the most popular ideas.

Assign an individual or committee to develop proposals for names or tag lines based upon the key asset. The name or tag line will express an identity for the community building project (Task 4.5).

> *Arrive at a vision for what the community will look like in twenty years after building upon its key asset.*    ACTION

AGENDA—Meeting 7

Task 4.3—Envision the future

Preparation
Circulate the draft scenario for review prior to the meeting.

Agenda
1. Review the scenario and discuss the implications of the key asset
2. Have small groups brainstorm future visions
3. Share ideas with larger group and consolidate
4. Discuss and conduct a preference vote on best ideas, if needed

Homework
Assign a committee to develop proposals for names or tag lines based upon the key asset.

TASK 4.4   Develop core strategies based upon your vision

Take a moment to read how Midville converted its key asset (birthplace of several widely known card games) into an industry made up of small entrepreneurial and civic enterprises, tourism, and social interaction.(See the sidebar Midville Community Task Force Results, page 191.) Recall examples of asset-based community building from Part 2 of this book. Peekskill reinvigorated its downtown by developing spaces where artists could live *and* work (Strategy 3: Attract Investment by Creating Live/Work Zones for Artists). Danville saved, and added to, its historic character by having artists mediate highway planning (Strategy 10: Broaden Participation in the Civic Agenda). San José enhanced its environment to welcome and retain a skilled workforce from around the globe (Strategy 1: Create Jobs).

When you develop your plan, you'll retain and build on your community's most important values and assets. As mentioned previously, conventional approaches to planning identify the problems, deficits, or challenges, and then ascertain what assets the community has to throw at them. Unfortunately, that approach usually depletes assets without gaining much noticeable improvement. The asset-based approach builds upon strengths in ways that result in positive change. Like Midville, the things your community values, identifies with, and possesses can be converted into new industries and activities that improve the economy and social fabric.

The ten creative community building strategies highlighted in Part 2 may or may not fit your community's plan. They have worked in many places besides the communities highlighted in this book. Therefore, chances are one or more will fit your community. If you think of new ones, not part of this book, articulate them and use them. You may have more success convincing others to adopt them if you can find examples of communities where similar strategies have worked. Review the list (Figure 1: Economic and Social Capital Development Strategies, page 19). Discuss which ones make sense for your community's values and assets and create a short list of core strategies.

Discuss the creative community building strategies that your group is best positioned to use. Post your vision and scenario side by side with your list of core strategies. A picture will emerge of how these strategies may best support your vision, although it may require more time to reflect upon and make sense of the ideas. If time allows, have participants write activities identified in the visioning on Post-it notes and stick them next to strategies. As your key asset and activities begin to cluster around strategies, you'll know which ones you're best equipped to focus on. A follow-up committee or plan writer can develop more detail around these activities later.

ACTION ▶   *Identify two to four strategies (at least one from the economic and one from social capital categories) that will be central to your plan.*

Midville Community Task Force Results

Key Asset: **Birthplace of several widely known card games**

Identity: **"The Town That Plays Together"**

The task force examining options for Midville took six weeks to play out scenarios and reach a unanimous decision. Of the six contenders on its short list of assets, the task force agreed that the invention of popular card games had the strongest connection to the community's values, culture, and way of life, and that this asset could be expressed in creative and inclusive ways.

Scenario and Relation to Values:

Card playing embodies community values of inventiveness, social gathering, and intellectual competition. As card games include a factor of chance, they also have a connection to the Native American culture that was dominant in the area a century-and-a-half earlier and that is still well represented.

The task force decided that the invention of games could be built upon in a manner that would embrace newer residents from Latin America and Asia, people from other agrarian cultures where social interaction is often based around game playing. Historical research confirmed the local legend of a long-since-demolished stagecoach stop where travelers and locals played cards and taught each other new games. This meeting ground nurtured invention and competition. The task force saw Midville's history of welcoming and learning from newcomers and travelers as a strength upon which to build.

The Vision:

The planning group foresaw regional card game playoffs called The Midville Shuffle, an annual contest to invent new games, and the commissioning of local artists to create playing cards. These activities could spawn cottage card manufacturing and sales, an Internet presence, a film series themed around card games, and the redevelopment of the legendary stagecoach stop, to be named The House of Cards. The stagecoach stop would be a place to host local celebrations and international card-playing tournaments, as well as to house the Last Chance Museum, including multicultural exhibits of playing cards and other games of chance.

The group agreed that first and foremost the identity would reinvigorate social gathering and interaction in Midville around a culturally based participatory activity. It would provide a sense of pride in the accomplishments of local citizens. It would be a broad, culturally based strategy to renew the economy. Further, the focus on social games that use symbols and numbers applied across many cultures, from pre-colonization to recent times, as there are similar games across many cultures. Finally, it was noted that such games strengthen participants' memory, math skills, teamwork,

Midville Community Task Force Results

strategic thinking, and other useful practices. They have the potential to bring artists and designers together with teachers and mathematicians, youth with adults, and so on.

Creative Community Building Strategies: Midville planners decided to employ two economic strategies and two social capital strategies: Stimulate Trade through Cultural Tourism and Diversify the Local Economy; and Broaden Participation in the Civic Agenda and Engage Youth. Other efforts including job creation and attracting and supporting artists would also be part of the picture in the long term, as would all the other social capital approaches.

Postscript:

The meteor shower and the native superhero were ultimately considered anomalies that would always serve as curiosities for locals and visitors, but were the result of outside forces. The idea for an astronomy center based upon the famous meteor shower was dismissed as requiring too much outside investment and expertise and was of limited local value. The fertilizer manufacturer briefly promoted the idea of a fertility festival, but was happier to get behind the promotional concept of fertile imaginations that birth inventions such as card games. "Gateway to the Wheat Belt" was also dismissed as not unique to Midville. Finally, the group felt that the river headwaters asset symbolized valuable resources leaving the community.

Midville's clarity on its values and connection to its history and multiple cultures manifested in social game playing. Branding itself as "The Town That Plays Together" provides powerful symbolic currency. It both connects people within its boundaries and attracts people and creative thinkers from well beyond.

The process of focusing on a raw vision demonstrates a kind of thinking rooted in cultural values and practices, finding what is not merely distinctive, but authentic and inclusive. The key was not simply that some card games were invented in Midville, but that social gathering around games was a widespread and valued practice that could continue to build a stronger community. That element best spoke of and to the culture of Midville. Seeing how it could also speak to outsiders was easy.

TASK 4.5   Name your identity

You've found the values and that key asset you believe community can be built around, you've come up with a description of what the community could look like, and you've selected your creative community building strategies. Now you have to articulate this identity in a few words.

"Home of . . .," "Birthplace of . . .," "The . . . Capital," "The . . . District," and "Gateway to . . ." are common ways people have named their communities. Some communities ultimately take on a shorter identity. For example, Portland, Oregon, has an area called The Pearl District. The area was once home to the pearl industry and is now bustling with many artists, cultural groups, restaurants, and the like. It has become known simply as "The Pearl."

A part of Brooklyn, New York, was once a virtually abandoned industrial waterfront area under the shadow of an enormous bridge. A major property owner and developer gave it the name DUMBO, standing for Down Under Manhattan Bridge Overpass. He gave free and low-cost space to edgy arts groups and artists. DUMBO stuck and rapidly became associated with the buzz about artists living and working there.*

A welcome sign outside Madison, Minnesota, reads "Lutefisk Capital USA." Madison hosts a lutefisk-eating contest every November.

A historically segregated portion of Coconut Grove, south of Miami, Florida, has been inhabited for several generations by immigrants of African descent from Jamaica, the Bahamas, and other Caribbean islands. The area has long been known as the Black Grove or the West Grove. Community leaders there implemented strategies to protect the longtime residents from predatory development and gentrification. To name the cultural assets of the community and retain its identity, some leaders proposed the designation "The Island District."

In essence, you are creating a brand name for your community. Volumes have been written about developing brand names for products and processes, and consultants earn extraordinary sums developing such names. But your community, working via the alliance you've assembled, should name its own identity. This name needs to be owned by the community.

It's *difficult* to come up with a clever name or phrase, especially when a group tries to write together. You know your group best—if things seem to flow well with the group, go ahead and brainstorm some identities. BE SURE that all the names reflect that key asset developed in Task 4.2. If the group does not work well this way, assign this task to an individual or small writing

---

* There's a downside to this story: the effort was so successful that property values rose quickly, driving artists and other low-income residents away. High-priced lofts and trendy restaurants are now established in the area.

committee. Have them bring back a list of *draft* names, and let the group choose the top one to three candidates. Use the same person or committee to revise again. Repeat the process until the group finds a name it can really get behind.

The name may come quickly, or it may seem to take forever, with the group finally settling on the one that the fewest people object to. Don't make the decision too precious. And *do not* let the naming process slow down the rest of your work! So long as the basic identity has been agreed to by the group, it can continue with other parts of this process while the "naming crew" continues to work on that perfect identity.

Rest assured that eventually, a very good name will emerge. Once you promote it, the broader community will eventually change it, shorten it, or sweeten it in some way. Don't be frustrated when this happens—it's a sure sign that the community has made the identity its own. No branding consultant can give you that.

Identities become powerful vehicles to stabilize, change, or build communities depending upon who is doing the naming and to what end. The old saying "Build it and they will come" could well be replaced by "Name it and they will come."

ACTION   *Decide on a name or phrase that describes your community identity.*

Summary

Your group made its way through the most difficult part of the process in this step. You looked back at the research and community mapping to assess what you've learned. Then you zeroed in on the most distinctive asset of your community, the one that you believe will rally civic energy and resources and move the community to become an even better place. You created a vision for the future, selected creative community building strategies to get it moving, and gave a name to the initiative. Now you're ready to see how all the pieces fit together, flesh out the activities, and put a plan on paper.

CHAPTER 8

Step 5: Craft a Plan That Brings the Identity to Life

I N STEP 4, YOU ARRIVED at your vision and identity. Now you must clarify what you believe you can best accomplish in measurable terms and put it into writing. This plan will spell out how your identity will result in real change and will propel your community forward with renewed imagination and energy.

In addition to providing a planning framework, this chapter focuses on outcomes, on building a case for what you want to make happen, and on having the tools to effectively measure and articulate outcomes. The support you'll need to further your efforts will come both from your ability to articulate the vision and from the outcomes you document as you move forward step by step. By harvesting the knowledge and experience you're generating, you'll influence future policy in your community and in others.

If you're reading this book, you've probably been through organizational planning, and perhaps community planning, in other roles. There are many good texts specifically on the subject of organizational planning, as well as consultants who routinely lead such processes.[118] If you are familiar with organizational planning, community planning is perhaps just a littler messier—there are more "moving parts" in the form of organizations and people in different sectors with distinct organizational cultures. The good news is that the format and language of plans are fairly consistent across government, nonprofit, and business sectors. There are different styles and different ways to measure progress, but the goal of any plan is to spell out, in plain language, where you're going, the steps you'll take to get there, and how you'll know when you've arrived. Given the level of involvement and change that your effort seeks to accomplish, it may be difficult to tie every idea up into a neat plan. Like the creative process itself, community building unfolds as you move forward; you learn as you go. But you do need to start with a plan.

This is one part of the process where a member of the group or a consultant can do a great deal of focused work in a relatively short time. You can't afford to lose momentum now, and you should schedule meetings to develop a plan at a brisk pace. A good plan writer can kick into gear here to capture all that's been said, translate it into plain terminology, and put it in a planning

Practitioners—community workers, arts administrators, and artists—must recognize that harvesting their knowledge and experience in a systematic way is key to the creation of solid grounded theory that can guide research and policy that will further their efforts. More than merely recognizing this reality, they will have to be key players.

— Jackson and Herranz[117]

framework. If you use a consultant or writer, it's best if he or she has been part of the planning process and understands the nuances and real spirit behind the words.

It's difficult to predict how efficiently your group will be able to complete Step 5. With good meeting preparation, facilitation, and writing—and quick agreement among the group members—it can be accomplished in as few as three meetings. It may also take more, which is not a negative reflection, only an indication that your group or community requires more time to process and take ownership of the plan.

There are six tasks in this step:

1. Create outcomes

2. Set goals

3. Attach measures to outcome targets

4. Generate a list of activities

5. Organize action steps and resource needs into a plan

6. Celebrate your work!

TASK 5.1   Create outcomes

With a vision and core strategies in place, you can begin to break that vision into smaller parts—discrete outcomes that will add up to make the vision real. It may be tempting at this point to focus on activities that the group wants to undertake to realize its vision. But it is more important to leap *over* these details to state the broad outcomes. All the things you want to do to get results aren't very meaningful if you don't know what results you want. Depending upon how smoothly your process has worked and how productive your group has been, you may have accomplished much of this during your visioning session. In which case, you can consolidate the results, review them at this meeting, and move into measures and benchmarks more quickly.

Outcomes flow directly from the vision but are more specific. They express where you're headed and what you really want to achieve; they describe the conditions that should exist when you've arrived. As with the vision, they should have a long horizon—ten to twenty years. They should be expressed in concise and meaningful terms, such as these sample outcome statements:

• Violent crimes drop by over 50 percent

• Retail, social and cultural activities expand to at least 18 hours a day

• Aesthetic improvements attract regional attention with customers from outside the ZIP code increasing by more than 300 percent

- Property crimes decline by at least 25 percent

- Up to 100 new units of housing are built or restored to use

- Use of city loan funds for façade improvements increases by at least 200 percent

- At least eight new businesses open that include retail and services useful to residents such as specialty hardware, hobby, housewares, full-service restaurants

- The renovated library/community center has expanded evening and week-end programming

(You also need to be able to measure these outcomes, compare them with the present condition, and map a course of activities to get there—something that you'll do in tasks 5.3 and 5.4.)

Elicit a series of outcomes from the group; write them down in list form.    ACTION

TASK 5.2   Set goals

In Task 5.1 you arrived at a list of desired outcomes. Now you need to organize them in ways that speak to the larger effort. These outcomes will be further articulated and put into measurable form after you write goal statements.

Some planners state broader goals first, then break out more specific outcomes or objectives around each one. The process described here is designed to tap creative thinking and starts with eliciting the outcomes people want to achieve first (as in sample outcomes 5.1), then clusters them and describes the goal that connects them.

Goal statements describe broad, long-term efforts that *lead to* a desired condition or outcome. They should be consistent with the overall direction and values of the project and the community. Goal statements are framed so that people can readily agree upon where they're going, even though any number of ways exist to get there.

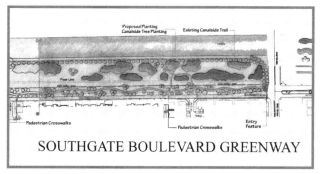

The city of Tamarac, Florida's proposed plan for Southgate Linear Park.

Your major outcomes will align in clusters, and each cluster will suggest a goal. Keep goal statements short, simple, and few in number (three to six). More than half (two to four) should address the outcomes you hope to see achieved; the balance should relate to the process and capacities needed to achieve the outcomes and sustain the effort.

The goal statement that emerged from the sample outcome cluster in 5.1 was:

Improve neighborhood safety and livability through expansion of social activity in the commercial corridor and development of a unique aesthetic character.

Other example goals include the following:

Achieve heightened levels of creativity and critical thinking skills in youth by providing them safe and supportive environments for self-expression.

Increase resources for growing program and institutional activities by expanding and diversifying revenue sources, efficient asset management, and sound fiscal practices.

Outcomes should be organized into no more than half a dozen clusters that will each represent a goal. Some outcome clusters will yield product-oriented, or programmatic, goals (for example, "new streetscaping puts our community on the map with a national 'most walkable cities' award"). Others will be about internal process, that is, how the group wants to function or how the group wants the community to function (for example, "the Business Improvement District generates sufficient revenues for all street and public space upkeep"). It is important to achieve a balance of both product- and process-oriented statements.

This clustering process can take place during a group meeting at which goal statements are articulated by the group and refined later. You or the group facilitator may be able to get agreement fairly quickly around which outcomes are related and make sense together. Alternatively, the leadership and facilitator can work on this task separately and report back for approval at a group meeting. Outcomes may shrink in number as they're consolidated and organized. If some outcomes make sense in more than one goal cluster, that's okay—but specific activities to move toward that outcome may differ.

Assuming one or more of the core strategies (Create Jobs, Stimulate Trade through Cultural Tourism, Promote Stewardship of Place) make sense for your effort, some of your goals may sound similar to them. Review your goals and outcomes to be sure they're in sync with your chosen core strategies and they function to achieve the overall change you'd like to see. You can go back and make revisions or additions as needed at this stage.

ACTION ▶ *Write three to six goal statements that encompass related outcomes.*

TASK 5.3   Attach measures to outcome targets

Now that you've grouped your outcomes and supported them with goal statements, you need to attach meaningful, quantifiable measurements to each of them. To do that, you need to establish the current baseline and then set a reasonable improvement goal. For instance, your farmers market now has thirty-five vendors. You want that number to double in five years. Or you want to see that your retail sales and related tax revenues grow faster than the norm for your area. So, you research and discover that sales tax revenue countywide increased 3 percent, while in your district it grew by only 2 percent. You set a goal to exceed the county benchmark in future years by 3 percent, showing that your community is doing better than the region.

Setting measurements involves four steps. First, you have to be sure you've clearly quantified the condition you're striving for. Then you have to establish the current condition. Next, set reasonable improvement expectations that tie to the outcomes you've established. Finally, you have to measure over time to demonstrate change.

While your resources for gathering and tracking data may be limited, one way to make the job easier is to use numbers that are already tracked by others. Public and private institutions track data regularly and, once you find the right sources, the work becomes simpler. Your city, county, local bank, or chamber of commerce may track business data and sales tax collections. Some census data is updated annually, but the ten-year figures also provide useful reference points, especially at ascertaining longer-term trends such as changes in population, specific demographics, incomes, types of occupations, and so forth. Your state, county, or city tracks data about traffic patterns, crime rates, health statistics, voting patterns, tax collections, property values, and new business licenses. Your schools track test scores, truancy, and graduation rates.*

When your outcomes are tied to larger social changes, they will be more meaningful to more people. For instance, you want more active pedestrian traffic on your commercial corridor. You may want safer conditions, and you may want more people who otherwise pass through to stop and patronize businesses. You might want more social interaction between the increasingly diverse populations. The indicators you choose to measure changes in these conditions could include retail sales activity, auto and pedestrian accidents, average traffic speeds on your thoroughfare, stranger-to-stranger crime rates, demographic trends in residential population, school enrollments, and voter participation from precincts in your neighborhoods. These statistics are all collected by someone else and are yours for the asking. Once you establish your outcomes and the indicators that help you measure them, and, once you find corresponding information sources, the hard work is done.

---

* For suggestions and sources to track various economic data, see *The Community Economic Development Handbook* by Mihailo Temali.

Down the road you will have a happy story to report to your partners, constituents, funders, and the press. For example:

> *It's been five years since we launched our cultural district with streetscape improvements, a multicultural festival and marketplace, youth programs, and a public art initiative. In that time, our community has experienced a 20 percent improvement in both traffic safety and crime, a 35 percent increase in sales tax collections, a 10 percent increase in voter participation, and a 5 percent improvement in school test scores.*

Wouldn't you just love to tell that story! Go ahead and take some credit. Leave the scientific "cause-and-effect" research to someone else.

Broader benchmarks are also important as a form of comparison. For instance, the crime rate in your city or state as a whole declined 10 percent, while in your area it declined 20 percent. Voter participation declined 5 percent in your last citywide election while in your neighborhoods it increased 10 percent. These kinds of comparisons say something that is equally, if not more, important.

Spend part of this meeting soliciting ideas from group members as to outcomes they'd like to see. Members from different sectors will have different kinds of benchmarks that they're familiar with and that are meaningful to them. Most of the nitty-gritty work of writing should take place in a small committee setting or with your plan writer who does the research and reports back to the group.

Worksheet 4: Set and Measure Outcomes, page 201, walks you through a few statements and questions that can help shape your stated outcomes. But first, revisit and rewrite the vision and bring it to a more concrete statement of outcomes. Ask your group to brainstorm a list of twenty to thirty such outcomes. Use the sidebar Midville's Outcomes, page 202, to become familiar with how to state an outcome. Post a large version of this sample worksheet at your meeting as a guide.

ACTION ▶ *Break down each outcome in measurable terms as in Worksheet 4: Set and Measure Outcomes, page 201.*

WORKSHEET 4   Set and Measure Outcomes

An outcome is a specific, observable, and achievable result that is consistent with your vision. Answer the following questions for each of your project's proposed outcomes.

1. Describe the specific community condition you want to see when the project has succeeded.

2. Describe indications that this success has occurred and how you will measure this success.

3. How long do you think it will take to achieve this outcome?

4. What current condition will you measure change against?

5. Estimate the incremental change that will get you there.

6. What comparison to a larger field or region can you make that would distinguish this effort?

7. Restate in summary form the outcome, how you'll measure it, and what it will require in incremental change to get there.

WORKSHEET 4   Set and Measure Outcomes

An outcome is a specific, observable, and achievable result that is consistent with your vision. Answer the following questions for each of your project's proposed outcomes.

Midville Outcome I:

1. Describe the specific community condition you want to see when the project has succeeded.

   The people of Midville spend more time working together volunteering in civic and community activities.

2. Describe indications that this success has occurred and how you will measure this success.

   On average, each resident contributes 2.4 volunteer hours per week.

3. How long do you think it will take to achieve this outcome?

   Seven years

4. What current condition will you measure change against?

   In 2004, residents contributed an average of 1.2 hours each week in volunteer time per data from the Volunteer Resource Center.

5. Estimate the incremental change that will get you there.

   Volunteer time will increase an average of 10% each year for seven years.

6. What comparison to a larger field or region can you make that would distinguish this effort?

   In the U.S. in 2002, it was estimated that the average time volunteered to civic activities was .75 hour per week.

7. Restate in summary form the outcome, how you'll measure it, and what it will require in incremental change to get there.

   Midville residents already contribute nearly double the national average in weekly volunteer time for civic activities. As a result of this project, they will double again what they give to an average of 2.4 hours per week.

Midville's outcomes continued

Midville Outcome II:

1. Describe the specific community condition you want to see when the project has succeeded.

   Midville Center is the hub for commercial and social activity in the tri-county area.

2. Describe indications that this success has occurred and how you will measure this success

   Commercial space will have a 90% occupancy rate; transactions and sales increase 400%.

3. How long do you think it will take to achieve this outcome?

   Ten years

4. What current condition will you measure change against?

   Commercial occupancy was at 45% in 2005; annual retail sales were estimated at $2.5 million.

5. Estimate the incremental change that will get you there.

   Occupancy will increase by an average of 7.5% each year; sales will grow by 15% per year.

6. What comparison to a larger field or region can you make that would distinguish this effort?

   Statewide, retail sales growth during the past decade was 5% per year.

7. Restate in summary form the outcome, how you'll measure it, and what it will require in incremental change to get there.

   As a result of this effort, Midville Center will be the vital regional hub of business and social activity, boasting 90% commercial occupancy and a four-fold increase in retail sales and sales tax receipts within the first 10 years.

TASK 5.4   Generate a list of activities

AGENDA—Meeting 10

Tasks 5.3 and 5.4—Attach measures to outcomes and generate a list of activities

Preparation
Copy and circulate goals, outcomes, and some ideas for benchmarks prior to the meeting. Write outcomes under each goal area on large sheets of paper for group review.

Agenda
1. Brainstorm and discuss measures and benchmarks for each outcome
2. Develop lists of specific activities that will lead to outcomes

Homework
Assign individuals, teams, or a writer to further flesh out the outcome statements and/or research and write up more detailed benchmarks. You might also do the same with lists of specific activities that will lead to outcomes.

With a vision, outcomes, measurements, and goals, you've got the bones of a great plan. Now it's time to flesh out those bones with activities your community will pursue. If your plan writer is sharp and your work groups did a good job in the earlier process, you've got a lot of material with which to start writing. In any event, you'll need to reconvene to talk through activities.

There's nothing magical about Task 5.4, and, like all creative work, it can seem a bit messy until it's all put together. You've created a list of outcomes and clustered them under goals. Now it's time to brainstorm the big list of programs or activities needed to make those goals reality. These activities will include things such as: *Create a loan program to assist qualified artists to purchase live/work spaces in Lowertown*, or *Begin a multicultural festival with involvement of all ethnic groups in Midville.*

Your group could work on this task together, or you could assign outcome clusters and goals to small groups and have them generate a list of activities for each goal. However you approach it, you will accumulate a long list of possible activities. Many of these will overlap, and some of them will actually accumulate under new outcomes and goals that should be added to the plan. Some activities will relate to accomplishing program outcomes and goals, and others will relate to providing the infrastructure needed to keep moving. Don't worry—just get a big list together.

Take time to digest and tinker with the details of the activities. Reduce overlaps, group like activities together, separate those that are truly strategic and effective from those that just seem to be "nice ideas," and otherwise organize the activities as concisely as possible, but don't try to convert them into a set of steps or a timeline—yet. Distribute the consolidated list of activities to your partners so they can study them. Bring the group back together around a focused agenda to prioritize and clarify activities. Refer to your asset inventory to be sure the activities are in sync with, or are building upon, the assets you identified.

 ACTION   *Generate a list of activities that use your assets to meet your outcomes.*

TASK 5.5   Organize action steps and resource needs into a plan

You're now closing in on completing your plan. This stage of the work is difficult to do in a large group setting. At this point, you may want to assign several individuals or small teams to each of the goal areas and lists of activities, and have them flesh out the action steps and resources necessary. Because different goal areas require different kinds of expertise, choose people from the group with the needed expertise to handle each goal area. Give them the job of better defining and then organizing the activities for each goal into succinct steps that move the project forward in a linear fashion.

Action steps should typically be of a scale or significance appropriate for six-month time horizons and include an estimate of resources needed for each step. The object here is to begin to figure out what you will need from the public, private, and nonprofit sectors to achieve these outcomes and to make the vision come alive. Resources might include facility donations, reduced loan costs for live/work spaces, zoning changes, publicity—the list does not need to be definitive, just the start toward understanding the resources and contributions the vision requires. Action steps and resources may sound like, "Secure city council approval to rezone properties on Oak Street as live/work spaces" or "Secure $25,000 in public and private sponsorships for Fall Festival."

If, like Paducah, Kentucky, you hope to attract creative people and enterprises into a forlorn part of town, the banker or community development officer in your alliance would be best equipped to write up the six to ten steps in the entitlement and financing process. However, that person might be paired with someone from your city development agency who can add or clarify the steps required to qualify for matching funds. Adding an artist to the team who can articulate the things that would make the package and the place attractive to other artists would also be an excellent idea.

Depending upon the level of working involvement of your group and the pace of your progress, you may delegate much of this task to a skilled volunteer or paid plan writer and then have that person bring a draft plan to the larger group for revision and approval.

One resource you will need to move forward with your plan is management. Some entity—or consortium of entities—has to keep the ball rolling. The planning group you've been working with, or many of its members, may become part of that entity; but, at this point, you need to decide who and what it is in specific terms. No one approach or type of group can be recommended. It depends upon the nature and scope of your plan and the role your partners have taken thus far—and want to take in the future.

AGENDA—Meeting 11*

Tasks 5.5 and 5.6—Organize action steps and resource needs into a plan and celebrate your work

Preparation
Assemble the work of teams and/or plan writer for group review. Circulate the draft prior to the meeting.

Agenda
1. Review, discuss, and refine the draft plan
2. Adopt the plan or schedule additional meetings and/or consultant work as needed
3. Acknowledge the excellent work of all involved!

Homework
Schedule and plan public announcement and celebration!

* *These steps may require more than one meeting and/or follow up by leadership, committees, or a consultant.*

You do want to be sure that whatever the entity, it continues to be broad based, able to work across sectors, and inclusive, and has the capacity to accommodate the values you've arrived at. Programs such as the National Trust for Historic Preservation's Main Street Program offer specific requirements and responsibilities for their affiliates—some of which may be useful as models.[119] Your planning group undoubtedly includes many good thinkers and experienced organization leaders. Tap one or more to design or designate an entity to oversee implementation of the plan.

At this point, people like to see results and may be itching to get moving. Busy people would rather review a draft and make additions or corrections than try to write it in committee. If there's general consensus and enthusiasm building, folks won't wait for the ink to dry before acting within their own spheres. If you do encounter stubborn disagreement over details, try to work them out privately with the objecting party so as not to drag the group down.

ACTION ▶   *Write a plan that includes values, vision, goals, measurable outcomes, activities, action steps, and resource needs.*

TASK 5.6   Celebrate your work!

People thrive on acknowledgment for what they've done. But you've entered into long-term work that's never done. You can't wait until the project is complete to give an award, have a celebration, or declare success. Look for occasions to recognize contributors and hard work now, personally and in front of an audience! At the conclusion of major steps, raise a toast, and acknowledge the contributions of committee members, volunteers, and supporters. The completion of this plan and its adoption by the planning group is one of those milestones.

At every meeting, acknowledge positive change taking place in the community, especially changes resulting from efforts of your planning partners. A change may have little or nothing to do with your planning process or project, but instinctively you know it's related, or it's the kind of thing you hope to see more of. *A new Mexican bakery opened. The theater group got an important grant. The East African resettlement program just welcomed fifty new immigrants. The Acme Community Development Corporation just received funding for its job training program.* Announce items like this at meetings and in your newsletter or periodic e-mail messages. Be inclusive. Paint a picture of a complex community that cares about its many parts.

When it comes to larger successes, symbolic or otherwise, be sure to conduct appropriate rituals—ribbon cuttings, groundbreakings, and so forth—and find a way to include people and cultural elements that give the event meaning to a wider audience. Of course, politicians and bankers like to be photographed with shovels at a groundbreaking. But what about the neighborhood kids, the newer immigrants who speak little English, or the artists living in the old warehouse? Include them and let them know that this ceremony celebrates the coming of a building that will house a bicycle co-op, teen video center, and farmers market featuring local artists and craftspeople. For a small fee, one of the artists will be happy to work with local kids to decorate their bicycles and stage a mini-parade around the site. Teens interested in working with the video center can be asked to make videos of the event. These activities will generate much more interesting photos or local TV coverage than the generic mayor and banker with a shovel. Who knows—you may get the mayor to ride her *own* decorated bicycle among the kids!

> *Celebrate completion of the plan; acknowledge people and their achievements on an ongoing basis.* ACTION

Summary

All your hard work has now come together into a dynamic plan to transform your community. You've got clear and concrete outcomes that you can measure as the project moves forward. You can also compare your progress with meaningful benchmarks and see how you're doing in relation to neighboring communities and others across the country. You've got detailed activities and action steps and you know roughly what kind of resources you'll need to move ahead. Your plan is in hand for all to see. You've accomplished an enormous amount of work!

And now that you've celebrated this stage, the real fun—and work—begins. You're ready to set things in motion, build support from all sectors of your community, and tell stories of success. You made many friends along the way who will now be there to make it all real. The next chapter provides tips for successful implementation in three essential areas: fundraising, public policy support, and telling your story.

CHAPTER 9

Securing Funding, Policy Support, and Media Coverage

THE PLAN YOU CREATED using Chapters 4–8 of this book is the basis for implementing your community building project. As every community and situation are distinct, it's impossible to provide guidance to actual implementation. However, there are critical issues to be aware of as you move into realizing the plan. The final chapter of this book provides tips in three areas that will be helpful as you move forward: funding, shaping policy, and telling your story.

Chapter 9 contains tips on how to organize yourself, how to think through your needs, how to take stock of the assets you do have, and how to position your project successfully with philanthropists, sponsors, public policy makers, and the media. A few caveats here: First, there are many wonderful books, videos, and guides to fundraising, public policy, and public relations, some of which are listed in the Bibliography on page 253. This chapter isn't a complete guide to any of these large topics—just some tips relative to this specific type of work. Second, this book is written from the vantage point of an organizer in the private nonprofit sector. If you are a policy maker or local government official, this chapter may not align precisely with your needs, but it should still contain valuable information for you or your project partners.

You and your partners already know a great deal about your community—its players and how it works. A project with feet in so many sectors, like the one you've created, will have a wide range of potential supporters. The trick is to show clear outcomes that correspond to both broader and more specific goals of your community. Being sure your alliance has members with experience in these different arenas is quite important. They can help position the project appropriately, frame it in the right terminology, and open the doors to decision makers.

> You can go to any city in America and find an arts organization creating vitality in every neighborhood. And leaders still don't get it. Arts and culture is the genesis of the revitalization of communities.
>
> —Pittsburgh Mayor Tom Murphy [120]

Tips to Secure Funding

Fundraising scares most people. However, for every project, it's essential. When you and many other reputable community leaders believe in what you're doing and show enthusiasm, you're halfway there. The other half is talking to the right people about the right thing at the right time. Having engaged such a broad base of leaders in the planning process as outlined earlier, you will have already brought together the people who *care* and the people who have (or control) the resources. Getting this latter group invested in the project through participation in planning will help shake loose their financial support. You should already have partners in your group who can take the lead in making appeals within their respective sectors to get the resources you need.

Public funding mechanisms, federal and state grants, and private philanthropy are becoming increasingly imaginative and complex. The creative community builder learns how to enlist help and navigate these waters. With rare exception, they are friendly waters, though they can become choppy if it's perceived that you're stepping on someone's toes or going after a pot of money that "belongs" to someone else. That's why all your partners need to be advocates and ambassadors for the project among local funders, and they need to understand how it advances their individual as well as community-wide interests. When it comes to public bonding, special assessments, or other municipal or state mechanisms, you need that expertise on board, just as you do when it comes to grantwriting, individual donor solicitation, corporate identity sponsorship, or special events. Tracking expertise in these areas was part of your asset inventory early in the planning process.

A key question here is, Who is going to apply for funding or be the conduit for development projects? This could be complicated or not, depending upon comfort levels in your community around collaboration. In Step 5, Task 5.5, you defined the management or oversight entity, but the management entity does not have to be the same entity or entities that receive and manage public and private funds.

One scenario is to set up a nonprofit and apply for tax-exempt status. This can be problematic in the short term. Some funders aren't comfortable entrusting funds to an untested entity. Public funding can have complicated requirements that are impossible for an organization with limited capacities.

Another scenario is to designate one existing nonprofit as the lead agency— one whose mission and structure are flexible and whose position in the community is well regarded.

A third is for existing organizations—including government agencies, businesses, and nonprofits—to each seek, secure, and manage funds for projects related to their area of expertise. At the same time, they create a coordinating consortium to oversee how all the pieces of this community building puzzle fit and function together.

You already have people with fundraising experience in your group. However you structure the fundraising entity or entities, the following four tips will help focus general fundraising skills in ways that promote creative community building efforts.

1. Appeal to funders through broad community interests

2. Find the fit between project outcomes and funders' interests

3. Look under the surface to see whose interests are served

4. Break your project into parts while retaining its holistic vision

Appeal to funders through broad community interests

TIP **1** Secure Funding

You have taken leadership in supplying and facilitating vision and cohesion for development in your community. Among your contributions are setting a tone of cross-sector collaboration and focusing on the community's special values and assets. If your current civic leaders and purse-string holders act with broad and common interests, your job will be easier. If not, you will need to continue to lead through unity around common interests and values, such as fairness, cultural equity, environmental and civic responsibility, and economic progress for all.

Options for financial support improve when you position your plan in these terms, and converse with other leaders on the level of broad values. Economic progress is a top goal for many leaders and needs to be a part of every plan. However, be sure your plan (and fundraising pitch) balances economic goals with social capital development and other values. Many communities have been ransacked by capital flight, environmental degradation, and cultural disregard. Fighting for something better by proposing community-based, culturally inclusive approaches with long-term, sustainable results may be outside the box, but is part of the process.

This being a practical world, this is easier said than done. The creative community builder cannot expect simple either-or answers. Therefore, you need to keep your eye on this larger picture while balancing the reality of getting the work done.

Find the fit between project outcomes and funders' interests

Learning to assemble puzzles is a useful skill in many areas of life. However, in real life, puzzles fit together in more than one way. The puzzle pieces you've developed through the process described in Part 3 will fit together in several ways depending upon how visionary, clever, and persuasive you can be. If your planning evolved organically, the task of finding the fit between outcomes, stakeholders, and funders is largely automatic. Your community's assets, identity, and aspirations have been articulated. You have a clear vision and smart plan of activities. You can ascertain your progress with meaningful improvement goals and benchmarks. Key players in the public, private, and nonprofit sectors worked together at the table to shape this strategic undertaking, and each is a passionate advocate who brings expertise and existing seedlings to nurture. You couldn't be much better positioned to leverage funds.

However, don't underestimate the power of inertia, territoriality, and the inability (or unwillingness) to venture into the unknown. These are forces to be cognizant of from the start, but they'll emerge most when it comes to dipping into known pots of money. People fear change or losing something to which they feel entitled. When the new, sexy project comes along, the older ones may put up barriers, sometimes in a passive-aggressive way.

You can find good fits and avoid conflict through several strategies. First, you can build trust around the group's sincere interest in community-wide improvement. This process is designed to do that—as much to get the "haves" to give up some power, as to get the "have-nots" to feel a sense of hope and empowerment. Those with a larger share of power and resources can gain by letting go. You need to help them see that. This is truly a case where the whole is greater than the sum of the parts.

Secondly, you can endeavor to steer the planning so that there's a multifaceted role for all interests. Look for ways that your alliance partners get invested in each others' interests. Obviously, the restaurant owner can see the benefit in a successful performing arts center, but can the members of a cycling club see how a successful after-school teen arts program can benefit them? If your plan calls for the youth to create imaginative public art or signposts for the bike trail, will the cycling group sponsor a benefit ride for the teen program? What if the youth win an award for designing the best bicyclist jersey and the riders teach bike and pedestrian safety courses for the kids? Imaginative ways to engage people, and to help them build a stake and relationships across interests, will help weave your effort into a stronger fabric.

Everyone, whether in the nonprofit, business, or government sector, has to stick to their mission and see results from their investments of time and money. Some people can see a more distant horizon and are willing to make longer-term investments. Such visionaries, willing to take more risk, reside in *every* sector. Don't limit your options by assuming, for example, that the local big-box store manager cares only for short-term profits or that the city council member just wants votes.

All this is to say that the project and its outcomes need to articulate how there's something for a wide range of interests. This will increase the chances that your undertaking will work and its members will invest in it and put their good names and their resources on the line to leverage additional support.

Look under the surface to see whose interests are served

TIP 3 Secure Funding

To understand whom to appeal to for what kind of support, you need to fathom who will benefit from which aspects of the project and in what ways. People are motivated by different things: civic pride, humanitarianism, public relations, or organizational or personal financial gain.

This is also a delicate part of the process, but not one to which you can afford to turn a blind eye. Ensuring that benefit is retained within your community and equitably distributed is part of the work. Examining who stands to gain from a revitalized community is important for a number of reasons, one of which is to figure out whom you can look to for funding. Dissecting your project's ultimate impacts will help you identify the right supporters for the right parts of the overall effort.

Most public and private sector leaders operate in an environment of scarcity and competition. Grand concepts are easier to discuss and agree upon, but lining up for appropriations, grants, and revenue streams is where the rubber hits the road. When it comes to philanthropic support, you need to learn about the particular philanthropist's interests and clarify where your project helps meet the philanthropy's goals. The same is true with corporate identity sponsors or public policy makers. While visibility is a common denominator, businesses are increasingly sophisticated about the kinds of things they want their identity associated with.

Among the larger motivators for both private and public investors, particularly regarding capital projects, are growth in real estate values and business activity. In culturally driven community development, these are generally among the major and most visible outcomes.

Escalation of real estate values is the double-edged sword of community revitalization, sometimes setting off gentrification. It helps attract investment and gives existing owners greater equity, although this is generally accompanied by a greater tax burden. It also squeezes out those on the economic margins. Higher housing and commercial leasing costs tend to give way to higher-income individuals and higher-margin businesses, such as franchise chains that homogenize community character. But real estate values are a symptom, not a cause, of this malaise.

The flip side is that the city, county, or state realizes higher sales and real estate tax revenues. Values rise because demand rises. As a result of your work, your community will become a more desirable one in which to live and do business. Possessing a clear analysis of these dynamics is essential to understanding the various motivations of your partners—and detractors. The job of the creative community builder is to understand, acknowledge, and balance them, giving an edge to the disenfranchised at every possible opportunity. Understanding whose interests will be furthered provides a road map for finding your base of political, financial, and human resource support.

TIP ❹ Secure Funding

Break your project into parts while maintaining its holistic vision

Your cross-sector, "interdisciplinary" planning group provided excellent opportunity to build the case for support for the whole project by getting support for each of its many pieces. As your plan turns to action, for the purpose of fundraising you'll have to break it down into parts—not conceptually, but in terms of budget items, activities, and outcomes—puzzle pieces that make up a whole.

Your planning partners come from a diverse range of interests that might include advancement of the arts, economic development, services for the elderly and youth, education, civic participation, historic preservation—the list could be very long. You'll wonder where this newfangled, culturally centered community project (that includes economic development, civic engagement, and neighborhood design) might fit among the interests of funding agencies that are typically concerned with only poverty, health, housing, or the arts. The good news is that your project fits in all, or at least many, of them. The bad news is most of the keepers of purse strings won't know how to relate to a project that crosses multiple areas of interest. The number of public and private philanthropies who appreciate—and can figure out how to support—broadly based creative community building efforts seems to be increasing. However, most still need you to articulate how the project converges with the goals of their specific interests.

Let's say you have a comprehensive neighborhood redevelopment project that includes an ethnic marketplace, youth mural painting projects, building façade improvements, and a citizen-led design effort for a new public recreation and multipurpose facility. You package two discrete projects (summer youth arts activities and Spanish language entrepreneur training) for private funders whose interests respectively are youth development and economic empowerment.

Then, you go to the city for business fix-up grants and to the park board for public participation funds for facility planning. They are all pieces of a larger strategy but would rarely be entertained together in a funding proposal. Now you've got potential funders for each, who may not be in the least interested in the other, but who might be thrilled to see that a consortium has formed a broader strategy where these are integral parts of a larger whole.

Through the process in previous chapters you've built a strategy from the ground up with the larger public benefit in mind. Now you're breaking it down and finding ways to build upon existing community projects. Consortium partners must be willing to approach their respective funding sources on behalf of some element of the project—in addition to their own needs. There is a delicate balance where each partner is looking to advance its own interests and at the same time be willing to bring its assets to the table and forge a win-win result.

Tips for Shaping Public Policy

Good public policy is crucial to creative community building projects. Part 1 of this book provided facts and arguments to help make the case for your efforts. Then, through the planning process, you've discovered and constructed other rationale especially relevant to the strengths and concerns of your community. Below are characteristics of policies that have helped others. These are followed by tips to approaching local government, an important public sector partner.

Creative community building requires a rarely seen level of collaboration across city agencies, levels of government, and private sector and community organizations. As such, you will likely find yourself blazing new trails or running up against obstacles rooted in inertia and tradition. These things you and your partners will learn to navigate, accumulating valuable information and skills in the process.

Every one of the twenty projects described in Part 2 required cooperation and action by public agencies or changes to local policy that enabled them to proceed with their projects. These may have been as simple as obtaining street permits and police escorts for a May Day parade or as complex as changing live/work zoning ordinances. They involved bringing to the same table officials in conservation, public space, schools, libraries, municipal finance, and cultural programming from city, county, and state levels.

It's important that when such relationships are established they're done so on a personal level as well as on institutional and policy levels. Skills honed and connections established through smaller, simpler activities can be parlayed into much larger undertakings. Long-term implications may grow to yield results well beyond the initial expectations. Employees or officials in one organization or agency, over time, will likely show up in another. They might then be in a position to be even more helpful. This is long-term community building, not achieving short-term ends regardless of who is in the way.

The willingness of the City of Peekskill to permit a few artist live/work spaces yielded not only a statewide housing demonstration project, but also a citywide economic development strategy based upon cultural assets. Minneapolis' In the Heart of the Beast Puppet Theatre rarely espouses ideas in the political mainstream. However, it has an unquestionable capacity to draw participation from across the racial and economic spectrum, and a solid commitment to its neighborhood. With these assets, and through relationships it forged with for-profit and nonprofit developers, philanthropies, banks, political leaders, and others, it expanded its role in real estate and community development. It has become both a symbolic and a real force in south Minneapolis.

Public agency staffers and political leaders can be advocates, and they can be obstacles. Having their support is critical, but such support can be facilitated by policies that favor creative approaches to building community. And policies are set by people.

A growing number of cities and towns have undertaken cultural planning during the past two decades. Often launched by arts councils or other public agencies, these plans are typically designed to elicit and rationalize greater support for those entities and for cultural institutions. A new generation of cultural planners is approaching the process with the broader community well-being at the center, ascertaining how to best apply the cultural and arts assets of the community to further economic, social, civic, and physical development and to solve community problems.

Canadian researchers have produced excellent work reviewing how cities in Canada, the United Kingdom, and Australia have planned for and developed policy around creative economy and creative community building initiatives.[121] Successful communities, in their observations, have learned the importance of balance between

- Local community roots *and* global cosmopolitan influences
- Heritage *and* novelty
- Large-scale flagship projects commanding international attention *and* smaller projects that replenish the creative base
- Formal high culture *and* informal street scenes
- Nonprofit artists *and* creative industry clusters
- Local knowledge *and* professional expertise
- Rule-based accountability *and* grassroots experimentation

- Holistic thinking *and* strategic action
- Neighborhood regeneration *and* social inclusion[122]

Cultural plans developed in U.S. cities share important characteristics. They

- Broadly define culture to include all ethnic/cultural groups and art forms
- Acknowledge and further the role of culture and art across the spectrum of civic affairs
- Engage a wide range of public agencies in supporting cultural strategies
- Invest in both capital and human cultural infrastructure
- Include supportive regulatory policy, personnel, and financial resources
- Provide support for art in public places (public art)
- Recognize, value, and support individual artists directly and indirectly
- Connect design as an art form to the arts community and community at large

A community planning meeting held by the East Windsor, CT, Watershed Conservation Commission to discuss a proposed housing development.

Other than establishing and funding an arts council, most municipal governments don't think of arts and culture as having a place in local government. The twenty examples prove the limits of such a narrow attitude. Policies, practices, and people attuned to the multiple ways that culture and the arts can enhance and help further all city goals are important. They can result in tremendous growth in both economic and social capital.

Policies that favor creative growth should emanate not only from the arts council. All kinds of policies and areas of government are relevant to this work. As your group considers how to make best use of policy to proceed, it should look across departments and agencies to those that address

- Cultural Affairs
- Economic Development
- Education
- Health
- Housing
- Human Resources
- Law Enforcement
- Libraries
- Parks and Recreation
- Planning and Development
- Transportation

A recent plan created for the City of Minneapolis looked specifically at ways in which arts and cultural assets of the city could be applied toward addressing the entire range of the city's established goals.[123] This plan appears in the sidebar Shaping City Plans to Leverage Cultural Assets on page 218.

The following five tips provide an overview of the process and landscape in which public policy is created on the local and state levels. They are adapted and condensed from an excellent step-by-step guide to lobbying and building capacity in the political arena, *The Lobbying and Advocacy Handbook for Nonprofit Organizations.*[124] The tips are

1. Be sure your partners are on board with the policy-shaping effort
2. Understand and target the appropriate arenas of influence
3. Get to know the people who influence policy
4. Use direct lobbying and grassroots mobilizing
5. Advocate with the executive branch

Shaping City Plans to Leverage Cultural Assets

A 2004 City Plan for Arts and Culture developed by the City of Minneapolis builds itself around a set of eight long-established city goals.

City Goal 1: *Build communities where all people feel safe and trust the city's public safety professionals and systems*

Arts and cultural activities are recognized as important tools for community development and neighborhood revitalization. Quite often, cultural activities (like free concerts in neighborhood parks and cultural facilities) are a forum through which neighbors meet neighbors, a critical step in what public safety professionals will testify is a basis for crime prevention—the arts in service of community building efforts.

City Goal 2: *Maintain the physical infrastructure to ensure a healthy, vital, and safe city*

The city's physical infrastructure includes its public arts works, historic theaters, and many cultural spaces, for which it has provided capital support and/or financing, as well as many streetscape and other built-environment elements that integrate cultural elements. The city has invested well over $100 million in physical cultural infrastructure over the last two decades, by far its most significant cultural investment. Cultural spaces and the economic and social activity they stimulate contribute to neighborhood and commercial corridor revitalization as well as to the health and safety of residents and visitors.

City Goal 3: *Deliver consistently high-quality city services at a good value to our taxpayers*

It is the overall intent of this plan that programs and services, proposed to be offered by various city departments and through partnerships, are of high quality and represent a "good value." Many efforts have been made in crafting the recommendations to avoid duplication and look for cost-effective ways to deliver services (e.g., by working with the Greater Minneapolis Convention and Visitors Association for promotion of arts and cultural opportunities, through its www.minneapolis.org web site and reduced ticket offers, thereby avoiding the need to create a duplicate site). Involvement of artists in providing services—from designing and fabricating building and streetscape fixtures to facilitating public involvement, delivery of training workshops, and design of communications materials—has proven to be a low-cost, innovative, and effective alternative in many cities, including Minneapolis.

City Goal 4: *Create an environment that maximizes economic development opportunities within Minneapolis*

Many of this plan's recommendations relate directly to economic and community development strategies (e.g., integrate and utilize arts and culture as a resource for economic develop-

Be sure your partners are on board with the policy-shaping effort

TIP  Shaping Public Policy

Before you do any kind of policy work, be sure that your task force—and the organizations that partners represent—supports the activity of shaping policy. The following points will help you secure this support:

1. Include opinion makers in your planning process

2. Keep up to date on *all* the important issues affecting your community

3. Know the PEOPLE involved in the process of policy making

4. Identify the right level or arena of government relevant to your issues

5. Know how government works in your community

ment). The nonprofit cultural sector generates over $269 million in economic activity annually that contributes to the vitality of neighborhoods throughout the city and also draws tourists (and visitor spending) to the city. Minneapolis' creative sector is also a key ingredient in the city's ability to attract and retain the talent and knowledge capital needed for the twenty-first-century economy.

City Goal 5: *Foster the development and preservation of a mix of quality housing types*

The city can maintain the presence of artists and their positive impact on community identity, vitality, and enhanced property values by ensuring that affordable housing and live/work space are available and accessible. Many cities have incorporated public art into affordable housing projects to enhance livability and value to neighborhoods.

City Goal 6: *Preserve and enhance our natural and historic environment and promote a clean, sustainable Minneapolis*

Public art and cultural activity animate public spaces—including parks, public buildings, and streetscapes—enhance their value and use, and reflect and celebrate community heritage and diversity. Many of Minneapolis' historic buildings—movie theaters, warehouses, churches, etc.—have been preserved and creatively adapted as cultural spaces, often with significant city investment and assistance.

City Goal 7: *Promote public, community, and private partnerships to address disparities and to support strong, healthy families and communities*

An entire recommendation in the plan is devoted to fostering collaborations and partnerships among arts and cultural organizations and between the cultural and other sectors in the

city. Most other recommendations and their accompanying objectives propose a range of partnerships. Cultural programs are now recognized as contributing to healthy youth development, neighborhood revitalization, healing, and other community building processes. The stimulus of arts and cultural collaborations should likewise be seen as an important strategy in sustaining and improving a vibrant cultural community.

City Goal 8: *Strengthen city government management and enhance community engagement*

As this plan has been crafted to specifically address the city's role in cultural development efforts, its overall intent is to strengthen "city government management" vis-à-vis cultural affairs. Enhancing community engagement, particularly in arts and cultural activities and offerings, is a primary objective, which calls for better overall promotion of the city's cultural opportunities.

6. Provide recognition to your supporters in the public arena

7. Have facts and stories at your fingertips about what difference policy work makes in your community

8. Know the implications of any policy changes you're seeking; no one likes surprises

9. Have examples from other places; show that with similar policy changes, the roof didn't fall in

10. Engage your partners and other friends of your project

11. Get to know your way around your city hall, county commission offices, and state capitol

12. Use the media only at opportune right times; don't blindside people who need to influence

13. Don't go with a hand out but with the offer of a hand

14. Look across the entire spectrum of agencies and interests

15. Find advocates on all levels within local and regional government

16. Avoid political alliances with a single party or leader

17. Alert people to change—or the need for change—that will affect their lives

TIP **2** Shaping Public Policy

Understand and target the appropriate arenas of influence

Your planning and implementation group will work to influence government decision makers in one of three arenas of influence. These are the legislative, executive, and judicial branches.

Legislative branch

Often the most effective action is shaping public policy through legislative lobbying. Legislatures create laws that impact all dimensions of human activity. Legislatures determine how government will collect revenues and how it will spend its resources. Use the legislative arena to influence funding priorities and appropriations decisions, shape broad policies, and pass laws that set the standards for use of cultural assets in community building activities.

Executive (administrative) branch

Some issues can be addressed most effectively at the administrative level, where the governor, county commissioner, or mayor can act with executive authority. If an executive can address your problem with an administrative order or an agency can change rules to solve a problem, then work with the executive branch of government. Remember that administrative agencies do more than make rules, develop policies, and implement programs. They also develop and propose legislation and budgets.

Judicial branch (courts)

For some long-debated and complex issues, the courts are the proper arena for influence. You can use litigation to meet objectives when legislative bodies have no authority to act or refuse to act; when federal, state, and local legislative decisions are contradictory; and when there is reason to believe that laws have been violated. Keep in mind that litigation is more costly than lobbying.

Multiple arenas

Sometimes you will want to work in multiple arenas for change. Your planning and implementation group should assess where decisions will be made about your issue and how you can have an impact in one or more of those arenas.

Get to know the people who influence policy

TIP **3** Shaping Public Policy

In addition to knowing the process for lawmaking, you must understand the people of the process. They are the decision makers who have the power to decide about your issues and who control the timing and tone of the debate. They include legislative leaders and staff, executive branch officials and staff, and others in the public affairs community: lobbyists, political analysts, media, researchers, and policy analysts, and engaged citizens. Remember that those who oppose you are also "people of the process" and need to be included in your assessment of all the important players surrounding your issue.

Plan a business-hours visit to your state capitol, county office, or city hall for members of your planning group plus any stakeholders you want to involve in your lobbying effort. Plan to visit with your own elected representative, if possible, to get acquainted. You will have a much easier time getting support for your positions if you have worked, ahead of time, to build relationships with legislators and administrators involved in your issues. Here are a few pointers to remember:

- Be of value to public officials. Know what issues they care about and become a reliable source of accurate information.

- Be a good host. During times when the legislature is not in session, invite legislators to visit your community and see what you do.

- Be a good listener. Meet early with key legislators, be respectful, and listen.

- Ask for help early. Public officials are much more likely to be invested in your community building project if they've been involved in it from the start.

- Understand the environment. It's politics. Show that you have strong constituent support for your project.

- Reward support. Whether you fail or succeed, thank those officials who supported you. When you do succeed, thank them in public and invite reporters.
- Stay in touch. Show public officials the positive outcome of their acts.
- Never burn bridges. Today's enemy may be tomorrow's ally.

Use direct lobbying and grassroots mobilizing

Whether your arena of influence is the state legislature, the county board, or the city council, your planning group will be most effective if you use a two-pronged approach: direct lobbying and grassroots mobilizing. *Direct lobbying* is the action that your task force takes to persuade elected and appointed officials to support your project. *Grassroots mobilizing* involves educating and activating the public to persuade elected and appointed officials to support your project.

Your community building task force has unique and valuable expertise and experience about your issues. Without this information, elected officials may make uninformed decisions. In direct lobbying, you provide information—data and anecdotes—that shapes the debate. When you tap your members, friends, and allies and reach out to the public, you mobilize people who care about the issue. Therefore, they are willing to share their concerns (and your task force's positions) with decision makers, especially their own elected officials.

Grassroots strategies can multiply your overall effectiveness. Grassroots lobbying involves first developing a base of supporters (including your most direct stakeholders but reaching out to many others as well), keeping them informed and updated, and then mobilizing those who care about the project and who are willing to have their voices heard. Your supporters can use their influence as constituents. This is a great advantage to your initiative. Constituents elect government officials and can hold them accountable on election day. In a representative democracy, constituents' voices are sure to be heard, and your supporters can be persuasive with those whom they elect.

Advocate with the executive branch

The executive, or administrative, branch of government plays a key role in shaping public policies that influence local community conditions. Governors, commissioners, and mayors can develop policy and funding proposals that shape priorities in all segments of community life. Therefore, you should have ongoing contact with executive branch officials, agency directors, and those staff within agencies who work in your program areas. These connections will allow you to seed discussions with information and issues that need to be addressed.

Have a systematic way of maintaining communications with the executive offices that deal with your issues. Send regular updates on your issue. Call with new information or progress reports on your legislative initiatives. Alert executive staff to anticipated attacks on positions that you share with the executive branch. Include staff in regular mailings about your community building project.

Finally, work to get to know the people at both the bottom and the top of the executive hierarchy.

Work from the bottom up

Continually work to have good relationships with the staff of the executive branch of government. You can have an impact on the policies they shape and their funding decisions, and you can persuade them to support your project in working with the legislative branch. Learn the organization of the chief executive's staff and the people in roles that affect your work. Positions that are usually most important are chief of staff, government relations director, and communications director (also called press secretary). Once you know the structure of the chief executive's office, learn about and meet with the staff. Acquaint them with your community building project and your public policy agenda.

Work from the top down

Create a good relationship with the chief executive. You will have a better chance of the chief executive's support if you make sure he or she has had a chance to understand your cause and looks to your alliance for reliable information. Know the responsibilities (such as budget proposal, annual reports, veto timelines, and so forth) of the chief executive and the timeline for carrying these out. Know the chief executive's priorities and positions on the issues that you care about. This information can be gathered from campaign statements, public statements while in office, and other public documents, including budget proposals and "State of the State," "State of the County," and "State of the City " addresses. If you meet with the chief executive or have him or her as a guest speaker at an event that you host, keep a record of his or her comments about your project and your issues. Most units of government have a web site that includes a section maintained by the chief executive's office. It may include biographical information as well as the official's vision and policy positions.

Tips for Getting Helpful Media Coverage

The stories of your community's vision, goals, and successes in leveraging its cultural assets make great news—and good publicity helps you build and maintain momentum for more success. At the same time, in doing this work you're contributing to a larger body of experience and knowledge. You can tell compelling stories based upon the data you've collected through your carefully constructed outcomes, measures, and benchmarks. These stories and data will serve you well in getting local, regional, and perhaps national attention for your efforts. They will also help you and others engaged in this work build a better case to influence public policy, philanthropy, and institutional practices.

Chances are someone in your consortium possesses communications, promotions, and/or media skills. If not, there are many resources on developing and managing communications strategies. Be sure you're clear on the kind of communications plan you need and have the tools to create. You may be promoting business or tourism as part of your project, or you may be promoting youth empowerment or good design practices. You may be advocating all of these, but this is not exactly a promotional campaign. You're selling your community's identity, you're attracting attention, you're influencing public policy, and you're recruiting supporters. One straightforward guide that addresses all these areas is the *Jossey-Bass Guide to Strategic Communications for Nonprofits.*[125] It includes overall planning, simple steps, and helpful examples.

The work you've done thus far in planning your project has prepared you well to move into strategic communications. In developing your overall communications plan, develop goals based upon your values, vision, mission, and outcomes. You're well on your way.

Here are the tips:

1. Find and cultivate storytellers and stories
2. Find ways to reach audiences strategic to your success
3. Collect, study, and *use* data that shows change
4. Use both stories and data
5. Tie news stories to outcomes
6. Tell stories with pictures
7. Learn from but don't copy your competition
8. Tell stories about overcoming obstacles

Find and cultivate storytellers and stories

Don't underestimate the power of the first-person story and word of mouth. The story of the family business back from the brink, or the youth rescued from a life of crime by art, has enormous power.

The most effective way to tell your story is to get people "with authority" to tell it for you. The news media—including papers, magazines, TV, and radio—are among the primary authorities you think of first. To have your mayor, county commissioner, chamber president, or school superintendent singing the praises of your project carries far more weight than your saying the exact same thing. But "authority" also means real people telling firsthand stories of transformation. Theirs are often the most powerful. To be featured (favorably) in a major daily or regional newspaper or magazine also helps. Clip and copy the piece and be sure to include it in any information you distribute about your project.

The day may arrive when a notable leader outside the project makes a speech or gives a press interview and takes credit for what you've done. When this happens, you'll know you're on the right track! Unless it's really egregious, don't argue, thank the person, and call on him or her to increase support. Seek out the good storytellers, as mentioned above, and empower them. Provide your storytellers, or prospective storytellers, with information kits that include narrative facts, statistics, and good images of your community and project activities. Include validation in the form of news clippings or statements from known figures outside the project.

A groundbreaking event for Plaza Verde, a 40,000-square-foot building adjacent to the Heart of the Beast Puppet and Mask Theatre in Minneapolis.

Storytelling is one of the skills you might have included on your strengths inventory and one you might have recognized among planning team members and the people you touch through implementing the project. It's a useful skill to track on your community asset inventory. Sometimes good storytellers come from the least expected places. You may come across an artist or a young person who can move an audience to tears with a personal anecdote about his or her profound life change. You might find a small business owner who can't praise your project enough for turning the tide on a generations-old business that was about to take the family into bankruptcy. Or you might meet a recent immigrant who is now a homeowner and who found great support from neighbors after getting to know them through a community festival or puppet-making workshop.

These kinds of stories told to the right audiences, along with supportive data about general economic and civic upswings, can put your project on the map.

Find ways to reach audiences strategic to your success

At least as important as the story you have to tell is the audience you're telling it to. Who are the people that will make a difference to you and your work? The answer depends upon your project and the community you're in. You uncovered likely audiences and allies when you made a list of potential partners and assets early in the planning process. As you expand your understanding of how decisions are made and how things get done, you'll gain a better understanding of the people you need to influence.

Depending upon your plan, the strategic audiences you want to influence might include local, regional, state, or federal policy makers—or they could be the local trendsetters, the hip and fabulous who will attract attention to your project. They may vary from stage to stage, and they may include a wide range of people. In fact, the wider the range, the more indication that your project is crossing sectors, professions, and interests.

For WaterFire Providence to transform that city, its artist-originator Barnaby Evans had to round up hundreds of volunteers to stack firewood, pilot boats, string audio cables, and pick up trash. He taps artists from downtown lofts, social service workers, carpenters, and fishers. Very importantly, he raises significant dollars from businesses, political leaders, and philanthropists. He needs ongoing cooperation from the tourist industry, unions, public employees, and teachers. He also mingles frequently with art historians, museum professionals, academics, and journalists.

Like the community mural artist described at the beginning of Part 3, outreach is part of being a successful creative community builder. Having a wide vision and reach and being able to communicate with diverse elements of your community are key. With your project, identify those essential individuals, professionals, or institutions. Figure out whom they listen to, what they read, what clubs or associations they belong to or frequent, what statistics drive their decisions. *Then be sure to provide the stories that will influence them to the media outlets they prefer, reinforcing the facts they find important.* Sometimes you have to ***emphasize*** stories about certain outcomes when addressing some audiences, while ***stressing*** different outcomes with others. The important thing is not to tell different or contradictory stories. Focus on the pertinent part of the story in the context of the whole story. Give the appropriate information and emphasis to the audience you need to connect with and influence.

Collect, study, and *use* data that shows change

Through the planning process, you've already identified what kind of data will illustrate your outcomes and help to make your case. Because you may be dealing with unfamiliar data, you may need to invest time in learning to read and interpret it, as well as learning what the trends are in that field and what the data means in a broader context. It's important to be comfortable talking about whatever subject the data addresses and about your project outcomes in relation to that data and relevant trends.

Understanding who your strategic audiences are, and the kinds of information they value, you're ready to make your case. In order to be truly meaningful, the story you're telling has to retain validity over time, and it has to relate to a broader context. You're telling a story of change, and change for which you can reasonably take credit. You're also telling a story of how these efforts make your community special. For example, you're demonstrating that civic engagement in your community increased at a significantly higher rate than in other communities of comparable size. Or that new business starts and success rates doubled since your project went online, compared to the decade before or compared to other cities in your region. Chart your audiences and the types of information they typically like to see, and then figure out how you can generate that information.

Use both stories and data

Some analysts argue that "stories trump data,"[126] and that's often the case. However, it's the left-right punch of *both* that provides the best shot at a knockout. You're in the strongest position when you can document the stories with facts. While it's important that your group includes good storytellers, it's equally important that it includes people who can gather the data that proves the good stories are *more* than just good stories. Appeal to both the fact lover and the story lover.

When it's difficult to use statistics to link your efforts to social and economic changes, rely more on stories and less on data. In some of the social development areas, fewer tools are available to measure outcomes. If the emphasis of your project, for example, is leadership development among youth, or stewardship of public space, they're tougher to quantify. In these cases, good anecdotes can carry the day. In regard to economic change, numbers are easier to come by, and, for most decision makers in that field, it's the numbers that tell the most compelling story.

TIP **3** Getting Helpful Media Coverage

TIP **4** Getting Helpful Media Coverage

TIP **5** Getting Helpful Media
Coverage

Tie news stories to outcomes

In Step 5, you developed quantifiable outcomes that stated the desired results of your efforts, and you devised ways to measure them. Of course, you also need to be prepared for the outcomes you didn't anticipate. These surprises—let's call them "evolving outcomes"—can sometimes be the best things that happen. You've connected your outcomes to broad issues that people care about. Then you found others who keep track of relevant data whose work you can cite to demonstrate you've made a difference. It's around these outcomes, expected and unexpected, that your facts and stories should be centered when you communicate with news reporters.

Look back at the projects profiled in the ten strategies listed in Part 2. The Pilsen/Little Village Information Center and Mexican Fine Arts Center Museum can point to the growth in sales tax collections in their neighborhoods as an indicator of success. The Penn Avenue Arts Initiative in Pittsburgh points to the number of new jobs created and the number of properties renovated and re-inhabited. The Massachusetts Museum of Contemporary Art, with the help of Williams College,[127] has examined changes in property values and new business starts in its depressed former mill town.

School test scores, neighborhood crime reports, and voter participation, in addition to economic indicators, such as building permits and new loans issued, are things you can connect to your work. Combine these changes with good anecdotes and photos to tell the story.

You can also tap into existing research and databases on patterns of change related to culturally driven development to help make your case. Putting good local stories together with academic research, as in this book, can have a powerful punch. At the same time, don't make wild claims. That will ultimately be to your disadvantage. Tell your story and provide valid indicators of change and let people draw their own connections.

TIP **6** Getting Helpful Media
Coverage

Tell stories with pictures

Taking pictures and assembling documentation of your project is extremely important—and it starts at the beginning! Don't assume that someone else will do it, and don't let it go undone. Invest in a digital camera. Keep it in your bag or briefcase. An amateur or professional photographer in your group might be willing to take photos at special events or document your community and the changes it undergoes. If you can afford to pay someone to photograph major events, do so. However, make it a habit to snap photos at your meetings, of your guest speaker or facilitator at work. Most importantly, be sure that someone takes photos of your community "before." Make the shoot as exhaustive as possible. Capture an image of each streetscape, each building, each intersection, anything that you envision will change. Be sure to get people in your shots!

Remember that last time you looked at photos of a familiar neighborhood or cityscape from 1910? The buildings, vehicles, and business signage are fascinating. The pictures you are taking now will be useful and of equal fascination in the years to come—and probably in a lot fewer than one hundred years. Your local library or historical society—whom you have already consulted in exploring your community's history—will likely be happy to collect meeting notes, promotional brochures, news articles, and other items that will tell the story of transformation in your community.

You are making history!

Learn from but don't copy your competition

TIP **7** Getting Helpful Media Coverage

Think about what your "competition" has likely told decision makers and the media in your, or a nearby, community. Then think about positioning your story in a fashion that illustrates your project's strengths. One competitor's story might involve the typical giant retail chain. Big Box Company arrived asking for environmental concessions, construction permits, and public infrastructure improvements so it could bring a megastore to the outskirts of your community. Big Box officials said that the company was investing millions of its own dollars in the community. They promised hundreds of "new" jobs, growth in local tax revenue, and charitable gifts to worthy community groups. They even ran TV commercials suggesting that their megastores are good for the natural environment.

A few years later, your community found its historic downtown virtually boarded up. Big Box Company made millions in profits *that have left your community*. It made token gifts to charities for which it extracted lots of publicity and political favors. Once productive farmland is now a vast parking lot with runoff polluting a stream that used to be a peaceful picnic spot. You have traffic congestion and roadways that are dangerous for pedestrians. You rarely bump into neighbors, except perhaps behind the wheel at a traffic light. Your community lost most of its family-run businesses with their hometown charm, businesses that spent their profits next door and in civic improvements. These have been replaced by unsatisfying minimum wage jobs with few, if any, benefits and a distant corporate entity sucking out profits and public resources. The wider highways, strip retailers, gas stations, and fast-food joints are indistinguishable from any other in North America. Your town's identity is lost. This is a familiar story from coast to coast.

The story you can tell is a happier one. You've invested in and rallied the special qualities of your community's people and the special features of your built and natural environment. Your approach has resulted in heightened civic pride, stronger locally owned business and social relationships, improved rather than overextended infrastructure, and a greater degree of entrepreneurial activity. Your community is engaged in the creative economy of the twenty-first century.

Tapping the cultures, strengths, natural environment, and identity of your community is long-term grassroots work. The stories of a variety of "big solutions" whether by Big Retail, Big Factory, Big Sports, or even Big Culture are stories about ransacking your environment, raiding your treasury, and usurping the identity of your place. They promise and sometimes seem to produce bigger solutions faster. They also result in bigger problems in only a few years. You'll have a different story to tell and you want to have both the bigger perspective to tell it from and the facts to back it up.

TIP ⑧ Getting Helpful Media Coverage

Tell stories about overcoming obstacles

While your stories, of course, will focus on how you've achieved your goals, good stories can also come from how you've overcome obstacles. Some people say there's no such thing as bad publicity, and it's true—most of the time. Occasional setbacks can be used in your favor if you spin them right, using them to rally support to overcome challenges. It also primes the media for a follow-up story when you can happily report that you've moved over another hurdle. In any event, your project has become more well known than before. Just be careful that your project doesn't appear constantly besieged or not in control of its own destiny.

Joseph Thompson, founder and director of MASS MoCA, tells a dramatic story of his institution's long and arduous birthing by projecting newspaper headlines that chronicle years of false starts. The on-again, off-again story of setback and perseverance is both moving and entertaining.

You might pitch stories of a parade or festival, announcement of a new development initiative, the reopening or re-activation of a once-cherished theater or park, a community conflict with a creative solution, or a phoenix rising from the ashes. If you can supply an editor or writer with solid information and good first-person sources or storytellers to make it more dramatic, you're ahead of the game.

Summary

Chapter 9 reviewed tips that will help position your project with funders, policy makers, and the media. Some of these tips may seem obvious, some not, but all are critical to take into account as you move into implementation mode. Raising money, gaining cooperation from all levels of government, and dealing with media—welcome and unwelcome—will be critical to your success. You have, or can learn elsewhere, the practical skills needed to undertake these crucial efforts. Several excellent sources of information have been cited.

This chapter concludes the third part of this book and provides a comprehensive guide to creative community building. The rest is up to you and the other creative and caring members of your community.

Endnotes for Part Three

[102] Landry, *The Creative City*, 191.

[103] John P. Kretzmann and John L. McKnight, *Building Communities from the Inside Out: A Path Toward Finding and Mobilizing a Community's Assets* (Chicago: ACTA Publications, 1993), 6–8.

[104] Paul Mattessich and Barbara Monsey, *Community Building: What Makes It Work* (Saint Paul, MN: Fieldstone Alliance, 1997).

[105] Arthur Himmelman, *Collaboration for a Change: Definitions, Decision-making Models, Roles, and Collaboration Process Guide* (Minneapolis: Himmelman Consulting, 2002), 3. Available at http://depts.washington.edu/ccph/pdf_files/4achange.pdf

[106] Mattessich and Monsey, *Community Building*, 19–49.

[107] Linda Hoskins and Emil Angelica, *The Fieldstone Nonprofit Guide to Forming Alliances: Working Together to Achieve Mutual Goals* (Saint Paul, MN: Fieldstone Alliance, 2005).

[108] Mattessich and Monsey, *Community Building*, 19–49.

[109] Ibid., 21–49.

[110] Available from Fieldstone Alliance, www.fieldstonealliance.org, 1-800-274-6024.

[111] Mattessich and Monsey, *Community Building*, 19–49.

[112] Jon Hawkes, *The Fourth Pillar of Sustainability: Culture's Essential Role in Public Planning* (Victoria, Australia: UniversityPress.com, 2004), 15.

[113] Mihailo Temali, *The Community Economic Development Handbook* (Saint Paul, MN: Fieldstone Alliance, 2002).

[114] Josh Kirschenbaum and Lisa Russ, *Community Mapping Using Geographic Data for Neighborhood Revitalization* (Oakland, CA: The Equitable Development Toolkit, PolicyLink, 2002). www.policylink.org

[115] Nancy Duxbury, *Creative Cities: Principles and Practices* (Ottawa, Ontario: Canadian Policy Research Networks, 2004), 3. www.cprn.org

[116] R. and M. Root-Bernstein, *Sparks of Genius: 13 Thinking Tools for the World's Most Creative People* (New York: Mariner Books/Houghton Mifflin Company, 1999).

[117] Maria-Rosario Jackson and Joaquin Herranz, *Culture Counts in Communities: A Framework for Measurement* (Washington, DC: Urban Institute, 2002), 43.

[118] Bryan Barry, *Strategic Planning Workbook* (Saint Paul, MN: Fieldstone Alliance, 1997); Craig Dreeszen, *The Community Cultural Development Planning Handbook* (Washington, DC: Americans for the Arts, 1998); James F. Krile, *The Community Leadership Handbook: Framing Ideas, Building Relationships, Mobilizing Resources* (Saint Paul, MN: Fieldstone Alliance, 2006).

[119] Suzanne G. Dane, *Main Street Success Stories: How Community Leaders Have Used the Main Street Approach to Turn Their Downtowns Around* (Washington, DC: National Trust for Historic Preservation, 1997).

[120] Speaking at National Performing Arts Convention, Pittsburgh, PA, as quoted in the *Cincinnati Enquirer*, June 20, 2004.

[121] Duxbury, *Creative Cities*.

122 Neil Bradford, *Creative Cities: Structured Policy Dialogue Backgrounder* (Ottawa, Ontario: Canadian Policy Research Networks, 2004), 6–7. www.cprn.org

123 Arthur Greenberg and Bill Bulick, *City of Minneapolis Plan for Arts and Culture* (Minneapolis: AMS Planning and Research, 2004), 14. www.ci.minneapolis.mn.us/dca/docs/PlanforArtsCulture.pdf

124 Marcia Avner, *The Lobbying and Advocacy Handbook for Nonprofit Organizations* (Saint Paul, MN: Fieldstone Alliance, 2002). Used with permission.

125 Kathy Bonk, Henry Griggs, and Emily Tynes, *Jossey-Bass Guide to Strategic Communications for Nonprofits* (San Francisco: Jossey-Bass Publishers, 1999).

126 David O'Fallon, from a speech at Animating Democracy, a conference in Flint, MI, October 2003. A veteran of many battles with the Minnesota legislature, director of a statewide arts education center, a former National Endowment for the Arts program director, O'Fallon is now CEO of a large music education organization.

127 The Center for Creative Community Development is a joint research project of Williams College and MASS MoCA, led by economist Stephen Sheppard. See www.c-3-d.org

Afterword

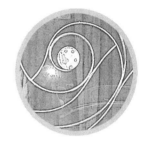

Creative community builders who work for the betterment of the place they call home deserve a spot among the ranks of great artists. Devising and bringing to life a community improvement project that is culturally centered and asset-based and involves people across a spectrum of professions and sectors is truly a creative act. Town by town, neighborhood by neighborhood, place by place, creative community builders like those described in this book are changing the ways communities think of themselves and position themselves in an emerging creative economy and multicultural world.

Whether the community builders in any given place consider themselves artists, their greatest allies and collaborators are artists and other people who possess skills as "intermediaries"—people who comfortably walk between the worlds of art, business, government, and the various institutions and associations organized around these and other sectors.

This book provided some guidance striding that path. It stressed the importance of focusing both on culture, in its broader definition, and on distinct local assets and characteristics. By recognizing and building upon cultural and other assets, the creative community builder harnesses the raw materials to leverage economic, social, civic, and physical transformation. And, since all fundamental social change is cultural, community builders have made changes that are sustainable and more in tune with the evolving conditions in their communities.

The stories from twenty communities across the United States show that creative approaches to engaging local cultural assets have brought about wonderful and lasting change in multiple ways in all sizes and types of community.

Rural highway reconstruction, incubating new arts groups with immigrant communities, putting craftspeople to work in housing redevelopment, and employing youth as radio journalists may be activities that seem to have little in common. Yet in each case, arts and cultural activities were used to build bridges and achieve successful results.

These stories, together with the planning steps in Part 3 , have provided you with tools to think anew about your community and the resources you and your neighbors have to work with. The steps combined a planning process that blends community organizing with creative exercises to elevate cultural sensibilities. The results will be different in every case.

This book may be your introduction to the field of creative community building or a reflection on work you've done yourself. The language and concepts, while more familiar in some other parts of the world, are new in the United States. The term creative community building has been used in other English-speaking countries for a decade or more. As a field of practice in the United States, it is only now being recognized. While there are notable pioneers whose work is still unparalleled, a field has not heretofore been acknowledged. One hope is that this book will help to better establish this field and practice.

You're now a part of this work and this field. You will bring about a heightened appreciation for the uniqueness of each person and each place. This will serve as the basis for transformation, for uplifting from within, and for creating more equitable and sustainable places for everyone to live, thrive, and exercise their creativity.

Glossary

501(c)(3)

A tax status of a nonprofit organization obtained from the Internal Revenue Service that allows tax-deductible gifts to the organization and exempts the organization from federal and state income taxes.

Animate/animation

To bring to life, to help members of a community find and fulfill active roles as participants in community and cultural life. An animateur (from French) is someone whose work is to aid people to associate their individual development with the development of their communities, and to mobilize their energies for participation in furthering that development.

Arts incubator

A space where arts organizations and artists are nurtured and supported. An incubator may include studios, shared equipment and facilities, office and meeting space, and galleries; it may offer workshops and training. Like business incubators, arts incubators are often set up in abandoned industrial buildings. An arts incubator can be an important component of cultural districts, community centers, downtown revitalization projects, and affordable housing for artists.

Assets

Individual, association, and organizational skills, talents, gifts, resources, and strengths that are shared with the community.

Asset-based community development (ABCD)

An approach to community building that emphasizes positive attributes of a community and its members, and generates community development goals and strategies focusing on these attributes rather than on the negatives or needs.

Asset mapping

A process of identifying and listing the institutions and formal and informal associations within a neighborhood, as well as unique facilities, programming, capacities, and goals these groups provide for the community. Surveying the skills, interests, and material assets of community members is an essential part of asset mapping, also known as a community capacity inventory.

Big-box development (or big-box retail)

Stores or other single-use structures that typically occupy more than 50,000 square feet, are box-like with few windows and surrounded or fronted by massive parking areas, and rely on auto-borne customers or visitors.

Brown fields

Building or development sites that were previously occupied by industries or other users that left behind environmental pollution or ruins requiring cleanup. (See also green fields or gray fields.)

Business improvement district (BID)

An area designated to benefit from special or supplemental fees or local property tax, generally earmarked for infrastructure, maintenance, and promotion efforts. Funds are used for such projects as main street signage and design standards, additional security personnel, parking management, and advertising, but can also be applied toward facade or other aesthetic improvements that support the creation of cultural or special districts.

Business incubator

Building where small and growing businesses can be nurtured and supported. Often set up in abandoned industrial buildings, they help cut costs through relatively cheap square-footage charges and shared equipment and basic support services. Often provide expertise and business assistance, and sometimes take on a certain "theme" focusing on a kind of clientele or business, such as design or technology.

Capacity building

The mobilization of individual and organizational assets within a community; the act of combining assets with others to achieve community building goals.

Charrette

A participatory planning and design process involving multiple stakeholders in public settings. Topical meetings, workshops, and commentary sessions are held to shape a strategic community design or re-design. Usually led by architects or design teams who draw plans for public review during an intensive three- to five-day process.

Community arts

(See informal arts and traditional arts.)

Community-based arts/artists

Led by professional artists or amateur practitioners, community-based arts include community members in the creation and/or interpretation of theater, dance, music, visual arts, crafts, or other artistic forms.

Community benefits agreements

Contractual agreements negotiated between a developer and community-based groups and/or a local government that guarantee amenities or dedicated resources to social, cultural, educational, and other uses within a development project.

Community cultural development

Initiatives undertaken by artists in collaboration with other community members to express identity, concerns, and aspirations through the arts and communications media, while building cultural capacity and contributing to social change.

Community development corporations (CDCs)

Nonprofit organizations dedicated to housing, business development, job training, and a variety of other community development activities. They generally serve specific neighborhoods and include community representatives in their governance. During the past thirty-five years, thousands of CDCs have sprung up nationwide, and they sponsor training, management, and resource development networks. (See Enterprise Community Partners and Local Initiatives Support Corporation in References to Organizations and Agencies, page 249.)

Community economic development

A strategy by which local development organizations initiate and generate their own solutions to local economic problems and thereby build long-term community capacity and foster the integration of economic, social, and environmental objectives.

Community organizer

A person who guides the process of community building and advocacy through rallying citizens to organize around common issues.

Community Reinvestment Act (CRA)

A federal program requiring banks and other lending institutions to devote a percentage of their lending to community development activities in lower-income communities within their service areas. It has been hugely successful leveraging billions in urban neighborhoods.

Creative class

A term used to describe a growing portion of the labor force engaged in a wide range of intellectual and creative endeavors. Also used to describe a group that exerts significant influence and is known for trend-setting.

Creative economy

A productive and growing sector of the economy that includes, but is not limited to, the arts, media, publishing, architecture, and design. This sector is sometimes credited with driving, influencing, or attracting other industries.

Cultural democracy

A principle assuming the equality, equal treatment, and equal participation of all cultures; a process of assisting communities and individuals to learn, express, and communicate in multiple directions, not merely from the top—the elite institutions of the dominant culture—down. (See also cultural equity.)

Cultural (or arts) districts

Designated or informal areas containing multiple arts organizations or facilities for the purpose of creating a critical mass of activity to draw and support other retail and service businesses, sometimes providing the core of cultural tourism or other economic development strategies. (See also district designations.)

Cultural equity

Describes the goal of artists, organizers, and advocates to redress and correct imbalances that historically favored a dominant culture, often by working to ensure a fair share of recognition and resources for practices and institutions that focus on nondominant (non-European) cultures.

Cultural resources

A broad range of institutions and community associations including, but not limited to, museums, galleries, theaters, public parks, libraries, historical societies, ethnic associations, public arts installations, and so on.

Cultural tourism or cultural heritage tourism

Travel based upon interaction with both the human-built and natural environment as a means to learn about and experience the arts, heritage, and special character of a place.

Density

The number of people, housing units, or structures per unit of land.

Design codes or guidelines

Formal requirements or guidelines pertaining to architectural style and relationships between structures and rights of way, sometimes encoded in local ordinances; may include accessibility as well as building type or style.

District designations

Areas within a municipality given special zoning, funding, or regulatory considerations by local government and usually identified by signage, maps, special tours, or other means. Districts might highlight arts, artists, culture, dining, history, technology, or other special purposes, as in Historic District or Arts District.

Double bottom line

A return on investment that includes economic and social and/or environmental benefits. Also called dual bottom line.

Empowerment

Recognition and use of the power that all people have; typically involves people working together to build, take, or somehow accrue power leading to self-determination.

Entitlements

The necessary permissions needed to use property or to build upon or alter property as desired; may include environmental, land use and zoning, historic, or other special requirements from local, state, or federal agencies.

Facilitator

A person or group who supports another person or group by assisting them in discovering, developing, and realizing their own direction, goals, and outcomes.

Gentrification

The rapid escalation of real estate prices, rents, property taxes, or condominium conversion that results in dislocation of poor and working-class residents who have been longer-term residents of that area. It can also refer to the revitalization of a neighborhood or area in which abandoned and underutilized properties are upgraded and economic prosperity is fostered.

Geographic information system (GIS)

Capturing and manipulating data from maps and aerial and/or satellite photos for analysis and planning; overlaying data about a geographic area to determine relationships of people and uses to inform planning and policy.

Gray fields

Building or development sites that were previously developed and occupied by commercial or mixed uses but have gone fallow, as in dead shopping malls. (See also brown fields and green fields.)

Green fields

Building or development sites that were previously undeveloped, as in a natural state or used in agriculture or recreation. (See also brown fields and gray fields.)

High art or fine art

High art is often associated with higher social class or wealth. Examples include opera, ballet, and orchestral music. Renaissance painting and other art forms with a long history in Western European culture, as well as comparable forms in other world cultures.

Historic preservation

To retain the qualities of buildings or places that reflect their history. Can involve the designation of structures or areas as historic through local, state, or federal agencies. A common strategy in revitalization, beginning with the restoration of existing physical elements and building physically and/or thematically upon those qualities.

Homeowner associations (HOAs)

Voluntary or deed-restricted entities in which adjacent or common property owners share in decision-making and management responsibilities. These include levying fees for maintenance and setting policies regarding use and aesthetic appearance, such as paint colors or noise. Condominium associations, cooperatives, and gated communities are the most common.

Indicators

A series of measured community attributes—such as school dropout rates, air quality, acres of underused land, health coverage—that are used to identify and monitor progress on various aspects of community transformation efforts.

Infill development

Building or rebuilding of active properties in vacant or underutilized real estate in between existing or occupied buildings, usually in partially abandoned urban areas, but increasingly in suburban areas typified by sprawl.

Informal arts

The many cultural practices that are carried out in settings such as homes, churches, restaurants, cafes, parks, street corners, or other public spaces, generally outside "formal" cultural institutions; includes games, music, storytelling, dance, sewing, and rituals.

Infrastructure

Roads, sewers, and other utilities that are usually tax supported and upon which habitation is dependent. Generally also includes parks, schools, and other public facilities.

Intermediaries

(1) Individuals who translate and build functional relationships between people or organizations in different industries or sectors. (2) Organizations that represent other organizations in fundraising, fund distribution, and establishing industry standards.

Learning community

A group of people who value the process of collective discovery and are comfortable living and functioning within the process of seeking resolution.

Leverage and leveraged assets

The capacity to move resources, people, institutions, or policy in a desired direction from a strategic position; usually using limited resources at one's disposal to move greater resources and thereby multiply one's impact.

Live/work housing

A building or complex designed, zoned, and otherwise designated to be used for both residences and commercial or light industry. Often refers to space used by artists as studio, office, and living accommodations. Zoning codes often do not permit mixing these uses thus requiring special dispensation or changes in zoning.

Local arts agency or council

City, county, or regional nonprofit advocacy and/or funding entity focused on supporting local arts organizations, artists, and partnerships; often an arm of local government, sometimes independent with public and/or private funding.

Master plan

A design-based document that sets out long-term scenarios for a neighborhood, community, or campus.

Microbusiness, microenterprise, or small business

Very small businesses, operated by local entrepreneurs. Microbusinesses usually have less than $100,000 in sales and fewer than five employees; small businesses up to $5 million in sales.

Microlending

Lending resources to start up microenterprises and microbusinesses or catalytic projects that test innovative ideas or help reposition individuals or organizations to enter new business activities.

Mixed use

Multiple land uses, such as residential, retail, office, and light manufacturing adjacent to or integrated within a single development, structure, or land parcel.

Mobilizing assets

The process of linking unique assets in a community to locally relevant community development goals. This process may take the form of local institutions providing new social services through their already well-attended facilities, or local associations reaching new populations by tapping the networks of other associations, or individuals with particular skills connecting to other people with interests in learning those skills.

New urbanism

A philosophy and practice of planning and architecture typified by mixed-use, walkable, and transit-oriented design; similar to traditional or older urban communities; a "brand" of sorts promoted by the Congress for New Urbanism.

NIMBY

Derived from the saying "Not In My Back Yard," and referring to people who may favor a program, development, or change but only if it is not located near them.

Nonprofit

A corporate structure governed by state law in which activities are driven by social purpose rather than financial gain. Ownership is vested in the entity itself and governed by a volunteer board of directors. Nonprofits are generally, but not necessarily, "tax-exempt" under local, state, or federal tax statutes. When federally tax-exempt, they can accept charitable contributions that are tax-deductible for the giver. (See also 501(c)(3).)

Pedestrian friendly

City or town design oriented to walking. Scale, amenities, automobile traffic patterns, signage, and mixed uses make a place welcoming and conducive to travel by foot.

Pivot points

Commercial districts, microbusinesses, workforces, and job opportunities that are ripe for catalyzing larger change. Sometimes designated districts or zones are a next step to recognize and bring ripe activities together and propel them to another economic level. (See also leverage and leveraged assets.)

Place making

The process of creating a special purpose and/or identity for a particular location. Might include a public park, commercial intersection, or other widely used place. Usually involves residents, neighbors, planners, designers, and public officials in designing, planning, building, and/or animating a place.

Public art

Refers to artistic creations created or placed in public spaces and usually paid for, at least in part, with public funds. Sculptures, murals, and artist-designed building amenities are most common, but the term increasingly refers to the process of engaging members of the public in both permanent and temporary (or event-based) arts projects.

Public-private partnerships

Collaborations between public and private entities where substantive resources are provided by both, and public benefit is served along with the prospect of private gain.

Public process

Recognized, open involvement of affected parties in local policy and governmental decision making.

Site control

A term in real estate development that denotes legal control over a parcel. This might include outright ownership but can also involve a contractual relationship that leads to ownership or to the authority to use the parcel and to transfer ownership. (See also entitlements.)

Smart growth

Policies and practices that ensure decisions about development result in well-planned and environmentally friendly growth patterns that protect open space, revitalize communities, provide transportation options, and maintain affordable housing.

Sprawl

The spread of urban or suburban development beyond the edges of historically defined areas without comprehensive regional planning; includes large, low-density residential development and separation between commercial and residential uses; the opposite of smart growth.

State arts agency or council

All fifty U.S. states have a state-government-affiliated agency for financial and technical support of individual artists or nonprofit arts organizations and activities; sometimes combined with tourism promotion.

Sustainable development

Development with the goal of preserving environmental quality, natural resources, and livability for present and future generations; initiatives to ensure efficient use of resources.

Tax abatement

An agreement by local taxing authorities to forgo collection of taxes on particular real estate or transactions for a designated period to provide incentive for investment or increased business activity.

Tax credits—low-income housing, historic, new market

A legal transference of tax deductions in exchange for a sanctioned activity. This could include construction of low-income housing, preservation of historic properties, or investment in a neighborhood with a difficult economy. Tax credits are awarded to the developer of record but may be transferred or sold for a fee. Nonprofit developers often sell the tax credits to a nonprofit and use funds for the sanctioned purpose.

Tax increment financing (TIF)

Public investment usually provided to a developer in a designated TIF area based on the assumption of future tax revenues. A city may loan or grant a developer funds to complete a project, paid back to the city through future tax revenues from the project.

Traditional arts

Long-standing practices in community settings of the creation and celebration of cultural practice of special relevance to that community. Practitioners may be amateur or professional artists who conduct their work in neighborhood, family, or ethnic community settings. Traditional arts usually include the preservation, practice, and reproduction of historic forms specific to regions or ethnic groups.

Traditional neighborhood design (TND)

Building and town plans that reflect older-style street grids with mixed-use buildings and residences revolving around public spaces and/or civic buildings. (See also transit-oriented development and new urbanism.)

Transit-oriented development (TOD)

A residential and commercial area designed to maximize access by public mass transit; usually a higher-density, mixed-used development with a rail or bus station at or near its center; a traditional urban neighborhood.

Unincorporated arts

Nonprofessional and loosely organized groups that might include church choirs, poetry slams, recitals, music ensembles, quilting guilds, reading groups, and other volunteer-run groups. (See also informal arts.)

Walkable community

Towns or neighborhoods that are conducive to walking; contain a wide variety of retail, service, residential, and employment opportunities within easy walking distance, often defined as a quarter-mile. (See also pedestrian friendly.)

References to Organizations and Agencies

American Association of Museums
1575 Eye Street NW, Suite 400
Washington, DC 20005
(202) 289-1818
www.aam-us.org
Museum information, networking, research, advocacy

Americans for the Arts
1000 Vermont Avenue NW,
6th Floor
Washington, DC 20005
(202) 371-2830
www.artsusa.org
Local arts councils, policy, research, networking

Arts & Business Council Inc.
One E. 53rd Street, 2nd Floor
New York, NY 10022
(212) 223-2787
www.artsandbusiness.org
Volunteerism, business partnerships, leadership development

Arts Education Partnership
One Massachusetts Avenue NW,
Suite 700
Washington, DC 20001
(202) 326-8693
www.aep-arts.org
Arts education research, networking, promotion

Arts Extension Service
University of Massachusetts
100 Venture Way, Suite 201
Hadley, MA 01035
www.umass.edu/aes
Training, publications, consulting on local arts development

Artspace Projects Inc.
250 N. Third Avenue, Suite 500
Minneapolis, MN 55401
(612) 333-9012
www.artspaceprojects.org
Development and management of artist housing and arts organization space

Asset-Based Community Development (ABCD) Institute
Institute for Policy Research
Northwestern University
2040 Sheridan Road
Evanston, IL 60208
(847) 491-8712
http://www.northwestern.edu/ipr/abcd.html
Organizational development and microenterprise

Association for Community Health Improvement
180 Montgomery Street,
Suite 1520
San Francisco, CA 94104
(415) 248-8408
www.healthycommunities.org
Community health education, networking and tools

Association of Performing Arts Presenters
1112 16th Street NW, Suite 400
Washington, DC 20036
(888) 820-2787
www.artspresenters.org
Funding, continuing education, advocacy for arts presenters

Center for Arts and Culture
4350 N. Fairfax Drive, Suite 740
Arlington, VA 22203
(703) 248-0430
www.culturalpolicy.org
Research, information on arts and culture policy

Centre for Creative Communities
118 Commercial Street
London, UK E1 6NF
+44 (0) 20 7247 5385
www.creativecommunities.org.uk
Cross-sector cultural and community development research, information, networking

Center for Rural Strategies
46 E. Main Street
Whitesburgh, KY 41858
(606) 632-3244
www.ruralstrategies.org
Rural economic, environmental, and cultural development and policy

CharretteCenter Inc.
3346 Hennepin Avenue, Suite 200
Minneapolis, MN 55408
(612) 823-1966
www.charettecenter.org
Commercial district revitalization, community planning and design

Community Arts Network/ Art in the Public Interest
P.O. Box 68
Saxapahaw, NC 27340
(336) 376-8404
www.communityarts.net
Information exchange, critical dialog in community-based art

Congress for the New Urbanism
The Marquette Building
140 S. Dearborn Street, Suite 310
Chicago, IL 60603
(312) 551-7300
www.cnu.org
Neighborhood planning, design, and policy

Connecticut Assets Network
530 Silas Deane Highway, Suite 220
Wethersfield, CT 06109
(860) 571-8463
www.ctassets.org
Asset-based strategies, training, and networking

Corporation for Enterprise Development (CFED)
777 N. Capital Street NE, Suite 800
Washington, DC 20002
(202) 408-9788
www.cfed.org
Microenterprise, public policy

Development Training Institute
3300 N. Ridge Road, Suite 100
Ellicott City, MD 21043
(410) 418-5181
www.dtinational.org
Real estate and neighborhood economic development training and leadership development

Enterprise Community Partners
10227 Wincopin Circle, Suite 800
Columbia, MD 21044
(410) 964-1230
www.enterprisecommunity.org
Workforce real estate and workforce development

Fannie Mae Foundation
4000 Wisconsin Avenue NW
North Tower, Suite 1
Washington, DC 20016
(202) 274-8000
www.fanniemaefoundation.org
(see Knowledgeplex)
Community development information and resources, primarily focused on housing

Foundation Center
79 Fifth Avenue
New York, NY 10003
(212) 620-4230
www.fdncenter.org
Fundraising and organizational development information

Good Jobs First
1616 P Street NW
Washington, DC 20036
(202) 232-1616
www.goodjobsfirst.org
Community benefits agreements, fair employment, economic development

Kauffman Center for Entrepreneurial Leadership
c/o Ewing Marion Kauffman Foundation
4801 Rockhill Road
Kansas City, MO 64110
(816) 932-1000
www.emkf.org
Entrepreneurial development

Knight Program in Community Building
University of Miami
School of Architecture
P.O. Box 249178
Coral Gables, FL 33124
(305) 284-4420
www.arc.miami.edu/knight/
Integrated community planning and design

Leveraging Investments in Creativity (LINC)
11 Beacon Street, Suite 710
Boston, MA 02108
(617) 227-1393
www.lincnet.net
Artist support, housing, arts-based economic development

**LISC (Local Initiatives
Support Corporation)**
501 Seventh Avenue
New York, NY 10018
(212) 455-9800
www.liscnet.org
(see local affiliate offices)
*Housing development and
commercial district revitalization*

**Mayors' Institute on
City Design**
1620 Eye Street NW, 3rd Floor
Washington, DC 20006
(202) 463-1390
www.archfoundation.org/micd
*Integrated design policy for
economic revitalization*

**National Business
Incubation Association**
20 E. Circle Drive
Athens, OH 45701
(740) 593-4331
www.nbia.org
Business incubators

**National Community
Reinvestment Coalition**
727 15th Street NW, Suite 900
Washington, DC 20005
(202) 628-8866
www.ncrc.org
*Commercial district revitalization,
microenterprise*

**National Congress for
Community Economic
Development (NCCED)**
1030 15th Street NW, Suite 325
Washington, DC 20005
(202) 289-9020
www.ncced.org
*Economic and community
development*

**National Endowment
for the Arts**
1100 Pennsylvania Avenue NW
Washington, DC 20506
(202) 682-5400
www.nea.gov
Funding, information, research

**National Housing Institute
and Shelterforce**
460 Bloomfield Avenue,
Suite 211
Montclair, NJ 07042
(973) 509-2888
www.nhi.org
Affordable housing

**National Trust
Main Street Center**
National Trust for Historic
Preservation
1785 Massachusetts Avenue NW
Washington, DC 20036
(202) 588-6219
www.mainst.org
Commercial district revitalization

NeighborWorks America
1325 G Street NW, Suite 800
Washington, DC 20005
(202) 220-2300
www.nw.org
*Community and economic
development*

**New York Foundation
for the Arts**
155 Avenue of the Americas,
14th Floor
New York, NY 10013
(212) 366-6900
www.nyfa.org
*National resource and information
network for and about individual
artists*

**Partners for Livable
Communities**
1429 21st Street NW
Washington, DC 20036
(202) 887-5990
www.livable.com
*Integrated cultural, economic, and
place-making strategies*

PolicyLink
101 Broadway
Oakland, CA 94607
(510) 663-2333
www.policylink.org
*Research, policy and equitable
development*

**Pratt Center for Community
Development (formerly
PICCED)**
379 DeKalb Avenue
Brooklyn, NY 11205
(718) 636-3486
www.prattcenter.net
*Community design, economic
development, housing, and policy*

Project for Public Spaces
700 Broadway, 4th Floor
New York, NY 10003
(212) 620-5660
www.pps.org
Public markets, public space design

ShoreBank
7936 S. Cottage Grove
Chicago, IL 60619
(800) 905-7725
www.sbk.com
*Community development lending
and organization development*

Social Impact of the Arts Project (SIAP)
University of Pennsylvania
School of Social Policy & Practice
3701 Locust Walk
Philadelphia, PA 19104
(215) 898-5528
www.ssw.upenn.edu/SIAP
Research on social and economic impacts of the arts on neighborhoods

Urban Design Alliance
70 Cowcross Street
London, England EC1M 6EJ
11 020 7251 5529
www.udal.org.uk
Design practices for sustainable urban communities

Urban Land Institute
1025 Thomas Jefferson Street
NW, Suite 500W
Washington, DC 20007
(202) 624-7000
www.uli.org
Real estate and commercial development

Volunteer Lawyers for the Arts
One E. 53rd Street, 6th Floor
New York, NY 10022
(212) 319-ARTS
www.vlany.org
Legal counsel

Bibliography

Adams, Don, and Arlene Goldbard, editors. *Community, Culture and Globalization*. New York: Rockefeller Foundation, 2002.

———. *Creative Community: The Art of Cultural Development*. New York: Rockefeller Foundation, 2001. (Out of print—a text-only version available from www.lulu.com/content/144730).

Bohl, Charles C. *Placemaking: Developing Town Centers, Main Streets and Urban Villages*. Washington, DC: Urban Land Institute, 2002.

Bye, Carolyn. *A New Angle: Arts Development in the Suburbs*. Minneapolis: McKnight Foundation, 2002.

Cleveland, William. *Art in Other Places: Artists at Work in America's Community & Social Institutions*. New York: Praeger, 1992.

Cuesta, Carlo M., Dana M. Gillespie, and Padraic Lillis. *Bright Stars: Charting the Impact of the Arts in Rural Minnesota*. Minneapolis: McKnight Foundation, 2005.

Dane, Suzanne G. *Main Street Success Stories: How Community Leaders Have Used the Main Street Approach to Turn Their Downtowns Around*. Washington, DC: National Trust for Historic Preservation, 1997.

Dreeszen, Craig. *The Community Cultural Development Planning Handbook: A Guide for Community Leaders*. Washington, DC: Americans for the Arts, 1998.

Florida, Richard. *The Rise of the Creative Class and How It's Transforming Work, Leisure, Community and Everyday Life*. New York: Basic Books, 2002.

Ford Foundation. *Downside Up: The Listening Tour Project*. New York: Asset Building and Community Development Program, Ford Foundation, 2003.

Fukuyama, Francis. *Trust: The Social Virtues and the Creation of Prosperity*. New York: Free Press Paperbacks, 1995.

Grams, Diane, and Michael Warr. "Leveraging Assets: How Small Budget Arts Activities Benefit Neighborhoods." Chicago, IL: Richard H. Driehaus Foundation and John D. and Catherine T. MacArthur Foundation, 2003.

Gratz, Roberta. *Cities Back from the Edge.* New York: Preservation Press, 1998.

———. *The Living City: How America's Cities Are Being Revitalized by Thinking Small in a Big Way.* Washington, DC: Preservation Press, 1994.

Graves, James Bau. *Cultural Democracy: The Arts, Community and the Public Purpose.* Chicago and Urbana, IL: University of Illinois Press, 2005.

Green, Gary Paul, and Anna Haines. *Asset Building and Community Development.* Thousand Oaks, CA: Sage Publications, 2002.

Grogan, Paul, and Tony Proscio. *Comeback Cities: A Blueprint for Urban Neighborhood Revival.* Boulder, CO: Westview Press, 2000.

Hawkes, Jon, *The Fourth Pillar of Sustainability: Culture's Essential Role in Public Planning.* Victoria, Australia: UniversityPress.com, 2004.

Hiss, Tony. *The Experience of Place.* New York: Vintage Books, 1990.

Huntington, Samuel P., and Lawrence E. Harrison, editors. *Culture Matters: How Values Shape Human Progress.* New York: Basic Books, 2000.

Jackson, Maria-Rosario, et al. "Investing in Creativity: A Study of the Support Structure for U.S. Artists." Washington, DC: Urban Institute, 2003. www.usartistsreport.org

Jackson, Maria-Rosario, and Joaquin Herranz. *Culture Counts in Communities: A Framework for Measurement.* Washington, DC: Urban Institute, 2002.

Jacobs, Jane. *Cities and the Wealth of Nations.* New York: Vintage Books, 1984.

———. *The Death and Life of Great American Cities.* New York; Vintage Books, 1961.

Kent, Fred, and Kathleen Madden. *How to Turn a Place Around: A Handbook for Creating Successful Public Spaces.* New York: Project for Public Spaces, 2000.

Kleiman, Neil Scott. "The Creative Engine." New York: Center for an Urban Future, 2002.

Korza, Pam, Barbara Schaffer-Bacon, and Andrea Assaf. *Civic Dialogue, Arts & Culture: Findings from Animating Democracy*. Washington, DC: Americans for the Arts, 2005.

Kretzmann, John P., and John L. McKnight. *Building Communities from the Inside Out: A Path Toward Finding and Mobilizing a Community's Assets*. Chicago: ACTA Publications, 1993.

Kunstler, James Howard. *The Geography of Nowhere*. New York: Touchstone, 1993.

Landry, Charles. *The Creative City: A Toolkit for Urban Innovators*. London: Earthscan Publications, 2000.

Markusen, Ann, and David King. "The Artistic Dividend: The Arts' Hidden Contribution to Regional Development," University of Minnesota, 2003. www.hhh.umn.edu/img/assets/6158/artistic_dividend.pdf

Mattessich, Paul, and Barbara Monsey. *Community Building: What Makes It Work*. Saint Paul, MN: Fieldstone Alliance, 1997.

McCarthy, Kevin F., Elizabeth H. Ondaatje, Laura Zakaras, and Arthur Brooks. *Gifts of the Muse: Reframing the Debate About the Benefits of the Arts*. Santa Monica, CA: RAND Corporation, 2004.

McKnight Foundation. *You Are Here: Exploring Art in the Suburbs*. Minneapolis: McKnight Foundation, 2005.

Mumford, Lewis. *The City in History*. New York: Harcourt Brace & World, 1961.

Ostrower, Francie. *Cultural Collaborations: Building Partnerships for Arts Participation*. Washington, DC: Urban Institute, 2003.

Partners for Livable Communities. "Cultural Heritage Tourism: How Communities Can Reinvent Their Future." Washington, DC: Unpublished paper, 2004.

———. *The Livable City: Revitalizing Urban Communities*. New York: McGraw Hill, 2000.

Pike, Matthew. *Can Do Citizens: Rebuilding Marginalised Communities*. London: Social Enterprise Services, 2003.

Plater-Zyberk, Elizabeth, Andres Duany, and Jeff Speck. *Suburban Nation: The Rise of Sprawl and the Decline of the American Dream*. New York: North Point Press, 2000.

Putnam, Robert. *Bowling Alone: The Collapse and Revival of American Community*. New York: Touchstone, 2000.

Putnam, Robert D., and Lewis M. Feldstein. *Better Together: Restoring the American Community*. New York: Simon & Schuster, 2003.

Rosenfeld, Stuart. "Crafting a New Rural Development Strategy," *Economic Development America*. Washington, DC: U.S. Department of Commerce Economic Development Administration, 2004.

Rowe, Peter G. *Civic Realism*. Cambridge, MA: MIT Press, 1997.

Stern, Mark J. "Performing Miracles." Center for an Urban Future, 2002. www.nycfuture.org/content/reports/report_view.cfm?repkey=86

Temali, Mihailo. *The Community Economic Development Handbook*. Saint Paul, MN: Fieldstone Alliance, 2002.

Walker, Chris, Maria-Rosario Jackson, and Carole Rosenstein. *Culture and Commerce: Traditional Arts in Economic Development*. Santa Fe, NM: The Fund for Folk Culture and the Urban Institute, 2003.

Weatherford, Jack. *Savages and Civilization*. New York: Fawcett Columbine, 1994.

Whyte, William H. *The Social Life of Small Urban Places*. New York: Project for Public Spaces, 2001.

Zukin, Sharon. *The Cultures of Cities*. Malden, MA: Blackwell Publishers, 1995.

Index

f indicates figure
p indicates picture
w indicates worksheet

A

acknowledgment, giving, 206–207
ACT (Arts, Culture, and Trade)
    Roxbury, 53, 54–57, 61, 129*p*
action steps, 205–206
activities, brainstorming, 204
African American communities, 53,
    54–57, 61, 85, 89–92, 93
agendas
    civic, 76, 103–104, 113–121, 116
    first meeting, 169
    second meeting, 170
    third meeting, 172
    fourth meeting, 176
    fifth meeting, 185
    sixth meeting, 187
    seventh meeting, 189
    eighth meeting, 190
    ninth meeting, 198
    tenth meeting, 204
    eleventh meeting, 205
Alaska Common Ground, 113–114,
    117–120, 120*p*, 121
Alexandria, VA, 44, 48–52
Anchorage, AK, 113–114, 117–120,
    120*p*, 121
Angelica, Emil, 159
architecture, 7, 47, 88
art/arts
    artist in residence programs, 40
    community building impact of,
        11–12, 209
    components of public, 76
    and day-to-day life, 113
    defining, 158
    described, 5
    economic impact of, 6–9, 23–31,
        53–61
    events, 26, 47, 65, 69
    public participation in, 84

art/arts *(continued)*
    shaping city plans to leverage, 217,
        218–219
artist, defined, 47
artist live/work spaces
    economic development by creating,
        26, 44–52, 216
    enhancing property values with,
        67–70
    and gentrification, 63, 193
Artist Loft Program and Arts District
    (Peekskill, NY), 44, 45–48, 45*p*,
    52, 216
Artist Relocation Program (Paducah,
    KY), 62, 67–70, 71
Artists for Humanity (AFH), 95–98,
    98*p*, 102, 133*p*
Arts and Culture Indicators in Commu-
    nity Building Project (ACIP), 11
Artspace Projects, 44
Asheville, NC, 62–66, 66*p*, 70
asset-based community development
    collaborative nature of, xvi
    focus of, xvii, 17, 140, 145, 187
    strength of, 190
assets
    identifying, 142–143, 145, 146*w*–148*w*
    importance of local, 140–141
    of individual partners, 143, 144*w*,
        167, 172–173
    intangible, 139
    mapping, 175–176, 177*w*–179*w*, 180
    narrowing list, 185–186
    partners' relationship to, 155
    selecting key, 187–188
    shaping community plans to lever-
        age cultural, 216–219
    values compared to, 171
authenticity, 167

B

Baker City, OR, 76, 80–83
Barker, Frankie, 119
Barnett, Tom, 68

Barone, Mark, 67, 68
Becker, Jack, 76
bed-and-breakfasts, 39
benchmarks, 200
Berkeley, CA, 99–102, 99*p*
big-box solutions, 21, 44, 53
Bloomfield-Garfield Corporation, 25
bohemian environments, 6–7, 26
Boston, MA
    economic diversification, 53, 54–57,
        61, 129*p*
    engaging youth, 95–98, 98*p*, 102, 133*p*
Brain, David, 4
brain drain, 96
brainstorming, 189, 204
branding. *See* community identity
Brause, Jay, 118
Brooklyn, NY, 193
Broward County (FL) Cultural Affairs
    Division, 104, 108–112, 197*p*
Brown, Nathan, 69
budgets, 160, 163*f*
Bunge, Eric, 39

C

Carpenter, Peter, 119
celebrations. *See* events
census information, 174
Center for Creative Community
    Development (C3D), 59
Chicago, IL, 34–37, 42, 158
children. *See* youth
Children's Village (Minneapolis,
    MN), 104–108, 106*p*, 112
cities
    community identity, 193
    components of economic competi-
        tiveness, 26
    economic development through artist
        live/work spaces, 44, 48–52
    economic development through
        cultural tourism, 34–37, 42, 158
    economic diversification, 53–61, 158
    engaging youth in, 95–102

cities *(continued)*
  enhancing property values, 62–66,
    70
  gentrification in, 63, 193, 213–214
  increasing civic participation, 113–
    114, 117–120, 121
  increasing participation in cultural
    events, 84–93, 216
  jobs creation through local business,
    24–31
  promoting interaction in public
    spaces, 76, 77–80, 83
  promoting stewardship of place,
    104–108, 112
  shaping plans to leverage cultural
    assets, 217, 218–219
civic agenda, 76, 103–104, 113–121,
  116
civic participation
  in governance, 113–121
  using cultural events to increase,
    84–93
Coconut Grove, FL, 193
collaboration, xv–xvi, 153
collaborators, described, 154
collective efficacy. *See* social capital
common ground
  finding, 74
  and partners, 164
  youth as, 73, 94, 95, 104, 106–108
Commonweal Theatre Company,
  39–40, 41*p*, 128*p*
communication
  and culture, 5
  informal community, 76
  marketing by word-of-mouth, 40
  media, 36, 99–102, 224–230
  and rapidly changing population, 11
community
  culture creates, 9–10
  defining, 141–142
  described, 4
  identifying data and history,
    173–175
  sustaining, 1, 6–7, 44, 53
Community Action Street Team
  (CAST), 100
community development corporations
  (CDCs)
  described, 13
  diversifying local economy, 53,
    54–57, 61
  partnerships between, 25
community identity
  branding example, 34, 38–41, 42
  and cross-cultural relationships,
    104–108, 112
  effecting change using, 140, 141

community identity *(continued)*
  in global economy, 183
  importance of, 4, 53
  and local business, 21
  marketing, 183
  naming, 193–194
  public arts event to foster, 76,
    77–80, 83
  strengthening existing, 64
  suburban, 104, 108–112
community uniqueness
  assessing, 145, 146*w*–148*w*
  and development, 139
  strategies fitting, xvii, 17
concept papers, 149–150, 164
condominiumization. *See* gentrification
consultants, using, 184, 195–196
Cornucopia Arts Center, 40
creative-class workers, attracting,
  6, 7, 8–9
creative community building, xv, 5, 236
creative economy, 6–9
Cropp, Hal, 40
cross-cultural relationships
  among youth, 95–102
  building, 84–93
  and community identity, 104–108,
    112
Crossroads Center for the Creative and
  Performing Arts (OR), 81
cross-sector partnerships, 34–37, 42
culinary arts, 39, 40
cultural events, 30, 84–93, 218
cultural heritage tourism
  archaeological, 50
  benefits, 32, 33
  defined, 32
  example, 34, 38–41, 42
cultural organizations
  community building impact of,
    11–12, 209
  fostering, 29–30
cultural tourism
  economic development through,
    32–42, 65–66
  from public arts events, 79, 80
  see also cultural heritage tourism
culture
  creates community, 9–10
  defining, 158
  described, 4–5
  economic value of, 6–9, 23, 219
  social connectedness across
    different, 10, 12
  see also art/arts
culture mavens, described, 155

D
Dafford, Robert, 69
Danville, VT, 113, 114–117, 120, 134*p*
data
  identifying community, 173–175
  sources, 174, 199, 228
  using in media coverage, 227
Davis, Dee, 33
Day of the Dead celebrations, 36–37
Delray Beach (FL) Cultural Loop and
  History Trail, xvii*p*, 85, 89–92,
  91*p*, 93
democracy, 113
de Tocqueville, Alexis, 3
DiBart, Ralph, 46
direct lobbying, 222–223
disinvestment, 24, 43, 62, 77
doers, described, 155
Dorsey, Jeffrey, 26
downtowns, improving, 45–48, 52, 67
Dugan, Gene, 118
DUMBO (Brooklyn, NY), 193
Duxbury, Nancy, 183

E
Earls, Felton, 73, 94
East Windsor, CT, 217*p*
economic development
  by creating artist live/work spaces,
    26, 44–52, 216
  through cultural tourism, 34–42,
    65–66
  by diversifying local economy,
    53–61
  by enhancing property values,
    62–71
  links with social capital develop-
    ment, 73
  through local business, 23–31, 44
  strategies overview, 19*f*
  values used in, 18
economy, creative, 6–9
education, 94
elderly communities, 63
electronic worksheets, 136
employment. *See* jobs creation
EpiCenter (Boston, MA), 96, 98*p*
ethnically diverse communities
  creating artist live/work spaces in,
    48–52
  engaging youth in, 95–102
  jobs creation in, 24–31
ethnic communities
  businesses serving, 26
  empowering, 34–37, 42
  participation in larger community
    by, 84–93

Evans, Barnaby, 77, 78
events
    acknowledging contributions/
        successes, 206–207
    art, 26, 47, 65, 69
    connecting immigrants to commu-
        nity, 30
    for economic diversification, 56
    ethnic, 36–37
    increasing civic participation in,
        84–93
    public art, 76, 77–80, 83
    and public safety, 218

F
facilitators, using outside, 184,
    188–189
family bonds, 7–8
Felder, Sara, 119
Feldstein, Lewis, 12
festivals. See events
Fine, Michelle, 94
First Night events, 77
Florida, Richard, 6–7, 26
Fooksman, Leon, 92
Foster, Deanna, 105, 107
Franzel, Johanna (Jones), 101
Friendship Development Associates,
    Inc., 25
Fukuyama, Francis, 8, 94
funding
    securing, 28, 210–215
    and sense of ownership, 160
future. See vision

G
gentrification, 63, 193, 213–214
goals
    clarifying, 149–150
    measuring achievement, 199–200,
        201w–203w
    and outcomes, 197–198
    stating, 197
    types of, 198
governance
    importance to community of, 4
    influencing officials, 215–216,
        220–223
    and planning to leverage cultural
        assets, 216–219
    social capital development through
        participation in, 113–121
    types and social bonds, 7–8
grassroots mobilizing, 222–223
Gratz, Roberta Brandes, 53
Grondona, Mariano, 18
Guzmán, Juana, 35, 37

H
HandMade in America, 62–66, 66p, 70
Hawkes, John, 167
Heath, Shirley Brice, 94, 97
highways, 55, 76, 80–83, 113, 114–117,
    120
Himmelman, Arthur, 153
historical tourism. See cultural heri-
    tage tourism
homosexual issues, 113–114, 118–120, 121
Hope Community, Inc. (Minneapolis,
    MN), 104–108, 106p, 112
Hoskins, Linda, 159
housing
    economic development by creating,
        26, 44–52
    and gentrification, 63, 193, 213–214
    improving, 61–72
    integrating public space, 106
    mixed, 219
Hudnut, Bill, 53

I
immigrant communities
    empowering, 34–37, 42
    growth of, 95
incubator programs helping, 28–30
    participation in larger community
        by, 84–93
industrial decline, 24, 34, 43, 58, 77
infrastructure
    attracting investment in, 43
    components of, 4
    impact of physical, 7, 9–10
    rehabilitating historic, 61, 67–70, 71
    reusing physical, 52–61
Inglehart, Ronald, 113
Interfaith Council of Anchorage (AK),
    113–114, 117–120, 120p, 121
Intermedia Arts (Minneapolis, MN),
    106p, 107, 180p
intermediaries, described, 154
In the Heart of the Beast Puppet and
    Mask Theatre (HOBT), 85–88,
    87p, 93, 216, 225p
investments, attracting, 44–52
The Island District (Coconut Grove,
    FL), 193

J
Jackson, Maria-Rosario, 195
Jacobs, Jane, 6, 24
jobs creation
    through local business development,
        21, 23–31, 43–44
    trends in, 174
    for youth, 94, 96–98
Jones, Laurel, 30

K
Keefe, Mary, 105, 107
Kent, Fred, 103
Kertzer, David I., 79
Koskoff, Sharon, 92
Krens, Tom, 58
Kretzmann, John P., 140

L
Landry, Charles, 21, 139
Lanesboro Art Council (Lanesboro, MN),
    9p, 33p, 34, 38–41, 41p, 42, 128p
Latino Information Center (Chicago,
    IL), 34–37, 42
leadership capacity, identifying, 143,
    144w
leadership styles, 166
League of Women Voters, 94
Leo Adler Memorial Parkway, 76, 80–83
literacy promotion, 56
lobbying, direct, 222–223
local business
    decline, 54
    jobs creation by, 21, 23–31, 43–44
    strengthening, 37
Lowe, Rick, 90, 91
low-income communities
    and gentrification, 63, 193
    promoting stewardship of place,
        104–108, 112

M
Madden, Kathleen, 103
Madison, MN, 193p
Madison Park Development Corpora-
    tion (Boston, MA), 53, 54–57, 61,
    129p
management entity, 205–206, 210
mapping, 175–176, 177w–179w, 180
marketing by word-of-mouth, 40
marketplaces, 75, 84
Markusen, Ann, 7, 44
Marshall, Caroline, 103
Marshall, Lane L., 104
MASS MoCA (Massachusetts
    Museum of Contemporary Art),
    13p, 53, 57–61, 60p, 130p, 158
May Day Parade and Festival (Minne-
    apolis, MN), 85–88, 87p, 93
Mazurek, Stephen, 119
McDaniel, Lynda, 65
McKnight, John L., 140
measurements
    early tools, 11–12
    of outcome achievement, 199–200,
        201w–203w

media
ethnic, 36
getting coverage, 224–230
youth-run, 99–102
meetings
first, 168–169
second, 170–171
third, 172–175
fourth, 175–176, 177w–179w
fifth, 185–186
sixth, 187–188
seventh, 188–189
eighth, 190–192
ninth, 197–198
tenth, 204
eleventh, 205–206
planning, 159
Mexican Fine Arts Center Museum
(MFACM), 34–37, 42, 158
microenterprises. *See* local business
Minneapolis, MN
increasing civic participation
through cultural events, 85–88,
87p, 93, 216, 225p
promoting stewardship of place,
104–108, 106p, 112, 180p
shaping plans to leverage cultural
assets, 217, 218–219
momentum, building, 180
Moore, Gary, 92
movie theaters, vintage, 46, 88
Moynihan, Daniel Patrick, 5
multicultural communities
creating artist live/work spaces in,
48–52
engaging youth in, 95–102
jobs creation in, 24–31
Murphy, Tom, 209

N

National Association of Counties, 110
New York City
artist live/work spaces, 68
community branding, 193
gentrification, 63
North Adams, MA, 13p, 53, 57–61,
60p, 130p, 158

O

O'Leary, Ellin, 99
organizational culture, 8
outcomes
activities to achieve, 204–206
clusters of, 197–198
connecting media stories to, 228
described, 196–197

outcomes *(continued)*
measuring, 199–200, 201w–203w
and sustainable development, 184
outdoor activities, 38–39, 40–41,
81–83, 109–111
Out North Contemporary Art House
(Anchorage, AK), 117–120, 120p,
121
outside-the-box thinkers, described, 154
oversight entity, 205–206, 210
ownership, sense of
building, 31, 135
and funding, 160
impact of, 103

P

Paducah, KY, 62, 67–70, 71
Paramount Center of the Arts (Peekskill, NY), 46
partners
assets/strengths of, 143, 144w, 167,
172–173
building cohesion among, 170–171
consensus among, 183
developing expectations for, 136,
153, 159–161, 168
establishing commitment among,
168–169
establishing small teams, 205–206
fundraising by, 210
identifying potential, 154–155,
156w–157w, 164
recognition of contributions,
206–207
recruiting, 164–165
shaping public policy, 215–220
types, 154–155
Partners for Livable Communities, 33
The Pearl (Portland, OR), 193
Peavey Park Designs (Minneapolis,
MN), 104–108, 106p, 112
pedestrian-friendly spaces, 9, 38–39, 75
Peekskill, NY, 44, 45–48, 45p, 52, 216
Penn Avenue Arts Initiative (PAAI),
24–27, 27p, 31, 127p
Pilsen/Little Village Information Center (Chicago, IL), 34–37, 42, 158
Pineapple Grove Main Street (Delray
Beach, FL), 89–92, 91p, 93
Pittsburgh, PA, 24–27, 27p, 31, 127p
place-based communities, 4
place making, 76, 77–80, 83, 103
place marketing, 183
Plater-Zyberk, Elizabeth, 9
population
growth of immigrant communities, 95
impact of rapidly changing, 11
loss, 25, 43, 80–81

Porter, Michael E., 8
Portland, OR, 193
process-oriented goals, 198
product-oriented goals, 198
programmatic goals, 198
property values, enhancing, 62–71,
193, 213–214
Providence, Rhode Island, 76, 77–80,
77p, 83, 131p, 145p
public art components, 76
public policy, shaping, 215–222
public safety, 75, 218
public spaces
integrating housing in, 106
managing properly, 75, 84, 103
pedestrian friendly, 9, 38–39, 75
social capital development by promoting interaction in, 75–83
Putnam, Robert, 6, 7, 12

R

Raphael, David, 115–116
readiness review, 151, 165
recognition, giving, 206–207
recreation activities, 38–39, 40–41,
81–83, 109–111
religious values, 8
resource needs, 205–206
road projects, 55, 76, 80–83, 113,
114–117, 120
Rodgerson, Susan, 96
Root River State Trail System (Lanesboro, MN), 9p, 39
Rosenfeld, Stuart, 43
Rowe, Peter G., 103
rural communities
identity branding, 34, 38–41, 42
increasing civic participation, 113,
114–117, 120

S

same-sex couples, 113–114, 118–120, 121
San José (CA) Arts Incubator (SJAI),
24, 28–31
schedule changes, 136, 159
Sheppard, Stephen, 59, 62
Silas Green shows, 89
Silva, Candelaria, 56
small business. *See* local business
small business incubators, 24–31
Smyth, Laura, 94
social capital
described, 6
erosion, 113
synonyms, 73

social capital development
    through cultural events, 84–93
    and economic development, 73
    by engaging youth, 94–102
    importance of arts to, 7, 10–12
    through participation in civic
        causes, 113–121
    through promoting interaction in
        public spaces, 75–83
    through promoting stewardship of
        place, 103–112
    strategies overview, 19f
Southgate Linear Park Project (Tama-
    rac, FL), 104, 108–112, 197p
Stern, Mark J., 84
stewardship of place, promoting, 103–112
strategies
    for attracting investment, 44–52
    based on vision, 190–192
    for economic diversification, 53–61
    for engaging youth, 94–102
    for enhancing property values, 61–72
    focusing on uniqueness, xvii, 17,
        140, 145, 187, 190
    for increasing connections among
        communities, 84–93
    for increasing participation in gov-
        ernance, 113–121
    for jobs creation through local busi-
        ness, 24–31
    for obtaining funds for project,
        210–215
    overview, 19f
    for promoting interaction in public
        spaces, 75–83
    for promoting stewardship of place,
        103–112
    for stimulating cultural tourism,
        32–42, 65–66
suburbs
    increasing civic participation, 85,
        89–92, 93
    promoting stewardship of place,
        104, 108–112
support, building, 180
sustainable development, 184, 235
Swift, Jane M., 59
synthesizers, described, 155

T
tag lines, 189
Tamarac, FL, 104, 108–112, 197p
teenagers. See youth
Temali, Mike, 174
Testa, John G., 45, 47
Thompson, Joseph, 58, 59, 158

timeline, 136, 159, 162f, 183
Torpedo Factory Artists' Association
    (TFAA), 44, 48–52
Tortolero, Carlos, 35
tourism
    building on, 67–68, 69
    economic value of, 32
    negative results of, 42
    see also cultural heritage tourism;
        cultural tourism; events
towns
    enhancing property values, 62,
        67–70, 71
    promoting interaction in public
        spaces, 76, 80–83
transparency, 153
Transportation Enhancement Project
    (Danville, VT), 113, 114–117, 120,
    134p
travel. See tourism
trust. See social capital
turf issues, 158

U
Understanding Neighbors (Anchorage,
    AK), 113–114, 117–120, 120p, 121
Urban Institute, 11
U.S. Small Business Administration, 23

V
values
    clarifying, 149–150
    identifying community, 171
    and rapidly changing population, 11
    religious, 8
    used in economic development, 18
Van Landingham, Marian, 49, 51
Venturelli, Shalini, 8
Vermont Agency of Transportation
    (VTrans), 113, 114–117, 120, 134p
Vermont Arts Council, 113, 114–117,
    120, 134p
Villani, John, 43, 44
vision
    clarifying, 149–150
    creating outcomes to realize,
        196–197
    developing, 188–189
    strategies based on, 190–192
visionaries, described, 154
Voice of the River Project (Baker City,
    OR), 76, 80–83
voluntary associations, 3, 8

W
Walker, Chris, 32
Wasserman, Andrea, 115–116
WaterFire Providence (RI), 76, 77–80,
    77p, 83, 131p, 145p
Watershed Conservation Commission
    (East Windsor, CT), 217p
Weatherford, Jack, 6
Weber, Max, 8
Weis, Lois, 94
Weiss, Glenn, 90
Westchester Community College, 47
West End/Clingman Avenue Revi-
    talization Project (Asheville, NC),
    62–66, 66p, 70
Whyte, William H., 9, 75
working-class communities, 63, 84–93
worksheets, electronic copies, 136

Y
youth
    as common ground, 73, 94, 95,
        104, 106–108
    cultural activity benefits, 11
    developing cross-cultural relation-
        ships among, 95–102
    engaging ethnic, 36
    involving in civic agenda, 116
    local businesses to engage, 26
    out-migration, 80–81, 96
    promoting literacy among, 56
    social capital development through
        engaging, 94–102
Youth Radio, 99–102, 99p

More Fieldstone Alliance Resources

Get Free Management Tips!

Sign-up for *Nonprofit Tools You Can Use,* Fieldstone Alliance's free e-newsletter. In each issue (arriving twice a month), we feature a free management tool or idea to help you and your nonprofit be more effective.

Content comes from our award-winning books, our consultants' direct experience, and from other experts in the field. Each issue focuses on a specific topic and includes practical actions for putting the information to use.

More Resources Online

Visit www.FieldstoneAlliance.org for a full listing of all our books and services. Free materials include:

Articles

In-depth information on key nonprofit management issues. There are more than 70 great newsletter issues in the archive!

Assessment Tools

See how your organization or collaboration is doing relative to characteristics of a successful nonprofit.

Research Reports

See research that was done to inform our demonstration projects and consulting practice.

Related Books

The Community Economic Development Handbook

by Mihailo Temali

A concrete, practical handbook to turning any neighborhood around. It explains how to start a community economic development organization and then lays out the steps of four proven and powerful "pivot-points" for revitalizing inner-city neighborhoods.

288 pp 2002
Item 069369   ISBN 978-0-940069-36-7

The Community Leadership Handbook

Framing Ideas, Building Relationships, and Mobilizing Resources

by Jim Krile

Based on the best of Blandin Foundation's 20-year experience in developing community leaders—this book gives community members 14 tools to bring people together to make change.

240 pp 2006
Item 069547   ISBN 978-0-940069-54-1

Community Building: What Makes It Work

by Wilder Research Center

Reveals twenty-eight keys to help you build community more effectively. Includes detailed descriptions of each factor, case examples of how they play out, and practical questions to assess your work.

112 pp 1997
Item 069121   ISBN 978-0-940069-12-1

The Fieldstone Nonprofit Guide to
Conducting Community Forums

by Carol Lukas and Linda Hoskins

Provides step-by-step instruction to plan and carry out exciting, successful community forums that will educate the public, build consensus, focus action, or influence policy.

128 pp 2003
Item 069318   ISBN 978-0-940069-31-2

The Lobbying and Advocacy Handbook for Nonprofit Organizations

Shaping Public Policy at the State and Local Level

by Marcia Avner

The Lobbying and Advocacy Handbook is a planning guide and resource for nonprofit organizations that want to influence issues that matter to them. This book will help you decide whether to lobby and then put plans in place to make it work.

240 pp 2002
Item 069261   ISBN 978-0-940069-26-8

Collaboration Handbook

Creating, Sustaining, and Enjoying the Journey

by Michael Winer and Karen Ray

How to get a collaboration going, set goals, determine everyone's roles, create an action plan, and evaluate the results. Includes a case study of one collaboration from start to finish, helpful tips on how to avoid pitfalls, and worksheets to keep everyone on track.

192 pp 1994
Item 069032   ISBN 978-0-940069-03-9

1-800-274-6024 | www.FieldstoneAlliance.org